Explorations in
CORE MATH
for Common Core Grade 8

 HOUGHTON MIFFLIN HARCOURT

Table of Contents Grade 8

COMMON
CORE

▶ Chapter 1 Rational Numbers

Chapter Overview... 1

CC.8.NS.1	**1-1**	Rational Numbers.................................... 5
PREP FOR CC.8.EE.7b	**1-2**	Multiplying Rational Numbers 11
PREP FOR CC.8.EE.7b	**1-3**	Dividing Rational Numbers 15
PREP FOR CC.8.EE.7b	**1-4**	Adding and Subtracting with Unlike Denominators 19
CC.8.EE.7b	**1-5**	Solving Equations with Rational Numbers 23
CC.8.EE.7b	**1-6**	Solving Two-Step Equations 29
		Problem Solving Connections 35
		Performance Task.................................. 39
		Assessment Readiness 41

▶ Chapter 2 Graphs and Functions

Chapter Overview... **43**

PREP FOR CC.8.EE.8	**2-1**	Ordered Pairs 47
PREP FOR CC.8.SP.1	**2-2**	Graphing on a Coordinate Plane 51
CC.8.F.5	**2-3**	Interpreting Graphs............................... 55
CC.8.F.1	**2-4**	Functions.. 61
CC.8.F.4	**2-5**	Equations, Tables, and Graphs..................... 67
		Problem Solving Connections 71
		Performance Task.................................. 75
		Assessment Readiness 77

Chapter 3 Exponents and Roots

Chapter Overview.. 79

CC.8.EE.1	3-1	Integer Exponents 83
CC.8.EE.1	3-2	Properties of Exponents............................... 87
CC.8.EE.3	3-3	Scientific Notation 93
CC.8.EE.4	3-4	Operating with Scientific Notation.................... 99
CC.8.EE.2	3-5	Squares and Square Roots............................. 105
CC.8.NS.2	3-6	Estimating Square Roots 111
CC.8.NS.1	3-7	The Real Numbers 117
CC.8.G.7	3-8	The Pythagorean Theorem 121
CC.8.G.6	3-9	Applying the Pythagorean Theorem and Its Converse 127
		Problem Solving Connections 131
		Performance Task.................................... 135
		Assessment Readiness 137

Chapter 4 Ratios, Proportions, and Similarity

Chapter Overview.. 139

PREP FOR CC.8.EE.5	4-1	Ratios, Rates, and Unit Rates........................ 143
PREP FOR CC.8.EE.5	4-2	Solving Proportions 147
CC.8.G.5	4-3	Similar Figures 151
CC.8.G.3	4-4	Dilations 157
		Problem Solving Connections 163
		Performance Task.................................... 167
		Assessment Readiness 169

Chapter 5   Geometric Relationships

Chapter Overview.. 171

PREP FOR **CC.8.G.1**   **5-1** Angle Relationships 175

CC.8.G.5   **5-2** Parallel and Perpendicular Lines...................... 179

CC.8.G.5   **5-3** Triangles 185

PREP FOR **CC.8.G.3**   **5-4** Coordinate Geometry 191

PREP FOR **CC.8.G.2**   **5-5** Congruence 195

CC.8.G.3   **5-6** Transformations 199

CC.8.G.1   **5-7** Similarity and Congruence Transformations 205

CC.8.G.2   **5-8** Identifying Combined Transformations 209

Problem Solving Connections 217

Performance Task.................................... 221

Assessment Readiness 223

Chapter 6   Measurement and Geometry

Chapter Overview.. 225

PREP FOR **CC.8.G.9**   **6-1** Circles 229

CC.8.G.9   **6-2** Volume of Prisms and Cylinders 235

CC.8.G.9   **6-3** Volume of Pyramids and Cones....................... 239

CC.8.G.9   **6-4** Spheres 243

Problem Solving Connections 247

Performance Task.................................... 251

Assessment Readiness 253

Chapter 7   Multi-Step Equations

Chapter Overview **255**

PREP FOR CC.8.EE.7   **7-1**   Simplifying Algebraic Expressions 259

CC.8.EE.7b   **7-2**   Solving Multi-Step Equations 265

CC.8.EE.7   **7-3**   Solving Equations with Variables on Both Sides 271

CC.8.EE.8   **7-4**   Systems of Equations 277

Problem Solving Connections 283

Performance Task 287

Assessment Readiness 289

Chapter 8   Graphing Lines

Chapter Overview **291**

CC.8.F.4   **8-1**   Graphing Linear Equations 295

CC.8.EE.6   **8-2**   Slope of a Line 299

CC.8.F.4   **8-3**   Using Slopes and Intercepts 305

CC.8.F.4   **8-4**   Point-Slope Form 313

CC.8.EE.5   **8-5**   Direct Variation 317

CC.8.EE.8   **8-6**   Solving Systems of Linear Equations by Graphing 321

Problem Solving Connections 327

Performance Task 331

Assessment Readiness 333

Chapter 9   Data, Prediction, and Linear Functions

Chapter Overview **335**

CC.8.SP.1	**9-1**	Scatter Plots 339
CC.8.SP.3	**9-2**	Linear Best Fit Models 345
CC.8.SP.4	**Ext**	Patterns in Two-Way Tables 351
CC.8.F.3	**9-3**	Linear Functions 355
CC.8.F.2	**9-4**	Comparing Multiple Representations 361
		Problem Solving Connections 367
		Performance Task 371
		Assessment Readiness 373

Learning the Standards for Mathematical Practice

The Common Core State Standards include eight Standards for Mathematical Practice. Here's how *Explorations in Core Math Grade 8* helps you learn those standards as you master the Standards for Mathematical Content.

① Make sense of problems and persevere in solving them.

In *Explorations in Core Math Grade 8*, you will work through Explores and Examples that present a solution pathway for you to follow. You are asked questions along the way so that you gain an understanding of the solution process, and then you will apply what you've learned in the Try This and Practice for the lesson.

3 EXAMPLE   Writing a Number in Standard Notation

Write each number in standard notation.

A 4.18549×10^{12}

   What is the exponent of the power of 10? _____

   Which direction should you move the decimal point? _____

   Place the decimal point. Add placeholder zeros if necessary.

   — — — — — — 4 1 8 5 4 9 — — — — — — — —

   The number 4.18549×10^{12} written in standard notation is _____ .

B 2.568×10^{-6}

   What is the exponent of the power of 10? _____

   Which direction should you move the decimal point? _____

   Place the decimal point. Add placeholder zeros if necessary.

Write each number in standard notation.

9. 4×10^5 _____

10. 1.8499×10^9 _____

11. 8.3×10^{-4} _____

12. 3.582×10^{-6} _____

② Reason abstractly and quantitatively.

When you solve a real-world problem in *Explorations in Core Math Grade 8*, learn to represent the situation symbolically by translating the problem into a mathematical expression or equation. You will use these mathematical models to solve the problem and then state your answer in terms of the problem context. You will reflect on the solution process in order to check your answer for reasonableness and to draw conclusions.

1 EXPLORE   Solving Equations by Combining Like Terms

A soccer club spent $97.50 on trophies from a custom trophy company. The cost of manufacturing *x* custom trophies is $18.50 for the setup cost, plus $12.50 per trophy. To ship the trophies, the company charges a standard fee of $4 per order plus $2.50 per trophy. How many trophies did the soccer club order?

A   Write an expression representing the **cost of manufacturing**.

   Setup cost   +   Cost for *x* trophies

   [   ]   + $12.50x$

B   Write an expression representing the **cost of shipping**.

   Standard fee   +   Cost for *x* trophies

   [   ]   +   [   ]

C   Write an equation that can be solved to find the number of trophies the soccer club ordered.

   Cost of manufacturing   +   Cost of shipping   =   Club's total cost

   [   ]   +   [   ]   =   [   ]

D   Solve your equation for *x*.

REFLECT

1.   How can you check your answer?

③ Construct viable arguments and critique the reasoning of others.

Throughout *Explorations in Core Math Grade 8* you will be asked to make conjectures, construct a mathematical argument, explain your reasoning, and justify your conclusions. Reflect questions offer opportunities for cooperative learning and class discussion. You will have additional opportunities to critique reasoning in Error Analysis problems.

2b. **Conjecture** Do you think that the value of r in the point $(1, r)$ is always the unit rate for any situation? Explain.

7. **Error Analysis** A student claims that the equation $y = 7$ is not a linear equation because it does not have the form $y = mx + b$. Do you agree or disagree? Why?

④ Model with mathematics.

Explorations in Core Math Grade 8 presents problems in a variety of contexts such as as science, business, and everyday life. You will use mathematical models such as expressions, equations, tables, and graphs to represent the information in the problem and to solve the problem. Then you will interpret your results in the problem context.

2 **EXPLORE** **Comparing a Table and an Equation**

Josh and Maggie buy MP3 files from different music download services. With both services, the monthly charge is a linear function of the number of songs downloaded. The cost at Josh's service is described by $y = 0.50x + 10$ where y is the cost in dollars and x is the number of songs downloaded.

Cost of MP3s at Maggie's Music Service					
Songs, x	5	10	15	20	25
Cost ($), y	4.95	9.90	14.85	19.80	24.75

A Find the unit rate of each function.

Josh: _____ Maggie: _____

B Which function has the greater rate of change? What does that mean in this context?

C Write an equation in slope-intercept form to describe the cost at Maggie's music service.

$y = mx + b$

$\boxed{} = \boxed{} \cdot \boxed{} + b$ *Substitute for y, m, and b.*

$\boxed{} = \boxed{} + b$ *Subtract the number that is added to b from both sides.*

$\underline{-\boxed{} \quad -\boxed{}}$

$\boxed{} = b$

$y = \boxed{} x + \boxed{}$

D Describe each service's cost in words using the meanings of the slopes and y-intercepts.

REFLECT

⑤ Use appropriate tools strategically.

You will use a variety of tools in *Explorations in Core Math Grade 8,* including manipulatives, paper and pencil, and technology. You might use manipulatives to develop concepts, paper and pencil to practice skills, and technology (such as graphing calculators, spreadsheets, or geometry software) to investigate more complicated mathematical ideas.

1 EXPLORE Applying Translations

The triangle is the preimage (input). The arrow shows the motion of a translation and how point *A* is translated to point *A'*.

A Trace the triangle on a piece of paper. Slide point *A* of your traced triangle down the arrow to model the translation.

B Sketch the image (output) of the translation.

C Describe the motion modeled by the translation.
   Move _____ units right and _____ units down.

D Complete the ordered pairs to describe the effect of the translation on point *A*.
   $(1, 11)$ becomes $\left(1 + \boxed{\ }, 11 + \boxed{\ }\right) = \left(\boxed{\ }, \boxed{\ }\right)$

E You can give a general rule for a translation by telling the number of units to move up or down and the number of units to move left or right. Complete the ordered pairs to write a general rule for this transformation.
   $(x, y) \rightarrow \left(x + \boxed{\ }, y + \boxed{\ }\right)$

1 EXPLORE Sum of the Angle Measures in a Triangle

There is a special relationship between the measures of the interior angles of a triangle.

A Draw a triangle and cut it out. Label the angles *A*, *B*, and *C*.

B Tear off each "corner" of the triangle. Each corner includes the vertex of one angle of the triangle.

C Arrange the vertices of the angle around a point so that none of your corners overlap and there are no gaps between them.

1 EXPLORE Parallel Lines and Transversals

Use geometry software to explore the angles formed when a transversal intersects parallel lines.

A Construct a line and label two points on the line *A* and *B*.

B Create point *C* not on $\overleftrightarrow{AB}$. Then construct a line parallel to $\overleftrightarrow{AB}$ through point *C*. Create another point on this line and label it *D*.

⑥ Attend to precision.

Precision refers not only to the correctness of arithmetic calculations, algebraic manipulations, and geometric reasoning but also to the proper use of mathematical language, symbols, and units to communicate mathematical ideas. Throughout *Explorations in Core Math Grade 8* you will demonstrate your skills in these areas when you are asked to calculate, describe, show, explain, prove, and predict.

REFLECT

4a. Scientists captured and released a whale shark that weighed about 6×10^5 units. Circle the best choice for the units this measurement is given in: ounces/pounds/tons.

4b. Explain how you chose a unit of measurement in **4a.**

_____

_____

_____

2c. Use your answers to **2a** and **2b** to explain whey there is only one cube root of a positive number.

_____

_____

_____

⑦ Look for and make use of structure.

⑧ Look for and express regularity in repeated reasoning.

In *Explorations in Core Math Grade 8,* you will look for patterns or regularity in mathematical structures such as expressions, equations, operations, geometric figures, and diagrams. You will use these patterns to generalize beyond a specific case and to make connections between related problems.

2 EXPLORE   Applying Properties of Integer Exponents

A Complete the following equations.

$3 \cdot 3 \cdot 3 \cdot 3 \cdot 3 = 3$

$(3 \cdot 3 \cdot 3 \cdot 3) \cdot 3 = 3 \qquad \cdot 3 \qquad = 3$

$(3 \cdot 3 \cdot 3) \cdot (3 \cdot 3) = 3 \qquad \cdot 3 \qquad = 3$

What pattern do you see when multiplying two powers with the same base?

Use your pattern to complete this equation: $5^2 \cdot 5^5 = 5$

Conjecture Write a general rule for the result of $a^m \cdot a^n$.

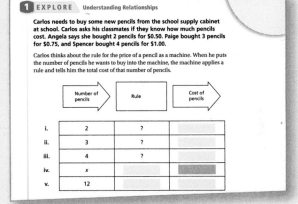

1 EXPLORE   Understanding Relationships

Carlos needs to buy some new pencils from the school supply cabinet at school. Carlos asks his classmates if they know how much pencils cost. Angela says she bought 2 pencils for $0.50. Paige bought 3 pencils for $0.75, and Spencer bought 4 pencils for $1.00.

Carlos thinks about the rule for the price of a pencil as a machine. When he puts the number of pencils he wants to buy into the machine, the machine applies a rule and tells him the total cost of that number of pencils.

	Number of pencils	Rule	Cost of pencils
i.	2	?	
ii.	3	?	
iii.	4	?	
iv.	x		
v.	12		

H&S Graphics, Inc/

Rational Numbers

Chapter Focus

You will write rational numbers as decimals and fractions. You will multiply and divide rational numbers. The sums and differences of fractions with unlike denominators will be found using common denominators. Finally, you will solve equations containing rational numbers.

Chapter at a Glance

COMMON CORE

Lesson		Standards for Mathematical Content
1-1	Rational Numbers	CC.8.NS.1
1-2	Multiplying Rational Numbers	PREP FOR CC.8.EE.7b
1-3	Dividing Rational Numbers	PREP FOR CC.8.EE.7b
1-4	Adding and Subtracting with Unlike Denominators	PREP FOR CC.8.EE.7b
1-5	Solving Equations with Rational Numbers	CC.8.EE.7b
1-6	Solving Two-Step Equations	CC.8.EE.7b
	Problem Solving Connections	
	Performance Task	
	Assessment Readiness	

CHAPTER 1

Unpacking the Standards

Understanding the standards and the vocabulary terms in the standards will help you know exactly what you are expected to learn in this chapter.

CHAPTER 1

COMMON CORE CC.8.NS.1

Understand informally that every number has a decimal expansion; the rational numbers are those with decimal expansions that terminate in 0s or eventually repeat. Know that other numbers are called irrational.

Key Vocabulary

rational number *(número racional)* Any number that can be expressed as a ratio of two integers.

irrational number *(número irracional)* A number that cannot be expressed as a ratio of two integers or as a repeating or terminating decimal.

What It Means to You

You will learn the definition of an irrational number. You will write rational numbers as decimals.

EXAMPLE

Write each fraction as a decimal. Then determine if the numbers are rational.

$$\frac{5}{4}$$

$$\begin{array}{r} 1.25 \\ 4\overline{)5.00} \\ -4 \\ \hline 10 \\ -8 \\ \hline 20 \\ -20 \\ \hline 0 \end{array}$$

The remainder is 0. This is a terminating decimal.

The fraction $\frac{5}{4}$ is equivalent to the decimal 1.25. Both are rational numbers.

$$-\frac{1}{6}$$

$$\begin{array}{r} 0.16\overline{6} \\ 6\overline{)1.0000} \\ -6 \\ \hline 40 \\ -36 \\ \hline 40 \\ -36 \\ \hline 40 \end{array}$$

Leave the negative sign off while dividing.

The pattern repeats.

The fraction $-\frac{1}{6}$ is equivalent to the decimal $-0.1\overline{6}$. Both are rational numbers.

COMMON CORE CC.8.EE.7

Solve linear equations in one variable.

Key Vocabulary

linear equation *(ecuación lineal)*
An equation whose solutions form a straight line on a coordinate plane.
variable *(variable)* A symbol used to represent a quantity that can change.

What It Means to You

You will solve equations.

EXAMPLE

The Kuhr family spent $52.00 for circus tickets. This cost included a $3.25 service fee for the order, and the circus tickets cost $9.75 each. How many tickets did the Kuhrs buy?

Let t represent the number of tickets bought.

Total cost	=	Tickets	+	Service Fee
52.00	=	9.75t	+	3.25

$$52.00 = 9.75t + 3.25$$
$$\underline{-\ 3.25 \qquad\quad -\ 3.25}$$
$$48.75 = 9.75t$$

$$\frac{48.75}{9.75} = \frac{9.75t}{9.75}$$

$$5 = t$$

The Kuhrs bought 5 tickets.

COMMON CORE CC.8.EE.7b

Solve linear equations with rational number coefficients, including equations whose solutions require expanding expressions using the distributive property and collecting like terms.

Key Vocabulary

coefficient *(coeficiente)* The number that is multiplied by the variable in an algebraic expression.
Distributive Property *(Propiedad distributiva)* For all real numbers a, b, and c, $a(b + c) = ab + ac$, and $a(b - c) = ab - ac$.

What It Means to You

You will solve equations using properties of equality and operations.

EXAMPLE

Solve the equation for x.

$$4(x - 5) + 7 = 35$$
$$4x - 20 + 7 = 35$$
$$4x - 13 = 35$$
$$4x - 13 + 13 = 35 + 13$$
$$4x = 48$$
$$\frac{4x}{4} = \frac{48}{4}$$
$$x = 12$$

CHAPTER 1

Key Vocabulary

rational number *(número racional)* Any number that can be expressed as a ratio of two integers.

repeating decimal *(decimal periódico)* A decimal in which one or more digits repeat infinitely.

terminating decimal *(decimal finito)* A decimal number that ends, or terminates.

 MATHEMATICAL PRACTICE The Common Core Standards for Mathematical Practice describe varieties of expertise that mathematics educators at all levels should seek to develop in their students. Opportunities to develop these practices are integrated throughout this program.

1. Make sense of problems and persevere in solving them.
2. Reason abstractly and quantitatively.
3. Construct viable arguments and critique the reasoning of others.
4. Model with mathematics.
5. Use appropriate tools strategically.
6. Attend to precision.
7. Look for and make use of structure.
8. Look for and express regularity in repeated reasoning.

CHAPTER 1

Rational Numbers
Going Deeper

Essential question: *How do you write rational numbers as decimals and as fractions?*

A **rational number** is a number that can be written as a ratio in the form $\frac{a}{b}$, where a and b are integers and b is not 0.

CC.8.NS.1

1 EXAMPLE Writing Fractions as Decimals

Write each fraction as a decimal.

A $\frac{1}{4}$

$$
\begin{array}{r}
0.2 \quad \\
4)\overline{1.0\,0} \\
-8 \\
2 \\
\end{array}
$$

Remember that the fraction bar means "divided by." Divide the numerator by the denominator.

Divide until the remainder is 0, adding zeros after the decimal point in the dividend as needed.

$\frac{1}{4} =$ _____

B $\frac{1}{3}$

$$
\begin{array}{r}
0.3 \quad \\
)\overline{1.0\,0\,0} \\
- \\
- \\
- \\
\end{array}
$$

Will this division ever end in a remainder of 0? Explain.

_____

Describe the quotient.

_____

When a decimal has one or more digits that repeat indefinitely, write the decimal with a bar over the repeating digit(s).

$\frac{1}{3} =$ _____

Write each fraction as a decimal.

1a. $\frac{5}{11}$ **1b.** $\frac{1}{8}$ **1c.** $\frac{4}{5}$

_____   _____   _____

REFLECT

1c. How do you write $1\frac{1}{4}$ as a decimal?

_____

1d. How do you write $2\frac{1}{3}$ as a decimal?

_____

The examples in ① show the two kinds of decimals that represent rational numbers.

- After the decimal point, there may be a finite number of digits. This is called a terminating decimal. 0.25 is a **terminating decimal**.

- After the decimal point, there may be a block of one or more digits that are not all zero that repeat indefinitely. This is called a repeating decimal. $0.\overline{3}$ is a **repeating decimal**.

Every rational number can be written as a terminating decimal or a repeating decimal.

CC.8.NS.1

2 EXAMPLE   **Writing Decimals as Fractions**

Write each decimal as a fraction in simplest form.

A   0.825

The decimal 0.825 means "825 thousandths." Write this as a fraction.

$$\frac{}{}$$

Then simplify the fraction.

$$\frac{825 \div }{1000 \div } = \frac{}{40}$$

$$0.825 = \frac{}{}$$

B $0.\overline{37}$

Let $x = 0.\overline{37}$. $0.\overline{37}$ has _____ repeating digits, so multiply each side of the equation $x = 0.\overline{37}$ by 10^2, or _____.

$$x = 0.\overline{37}$$
$$(100)x = (100)\,0.\overline{37}$$
$$100x = 37.\overline{37}$$

Because $x = 0.\overline{37}$, you can subtract x from one side and $0.\overline{37}$ from the other. ⟶

$$\underline{-x \quad -0.\overline{37}}$$
$$99x = 37$$

To solve for x, divide both sides of the equation by _____. Then simplify if necessary. ⟶

$$\frac{99x}{\boxed{}} = \frac{37}{\boxed{}}$$

$$x = \frac{\boxed{}}{\boxed{}}$$

$$0.\overline{37} = \frac{\boxed{}}{\boxed{}}$$

REFLECT

2a. How do you know that 0.825 and $0.\overline{37}$ can be written as fractions?

_____

_____

TRY THIS!

Write each decimal as a fraction in simplest form.

2b. 0.12 _____

2c. $0.\overline{57}$ _____

2d. 1.4 _____

PRACTICE

Write each fraction as a decimal.

1. $\dfrac{7}{8}$

2. $\dfrac{2}{3}$

3. $2\dfrac{4}{5}$

4. $\dfrac{23}{24}$

5. $\dfrac{17}{20}$

6. $\dfrac{18}{25}$

Write each decimal as a fraction in simplest form.

7. $7.\overline{4}$ _____

8. 0.56 _____

9. 0.45 _____

10. $0.\overline{93}$ _____

11. $0.\overline{54}$ _____

12. 6.02 _____

Compare. Write <, >, or =.

13. $\frac{4}{7}$ ⬤ $\frac{3}{8}$

14. $\frac{3}{4}$ ⬤ 0.75

15. 0.35 ⬤ $\frac{1}{3}$

16. $0.\overline{5}$ ⬤ $\frac{5}{9}$

17. 1.5 ⬤ $1\frac{3}{5}$

18. $\frac{2}{3}$ ⬤ 0.67

19. A $\frac{5}{16}$-inch-long bolt is used in a machine. What is the length of the bolt written as a decimal?

_____

20. The average width of a robin's egg is about 0.015 meter. Write this length as a fraction in simplest form.

_____

21. The weight of an object on the moon is $\frac{1}{6}$ its weight on Earth. Write $\frac{1}{6}$ as a decimal.

_____

22. Oxygen makes up about $\frac{3}{5}$ of the human body. Write $\frac{3}{5}$ as a decimal.

_____

23. On a test, Jerry answered 52 out of 60 questions correctly. What portion of Jerry's answers was correct? Write your answer as a decimal.

_____

24. Write $\frac{1}{9}$ and $\frac{2}{9}$ as decimals. Use the results to predict the decimal equivalent of $\frac{8}{9}$.

_____

25. The decimal equivalent of $\frac{1}{25}$ is 0.04, and the decimal equivalent of $\frac{2}{25}$ is 0.08. Without dividing, find the decimal equivalent of $\frac{6}{25}$. Explain how you found your answer.

_____

26. **Conjecture** A number that is not rational is called an irrational number. When written as a decimal, an irrational number is not _____

_____.

© Houghton Mifflin Harcourt Publishing Company

Additional Practice

Simplify.

1. $\frac{6}{9}$
2. $\frac{48}{96}$
3. $\frac{13}{52}$
4. $\frac{7}{28}$

_____

5. $\frac{15}{40}$
6. $\frac{4}{48}$
7. $\frac{14}{63}$
8. $\frac{12}{72}$

_____

Write each decimal as a fraction in simplest form.

9. 0.72
10. 0.058
11. $0.\overline{45}$
12. 2.1

13. 0.036
14. $0.\overline{7}$
15. 2.305
16. 0.0064

17. $0.\overline{31}$
18. 6.95
19. 0.016
20. 0.0005

Write each fraction as a decimal.

21. $\frac{1}{8}$
22. $\frac{8}{3}$
23. $\frac{14}{15}$
24. $\frac{16}{5}$

25. $\frac{11}{16}$
26. $\frac{7}{9}$
27. $\frac{4}{5}$
28. $\frac{31}{25}$

29. Write a fraction that cannot be simplified that has 24 as its denominator.

_____

© Houghton Mifflin Harcourt Publishing Company

Problem Solving

Write the correct answer.

1. Fill in the table below which shows the sizes of drill bits in a set.

2. Do the drill bit sizes convert to repeating or terminating decimals?

_____

13-Piece Drill Bit Set

Fraction	Decimal	Fraction	Decimal	Fraction	Decimal
$\frac{1}{4}$"		$\frac{11}{64}$"		$\frac{3}{32}$"	
$\frac{15}{64}$"		$\frac{5}{32}$"		$\frac{5}{64}$"	
$\frac{7}{32}$"		$\frac{9}{64}$"		$\frac{1}{16}$"	
$\frac{13}{64}$"		$\frac{1}{8}$"			
$\frac{3}{16}$"		$\frac{7}{64}$"			

Use the table at the right that lists the world's smallest nations. Choose the letter for the best answer.

3. What is the area of Vatican City expressed as a fraction in simplest form?

   A $\frac{8}{50}$ C $\frac{17}{1000}$

   B $\frac{4}{25}$ D $\frac{17}{100}$

Three of the World's Smallest Nations

Nation	Area (square miles)
Vatican City	0.17
Monaco	0.75
Nauru	8.2

4. What is the area of Monaco expressed as a fraction in simplest form?

   F $\frac{75}{100}$ H $\frac{3}{4}$

   G $\frac{15}{20}$ J $\frac{2}{3}$

5. What is the area of Nauru expressed as a mixed number?

   A $8\frac{1}{50}$ C $8\frac{2}{100}$

   B $8\frac{2}{50}$ D $8\frac{1}{5}$

6. The average annual precipitation in Miami, FL is 57.55 inches. Express 57.55 as a mixed number.

   F $57\frac{11}{20}$ H $57\frac{5}{100}$

   G $57\frac{55}{1000}$ J $57\frac{1}{20}$

7. The average annual precipitation in Norfolk, VA is 45.22 inches. Express 45.22 as a mixed number.

   A $45\frac{11}{50}$ C $45\frac{11}{20}$

   B $45\frac{22}{1000}$ D $45\frac{1}{5}$

Multiplying Rational Numbers
Going Deeper

Essential question: *How do you multiply rational numbers?*

1-2

video tutor

PREP FOR CC.8.EE.7b

1 E X A M P L E Multiplying Decimals

Pat's mom bought a new car for $19,055. After a year, its value depreciated to 0.8 of its original value. What was the value of the car after one year?

Multiply 0.8 × $19,055 to solve the problem.

Step 1: Multiply as you would with whole numbers.

$$
\begin{array}{r}
19{,}055 \\
\times\ \ \ \ 08 \\
\hline

\end{array}
$$

Step 2: Count the number of decimal places in each factor. Mark off the *same number* of decimal places in the product.

19,055 ⟵ ▢ decimal places

× 0.8 ⟵ ▢ decimal place

▢ ⟵ ▢ + ▢ = ▢ decimal place

After one year, Pat's mom's car had a value of _____.

REFLECT

1a. You can use estimation to check that your answer is reasonable. Round $19,055 to its greatest place value.

$19,055 ≈ ▢

0.8 × ▢ = ▢

Is the answer reasonable? Explain.

_____

1b. Why is rounding to the greatest place value an effective strategy for checking the solution to the car's value problem?

_____

_____

TRY THIS!

1c. Anya's $25,000 salary was multiplied by a factor of 1.25. What is her new salary?

_____

2 E X A M P L E   Multiplying Fractions

The evening temperature is decreasing at a rate of $1\frac{1}{2}$°F per hour. What will the change in temperature be in $4\frac{1}{2}$ hours, to the nearest whole degree?

Multiply the rational numbers $-1\frac{1}{2}$ and $4\frac{1}{2}$.

Step 1: Rename any mixed numbers as fractions greater than one.

$$-1\frac{1}{2} \times 4\frac{1}{2} = -\frac{}{} \times \frac{}{}$$

Step 2: Multiply numerators and denominators. Simplify, if possible, and round the answer to the nearest whole degree.

$$-1\frac{1}{2} \times 4\frac{1}{2} = -\frac{}{} = -6\frac{}{} \rightarrow \boxed{}$$

After $4\frac{1}{2}$ hours, the temperature change will be about _____ °F.

> **REFLECT**

2. Is your answer reasonable? How can you tell?

_____

_____

P R A C T I C E

Solve. Use estimation to check that your answers make sense.

1. What is the area of a classroom measuring 40 feet by 22.5 feet?

_____

2. What is the price of 1.8 lb of ground turkey priced at $4.30 per pound?

_____

3. For $\frac{1}{4}$ hour, Sam climbs down a mountain at a rate of 188 feet per hour. What integer describes his change in altitude?

_____

4. Fancy cat food is selling for $1.75 per pound. What will $2\frac{1}{2}$ pounds cost? Give your answer to the nearest cent.

_____

5. Elena earns $10/hour at her job. When she works more than 20 hours in 1 week, she is paid one and one-half times her normal rate. What does she earn in a week that she works 25 hours?

_____

6. One-half of the students in Richard's science class are girls. One-third of the girls in the class have blond hair. If 10 girls do not have blond hair, how many students are in Richard's science class?

_____

Additional Practice

Multiply. Write each answer in simplest form.

1. $8\left(\dfrac{3}{4}\right)$

2. $-6\left(\dfrac{9}{18}\right)$

3. $-9\left(\dfrac{5}{6}\right)$

4. $-6\left(-\dfrac{7}{12}\right)$

5. $-\dfrac{5}{18}\left(\dfrac{8}{15}\right)$

6. $\dfrac{7}{12}\left(\dfrac{14}{21}\right)$

7. $-\dfrac{1}{9}\left(\dfrac{27}{24}\right)$

8. $-\dfrac{1}{11}\left(-\dfrac{3}{2}\right)$

9. $\dfrac{7}{20}\left(-\dfrac{15}{28}\right)$

10. $\dfrac{16}{25}\left(-\dfrac{18}{32}\right)$

11. $\dfrac{1}{9}\left(-\dfrac{18}{17}\right)$

12. $\dfrac{17}{20}\left(-\dfrac{12}{34}\right)$

13. $-4\left(2\dfrac{1}{6}\right)$

14. $\dfrac{3}{4}\left(1\dfrac{3}{8}\right)$

15. $3\dfrac{1}{5}\left(\dfrac{2}{3}\right)$

16. $-\dfrac{5}{6}\left(2\dfrac{1}{2}\right)$

Multiply.

17. $-2(-5.2)$

18. $0.53(0.04)$

19. $(-7)(-3.9)$

20. $-2(8.13)$

21. $0.02(-4.62)$

22. $0.5(-7.8)$

23. $(-0.41)(-8.5)$

24. $(-8)(6.3)$

25. $15(-0.05)$

26. $(-3.04)(-1.7)$

27. $10(-0.09)$

28. $(-0.8)(-0.15)$

29. Travis painted for $6\dfrac{2}{3}$ hours. He received \$27 an hour for his work. How much was Travis paid for doing this painting job?

Problem Solving

Use the table at the right.

1. What was the average number of births per minute in 2001?

_____

Births	$4\frac{1}{5}$
Deaths	1.7

2. What was the average number of deaths per hour in 2001?

_____

3. What was the average number of births per day in 2001?

_____

4. What was the average number of births in $\frac{1}{2}$ of a second in 2001?

_____

5. What was the average number of births in $\frac{1}{4}$ of a second in 2001?

_____

Use the table below. During exercise, the target heart rate is 0.5–0.75 of the maximum heart rate. Choose the letter for the best answer.

6. What is the target heart rate range for a 14 year old?

   A 7–10.5

   B 103–154.5

   C 145–166

   D 206–255

Age	Maximum Heart Rate
13	207
14	206
15	205
20	200
25	195

Source: American Heart Association

7. What is the target heart rate range for a 20 year old?

   F 100–150

   G 125–175

   H 150–200

   J 200–250

8. What is the target heart rate range for a 25 year old?

   A 25–75

   B 85–125

   C 97.5–146.25

   D 195–250

Dividing Rational Numbers
Going Deeper

Essential question: *How do you divide rational numbers?*

PREP FOR **CC.8.EE.7b**

1 EXAMPLE Dividing Decimals

During their migration, salmon swim against the current. Suppose a salmon loses 0.6 mi of forward progress over the course of a day due to the downstream force of the water. On average, how many miles does the salmon lose per hour?

Divide 0.6 by 24 to solve the problem.

Step 1: Write the decimal point in the quotient.

$$\overset{\downarrow}{}$$
$$24\overline{)0.6}\ \ \ \text{(0. in quotient)}$$

Step 2: Divide as you would with whole numbers. Insert zeros as needed.

$$\overset{0.0}{24\overline{)0.600}} \leftarrow \text{Bring down zeros to continue the division.}$$

The salmon loses _____ mile per hour by swimming against the current.

TRY THIS!

1. What is $7.56 \div (-1.2)$? Why is the answer negative?

_____

PREP FOR **CC.8.EE.7b**

2 EXAMPLE Dividing Fractions

The area of a rectangular piece of land is $\frac{3}{4}$ square mile. The width of the land is $\frac{1}{2}$ mile. What is the length? (*Hint*: area = length × width)

To find the length of the piece of land, divide the area by the width.

Step 1: Rewrite the problem as multiplication using the reciprocal of the second fraction.

$$\frac{3}{4} \div \frac{1}{2} = \frac{3}{4} \times \frac{\ }{\ }$$

Step 2: Multiply and simplify.

$$\frac{3}{4} \times \frac{\ }{\ } = \frac{\ }{\ } = \frac{\ }{\ } = \frac{\ }{\ }$$

The length of the piece of land is _____ miles.

2a. How can you check your answer?

_____

TRY THIS!

2b. What is $-15 \div \left(-1\frac{1}{2}\right)$?

_____

PRACTICE

Solve. Check that your answers make sense.

1. What is $-24.3 \div (-4.5)$?

_____

2. What is $\frac{4}{9} \div \frac{-4}{9}$?

_____

3. The width of a classroom is 28.5 ft. Its area is 1,182.75 ft². What is its length?

_____

4. How many beads with a diameter of $1\frac{1}{2}$ cm are needed to make a bracelet 18 cm long?

_____

5. Halle is hiking down into a canyon. She descends 3,000 feet in $1\frac{3}{4}$ hours. To the nearest foot, what number shows her descent per hour?

_____

6. Doug spent $52 on 35 pounds of dog food. To the nearest cent, what is the price per pound?

_____

7. Cal's Cabs charges $4 for the first mile and $0.40 for each additional one-fifth mile. Al pays $7 for his ride. How far was the ride?

_____

8. Alex earns $12 an hour at his job. When he works more than 40 hours in 1 week, he is paid one and one-third his normal rate. How many hours does he work in a week in which he earns $576? Explain how you arrived at your answer.

_____

_____

_____

Additional Practice

Divide. Write each answer in simplest form.

1. $\dfrac{1}{5} \div \dfrac{3}{10}$

2. $-\dfrac{5}{8} \div \dfrac{3}{4}$

3. $\dfrac{1}{4} \div \dfrac{1}{8}$

4. $-\dfrac{2}{3} \div \dfrac{4}{15}$

5. $1\dfrac{2}{9} \div 1\dfrac{2}{3}$

6. $-\dfrac{7}{10} \div \left(\dfrac{2}{5}\right)$

7. $\dfrac{6}{11} \div \dfrac{3}{22}$

8. $\dfrac{4}{9} \div \left(-\dfrac{8}{15}\right)$

9. $\dfrac{3}{8} \div -15$

10. $-\dfrac{5}{6} \div 12$

11. $6\dfrac{1}{2} \div 1\dfrac{5}{8}$

12. $-\dfrac{9}{10} \div 6$

Find each quotient.

13. $24.35 \div 0.5$

14. $2.16 \div 0.04$

15. $3.16 \div 0.02$

16. $7.32 \div 0.3$

17. $87.36 \div 0.6$

18. $79.36 \div 0.8$

19. $4.27 \div 0.007$

20. $63.81 \div 0.9$

21. $1.23 \div 0.003$

22. $62.46 \div 0.09$

23. $21.12 \div 0.4$

24. $82.68 \div 0.06$

Evaluate each expression for the given value of the variable.

25. $\dfrac{18}{x}$ for $x = 0.12$

26. $\dfrac{10.8}{x}$ for $x = 0.03$

27. $\dfrac{9.18}{x}$ for $x = -1.2$

28. A can of fruit contains $3\dfrac{1}{2}$ cups of fruit. The suggested serving size is $\dfrac{1}{2}$ cup. How many servings are in the can of fruit?

Problem Solving

Use the table at the right that shows the maximum speed over a quarter mile of different animals. Find the time it takes each animal to travel one-quarter mile at top speed. Round to the nearest thousandth.

1. Quarter horse

_____

2. Greyhound

_____

3. Human

_____

4. Giant tortoise

_____

Maximum Speeds of Animals

Animal	Speed (mph)
Quarter horse	47.50
Greyhound	39.35
Human	27.89
Giant tortoise	0.17
Three-toed sloth	0.15

5. Three-toed sloth

_____

Choose the letter for the best answer.

6. A piece of ribbon is $1\frac{7}{8}$ inches long. If the ribbon is going to be divided into 15 pieces, how long should each piece be?

A $\frac{1}{8}$ in.   C $\frac{2}{3}$ in.

B $\frac{1}{15}$ in.   D $28\frac{1}{8}$ in.

7. The recorded rainfall for each day of a week was 0 in., $\frac{1}{4}$ in., $\frac{3}{4}$ in., 1 in., 0 in., $1\frac{1}{4}$ in., $1\frac{1}{4}$ in. What was the average rainfall per day?

F $\frac{9}{10}$ in.   H $\frac{7}{8}$ in.

G $\frac{9}{14}$ in.   J $4\frac{1}{2}$ in.

8. A drill bit that is $\frac{7}{32}$ in. means that the hole the bit makes has a diameter of $\frac{7}{32}$ in. Since the radius is half of the diameter, what is the radius of a hole drilled by a $\frac{7}{32}$ in. bit?

A $\frac{14}{32}$ in.   C $\frac{9}{16}$ in.

B $\frac{7}{32}$ in.   D $\frac{7}{64}$ in.

9. A serving of a certain kind of cereal is $\frac{2}{3}$ cup. There are 12 cups of cereal in the box. How many servings of cereal are in the box?

F 18

G 15

H 8

J 6

Adding and Subtracting with Unlike Denominators
Going Deeper

Essential question: *How do you add and subtract fractions with unlike denominators?*

video tutor

PREP FOR **CC.8.EE.7b**

1 EXAMPLE   Adding and Subtracting Fractions

Jorge took his dog Gracie on a walk. They walked $\frac{4}{5}$ mile north, a tenth of a mile east, a quarter-mile south, another $\frac{3}{4}$ mile east, and then half a mile north. There they stopped to rest. How far north of their beginning point did they stop?

Compute $\left(\frac{4}{5} - \frac{1}{4}\right) + \frac{1}{2}$ to solve the problem.

Step 1: Perform the subtraction.

$\frac{4}{5} - \frac{1}{4}$ *Find a common denominator: 5(4) = ⬜.*

$\frac{4}{5}\left(\dfrac{}{}\right) - \frac{1}{4}\left(\dfrac{}{}\right)$ *Multiply each fraction by a fraction equivalent to 1.*

   Rewrite with the common denominator.

Step 2: Perform the addition.

$\frac{11}{20} + \frac{1}{2}$ *Find a common denominator: ⬜.*

$\frac{11}{20} + \frac{1}{2}\left(\dfrac{}{}\right)$ *Multiply $\frac{1}{2}$ by a fraction equivalent to 1.*

$\frac{11}{20} + \dfrac{}{} = \dfrac{}{}$ *Rewrite with the common denominator.*

$\dfrac{}{} = \dfrac{}{}$ *Simplify.*

Jorge and Gracie were _____ miles north of where they started when they rested.

REFLECT

1a. You used the least common denominator of 5, 4, and 2 to rename the fractions. Why isn't 10 the LCD of 5, 4, and 2?

_____

1b. When you add or subtract fractions with unlike denominators you can use a common denominator, not just the LCD, to compute. What is a quick way to find a common denominator for any two fractions? *But*, what is a benefit of finding and using the LCD?

_____

_____

_____

TRY THIS!

1c. Gina bought 4 yards of fabric and used $2\frac{3}{4}$ yards of it. How much fabric did she *not* use? How much more will she need to make a scarf that requires $1\frac{2}{3}$ yards of fabric?

_____

1d. Leyla has $3\frac{3}{4}$ ounces of flour in a cup. She uses $2\frac{5}{9}$ ounces to cook dinner. She spills a quarter-ounce. How much flour does she have left?

_____

PRACTICE

Solve.

1. Cheng fenced in three sides of his backyard. How much fencing did he use?

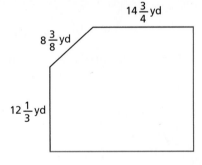

_____

2. An electrician needs a piece of wire exactly $\frac{2}{3}$ meter long. He has a piece of wire $\frac{7}{10}$ meter long. By how much should he shorten the piece of wire?

_____

3. Luke's swimming pool is a rectangle. Its perimeter is $42\frac{1}{3}$ yards. If the length of the pool is $12\frac{1}{2}$ yards, what is its width?

_____

4. A share of stock rose by a point and a half, dropped by $2\frac{1}{4}$ points, and rose again by $1\frac{2}{3}$ points. How much did the stock gain or lose in all?

_____

© Houghton Mifflin Harcourt Publishing Company

Additional Practice

Add or subtract.

1. $\dfrac{2}{3} + \dfrac{1}{2}$

2. $\dfrac{3}{5} + \dfrac{1}{3}$

3. $\dfrac{3}{4} - \dfrac{1}{3}$

4. $\dfrac{1}{2} - \dfrac{5}{9}$

5. $\dfrac{5}{16} - \dfrac{5}{8}$

6. $\dfrac{7}{9} + \dfrac{5}{6}$

7. $\dfrac{7}{8} - \dfrac{1}{4}$

8. $\dfrac{5}{6} - \dfrac{3}{8}$

9. $2\dfrac{7}{8} + 3\dfrac{5}{12}$

10. $1\dfrac{2}{9} + 2\dfrac{1}{18}$

11. $3\dfrac{2}{3} - 1\dfrac{3}{5}$

12. $1\dfrac{5}{6} + \left(-2\dfrac{3}{4}\right)$

13. $8\dfrac{1}{3} - 3\dfrac{5}{9}$

14. $5\dfrac{1}{3} + 1\dfrac{11}{12}$

15. $7\dfrac{1}{4} + \left(-2\dfrac{5}{12}\right)$

16. $5\dfrac{2}{5} - 7\dfrac{3}{10}$

Evaluate each expression for the given value of the variable.

17. $2\dfrac{3}{8} + x$ for $x = 1\dfrac{5}{6}$

18. $x - \dfrac{2}{5}$ for $x = \dfrac{1}{3}$

19. $x - \dfrac{3}{10}$ for $x = \dfrac{3}{7}$

20. $1\dfrac{5}{8} + x$ for $x = -2\dfrac{1}{6}$

21. $x - \dfrac{3}{4}$ for $x = \dfrac{1}{6}$

22. $x - \dfrac{3}{10}$ for $x = \dfrac{1}{2}$

23. Ana worked $6\dfrac{1}{2}$ h on Monday, $5\dfrac{3}{4}$ h on Tuesday and $7\dfrac{1}{6}$ h on Friday. How many total hours did she work these three days?

_____

Problem Solving

Write the correct answer.

1. Nick Hysong of the United States won the Olympic gold medal in the pole vault in 2000 with a jump of 19 ft $4\frac{1}{4}$ inches, or $232\frac{1}{4}$ inches. In 1900, Irving Baxter of the United States won the pole vault with a jump of 10 ft $9\frac{7}{8}$ inches, or $129\frac{7}{8}$ inches. How much higher did Hysong vault than Baxter?

_____

2. In the 2000 Summer Olympics, Ivan Pedroso of Cuba won the Long jump with a jump of 28 ft $\frac{3}{4}$ inches, or $336\frac{3}{4}$ inches. Alvin Kraenzlein of the United States won the long jump in 1900 with a jump of 23 ft $6\frac{7}{8}$ inches, or $282\frac{7}{8}$ inches. How much farther did Pedroso jump than Kraenzlein?

_____

3. A recipe calls for $\frac{1}{8}$ cup of sugar and $\frac{3}{4}$ cup of brown sugar. How much total sugar is added to the recipe?

_____

4. The average snowfall in Norfolk, VA for January is $2\frac{3}{5}$ inches, February $2\frac{9}{10}$ inches, March 1 inch, and December $\frac{9}{10}$ inches. If these are the only months it typically snows, what is the average snowfall per year?

_____

Use the table at the right that shows the average snowfall per month in Vail, Colorado.

5. What is the average annual snowfall in Vail, Colorado?

   A $15\frac{13}{20}$ in.   C $187\frac{1}{10}$ in.

   B 153 in.   D $187\frac{4}{5}$ in.

6. The peak of the skiing season is from December through March. What is the average snowfall for this period?

   F $30\frac{19}{20}$ in.   H $123\frac{4}{5}$ in.

   G $123\frac{3}{5}$ in.   J 127 in.

Average Snowfall in Vail, CO

Month	Snowfall (in.)	Month	Snowfall (in.)
Jan	$36\frac{7}{10}$	July	0
Feb	$35\frac{7}{10}$	August	0
March	$25\frac{2}{5}$	Sept	1
April	$21\frac{1}{5}$	Oct	$7\frac{4}{5}$
May	4	Nov	$29\frac{7}{10}$
June	$\frac{3}{10}$	Dec	26

Solving Equations with Rational Numbers
Going Deeper

Essential question: *How do you solve equations that contain rational numbers?*

Recall that to solve an equation you need to find a value for the variable that makes the equation true. This value is the solution.

Using the properties of equality helps you solve equations containing rational numbers.

CC.8.EE.7b

1 EXAMPLE   Using the Subtraction Property of Equality

Rebecca spent a total of $52.90 at the clothing store. She bought two things: a T-shirt for $19.95 and a pair of shorts. What did the shorts cost her?

You can write and solve an equation to solve the problem.

$c + \$19.95 = \$52.90$ *Write the equation. Let c = cost for a pair of shorts.*

$c + 19.95 = 52.90$ *Use the subtraction property of equality to isolate the variable.*
$\quad - \underline{} \quad - \underline{}$ *Subtract the same number from both sides of the equation.*

$c \quad = \underline{}$

The shorts cost _____.

TRY THIS!

1a. Two suitcases together weigh 82 pounds. One weighs 28.25 pounds. Write two equations you can use to find the weight of the other suitcase: one with decimals and one with fractions.

_____

1b. Explain how you can use the subtraction property of equality to solve the equation you wrote in **1a**.

_____

_____

1c. What is the solution to the equation? To the problem?

_____

_____

2 E X A M P L E **Using the Addition Property of Equality**

After driving for $2\frac{1}{2}$ hours, Alba estimated that it would be another $\frac{2}{3}$ hour before they would reach the lake. How long is the ride to the lake?

$t - \frac{2}{3} = 2\frac{1}{2}$	*Write the equation. Let t = driving time.*
$t - \frac{2}{3} = 2\frac{1}{2}$	*Use the addition property of equality to isolate the variable.*
$+ \underline{} + \underline{}$	*Add the same number to both sides of the equation.*
$t = 2\frac{1}{2} + \frac{2}{3} = \underline{} + \frac{2}{3}$	*Write mixed numbers as improper fractions.*
$t = \dfrac{}{6} + \dfrac{}{6}$	*Rename the fractions using a common denominator. LCD = 6*
$t = \dfrac{}{} = \underline{}\dfrac{}{}$	*Add and write as a mixed number.*

The ride to the lake is _____ hours long.

TRY THIS!

2. Explain how you can you use the addition property of equality to solve the equation $y - (-4.5) = 6.8$. Then solve it.

_____

_____

3 E X A M P L E **Using the Division Property of Equality**

Will and DeSean are slowly exploring an underwater cave. They have descended to a depth of -75 feet in 12.5 minutes. What is their rate of descent in feet per minute?

$12.5r = -75$	*Write the equation. Let r = rate of descent.*
$\dfrac{12.5r}{} = \dfrac{-75}{}$	*Use the division property of equality to isolate the variable. Divide both sides of the equation by the same number.*
$r = -75 \div $	*Divide.*
$r = $	

They descended at a rate of _____ feet per minute.

> The word descended indicates a *negative* amount.

3. Explain how you can you use the division property of equality to solve the equation $-\frac{2}{3}n = 16$. Then solve the equation.

_____

_____

CC.8.EE.7b

4 EXAMPLE Using the Multiplication Property of Equality

A stock that Carmen purchased lost, on average, $3.75 per share each week. If she held the stock for 4 weeks, what was her total loss, per share?

$\frac{m}{4} = -3.75$ *Write the equation. Let m = total stock loss.*

$\frac{m}{4} \times \underline{} = \frac{-3.75}{1} \times \underline{}$ *Use the multiplication property of equality to isolate the variable. Multiply both sides of the equation by the same number.*

$m = \frac{-3.75}{1} \times \underline{}$ *Multiply.*

$m = \boxed{}$

The total loss was _____ per share. ⟵ The word loss indicates a *negative* amount.

TRY THIS!

4a. Explain how you can you use the multiplication property of equality to solve the equation $\frac{w}{-2.25} = -12$. Then solve the equation.

_____

_____

REFLECT

4b. How are multiplication and division related? How can you use that relationship to solve equations involving these operations?

_____

_____

Tell which property of equality you would use to solve each equation.

1. $n + (-6.5) = 14.7$

2. $\dfrac{p}{0.3} = 1.5$

3. $b - 1\dfrac{5}{8} = \dfrac{-4}{5}$

_____   _____   _____

4. $\dfrac{r}{-4} = 2$

5. $-3t = 24$

6. $y + 5 = \dfrac{3}{5}$

_____   _____   _____

Solve by writing and solving an equation.

7. Jacob purchased a DVD player online. He paid $25.95 less than the price of the same item at a local store: $159. What did Jacob pay for his DVD player?

_____

8. Anna is $3\dfrac{1}{2}$ years older than her sister and 8 years younger than her brother. If Anna's brother is 19, how old is her sister?

_____

9. Jan and Mica are rock climbing in Yosemite National Park. Mica has descended 400 feet, which is 2.5 times as far as Jan has come down. What rational number expresses the change, in feet, of Jan's elevation?

_____

10. Anita and Miguel are deep sea diving off the coast of Mexico. Anita has dived to a depth of -6.5 meters. This is two-thirds as deep as Miguel's current depth. What rational number identifies Miguel's location beneath the ocean surface?

_____

11. **Error Analysis** Ivan says that the solution to the equation $6n = -19.2$ is -13.2. What is his mistake?

_____

_____

12. **Error Analysis** Kita estimates that the solution to the equation $4\dfrac{5}{6}y = 18$ is about $4\dfrac{1}{2}$. Is she right? Explain.

_____

_____

Additional Practice

Solve.

1. $x + 6.8 = 12.19$

2. $y - 10.24 = 5.3$

3. $0.05w = 6.25$

_____ _____ _____

4. $\dfrac{a}{9.05} = 8.2$

5. $-12.41 + x = -0.06$

6. $\dfrac{d}{-8.4} = -10.2$

_____ _____ _____

7. $-2.89 = 1.7m$

8. $n - 8.09 = -11.65$

9. $\dfrac{x}{5.4} = -7.18$

_____ _____ _____

10. $\dfrac{7}{9} + x = 1\dfrac{1}{9}$

11. $\dfrac{6}{11}y = -\dfrac{18}{22}$

12. $\dfrac{7}{10}d = \dfrac{21}{20}$

_____ _____ _____

13. $x - \left(-\dfrac{9}{14}\right) = \dfrac{5}{7}$

14. $x - \dfrac{15}{21} = 2\dfrac{6}{7}$

15. $-\dfrac{8}{15}a = \dfrac{9}{10}$

_____ _____ _____

16. A recipe calls for $2\dfrac{1}{3}$ cups of flour and $1\dfrac{1}{4}$ cups of sugar. If the recipe is tripled, how much flour and sugar will be needed?

_____

17. Daniel filled the gas tank in his car with 14.6 gal of gas. He then drove 284.7 mi before needing to fill up his tank with gas again. How many miles did the car get to a gallon of gasoline?

_____

Problem Solving

Write the correct answer.

1. In the last 150 years, the average height of people in industrialized nations has increased by $\frac{1}{3}$ foot. Today, American men have an average height of $5\frac{7}{12}$ feet. What was the average height of American men 150 years ago?

2. Jaime has a length of ribbon that is $23\frac{1}{2}$ in. long. If she plans to cut the ribbon into pieces that are $\frac{3}{4}$ in. long, into how many pieces can she cut the ribbon? (She cannot use partial pieces.)

3. Todd's restaurant bill for dinner was $15.55. After he left a tip, he spent a total of $18.00 on dinner. How much money did Todd leave for a tip?

4. The difference between the boiling point and melting point of Hydrogen is 6.47 °C. The melting point of Hydrogen is −259.34 °C. What is the boiling point of Hydrogen?

Choose the letter for the best answer.

5. In 2005, a sprinter won the gold medal in the 100-m dash in with a time of 9.85 seconds. His time was 0.95 seconds faster than the winner in the 100-m dash in 1900. What was winner's time in 1900?

   A 8.95 seconds

   B 10.65 seconds

   C 10.80 seconds

   D 11.20 seconds

7. After a morning shower, there was $\frac{17}{100}$ in. of rain in the rain gauge. It rained again an hour later and the rain gauge showed $\frac{1}{4}$ in. of rain. How much did it rain the second time?

   A $\frac{2}{25}$ in.   C $\frac{21}{50}$ in.

   B $\frac{1}{6}$ in.   D $\frac{3}{8}$ in.

6. The balance in Susan's checking account was $245.35. After the bank deposited interest into the account, her balance went to $248.02. How much interest did the bank pay Susan?

   F $1.01

   G $2.67

   H $3.95

   J $493.37

8. Two-third of John's savings account is being saved for his college education. If $2500 of his savings is for his college education, how much money in total is in his savings account?

   F $1666.67   H $4250.83

   G $3750   J $5000

Solving Two-Step Equations
Going Deeper

Essential question: *How do you solve equations that contain multiple operations?*

To solve an equation containing more than one operation applied to the variable, you typically *undo the operations* in *reverse* order. You undo addition and subtraction *before* you undo multiplication and division.

CC.8.EE.7b

1 EXAMPLE Solving a Two-Step Equation Containing Decimals

Remy has $447.50 in a savings account. Each week he deposits $7.50 from his earnings at his after-school job into the account. In how many weeks will Remy have $500 in his savings account?

A Write a two-step equation to represent the situation.

Let w = number of weeks Remy makes deposits.

$7.50w + 447.50 = 500$

B Use a table to help you solve the equation.

First, list the operations in the equation *by the order in which they are applied* to the variable.

Then, undo the operations in the equation in the *reverse* order.

Operations in the Equation	To Solve
1. First, w is _____ by 7.50.	**3.** First, _____ 447.50 from both sides of the equation.
2. Then, 447.50 is _____.	**4.** Then, _____ both sides by 7.50.

C Apply the steps in the "To Solve" column to solve the equation.

$$7.50w + 447.50 = 500$$
$$- \boxed{} \quad - \boxed{}$$
$$7.50w = \boxed{}$$

Use the subtraction property of equality. Subtract.

$$\frac{7.50w}{\boxed{}} = \frac{\boxed{}}{\boxed{}}$$

Use the division property of equality. Divide.

$$w = \boxed{}$$

It will take Remy _____ weeks to have $500 in his savings account.

TRY THIS!

Solve each problem by writing and solving a two-step equation.

1a. The length of a backyard is 22 meters. That is 20 feet less than 3.5 times the width of the yard. How wide is the backyard?

_____

1b. The temperature in an Arctic village is –35°F. That is 10° warmer than 1.5 times as cold as it is in an Alaskan town. What is the temperature in the Alaskan town?

_____

REFLECT

1c. For each problem above, tell which operations are applied to the variable and in what order. Then tell what operations you used to undo them, and in what order you used them.

_____

_____

_____

CC.8.EE.7b

2 EXAMPLE Solving a Two-Step Equation Containing Fractions

Mo studied 40 minutes for an exam. That is 8 minutes longer than $\frac{1}{4}$ the number of minutes Leon studied. For how long did Leon study?

A Write a two-step equation to represent the situation.

Let m = number of minutes Leon studied for the exam.

$\frac{1}{4} m + 8 = 40$

B Use a table to help you solve the equation.

Operations in the Equation		To Solve	
1. First, m is _____ by ___.		**3.** First, _____ 8 from both sides of the equation.	
2. Then, ___ is _____.		**4.** Then, _____ both sides by ___.	

C Apply the steps in the "To Solve" column to solve the equation.

$\frac{1}{4}m + 8 = 40$ *Use the subtraction property of equality to isolate the variable.*

$-\boxed{} \quad -\boxed{}$ *Subtract the same number from both sides of the equation.*

$\frac{1}{4}m = \boxed{}$

$\boxed{} \times \frac{1}{4}m = 32 \times \boxed{}$ *Use the multiplication property of equality to isolate the variable.*

$m = \boxed{}$ *Multiply both sides of the equation by the same number.*

Leon studied for _____ minutes.

TRY THIS!

Solve each problem by writing and solving an equation.

2a. Leonard sold 15 tickets to his band's concert. That is 5 fewer than half of the number Vera sold. How many tickets did Vera sell?

_____

2b. Dimitri did 18 push-ups. That is 12 more than one-fifth the number Avi did. How many push-ups did Avi do?

_____

REFLECT

2c. For each problem above, tell *which operations* are applied to the variable and *in what order*. Then tell what operations you used to undo them, and in what order you used them.

_____

_____

_____

PRACTICE

Tell which operations you will use and in which order you will use them to solve each equation.

1. $4.5n + 22 = 50$ _____

2. $2\frac{3}{4}y - 6 = 10$ _____

3. $25.5 = 2x + 2.75$ _____

Pedro runs a pedicab business that charges customers for rides through the park and around the city. The advertisement shows Pedro's prices.

Go with Pedro's Pedicabs!
Low, Low Prices! Friendly Drivers! Comfy Seats!
$30 for first hour

$7.50 for each additional 15 minutes

$2.50 for blanket rental

NO CHARGE for driver's jokes!

Tipping appreciated ↑↑

"…the best ride of my life!" Andy, from Dallas, TX

---

4. What is the cost of a 2-hour pedicab ride with Pedro's Pedicabs?

_____

5. What is the total price of a 2.25-hour drive with a tip of $15?

_____

6. The Suarez family took a pedicab ride with Pedro's Pedicabs. With a blanket rental and a $10 tip, the price of their ride came to $57.50. How long was their ride?

_____

7. Elden took a ride for $1\frac{3}{4}$ hours. He gave a $10 tip. Marla's ride was a half-hour longer than Elden's. She left no tip. Whose ride cost more? How much more?

_____

Solve by writing and solving an equation.

8. If you add 8 to a number divided by 5, the sum is 8. What is the number?

_____

9. Fred is 3 years more than two and one-half times his sister's age. If Fred is 18, how old is his sister?

_____

10. Five dollars more than half the price of a sweater is equal to $40.39. What is the full price of the sweater?

_____

11. Four bags of dry dog food plus 8.5 pounds of dry cat food weigh 17.5 pounds in all. How many pounds does each bag of dog food weigh?

_____

12. Make a Conjecture You know that one way to solve the equation $2n - 8 = 2.8$ is to undo operations applied to the variable:

- First add 8 to both sides to undo the subtraction of 8.
- Then divide both sides by 2 to undo the multiplication by 2.

What other method can you think of to solve this two-step equation?

_____

_____

© Houghton Mifflin Harcourt Publishing Company

Additional Practice

1. The school purchased baseball equipment and uniforms for a total cost of $1762. The equipment costs $598 and the uniforms were $24.25 each. How many uniforms did the school purchase?

_____

_____

_____

_____

_____

_____

2. Carla runs 4 miles every day. She jogs from home to the school track, which is $\frac{3}{4}$ mile away. She then runs laps around the $\frac{1}{4}$-mile track. Carla then jogs home. How many laps does she run at the school?

_____

_____

_____

_____

_____

_____

Solve.

3. $\dfrac{a+5}{3} = 12$

4. $\dfrac{x+2}{4} = -2$

5. $\dfrac{y-4}{6} = -3$

6. $\dfrac{k+1}{8} = 7$

_____

_____

_____

_____

7. $0.5x - 6 = -4$

8. $\dfrac{x}{2} + 3 = -4$

9. $\dfrac{1}{5}n + 3 = 6$

10. $2a - 7 = -9$

_____

_____

_____

_____

11. $\dfrac{3x-1}{4} = 2$

12. $-7.8 = 4.4 + 2r$

13. $\dfrac{-4w+5}{-3} = -7$

14. $1.3 - 5r = 7.4$

_____

_____

_____

_____

15. A phone call costs $0.58 for the first 3 minutes and $0.15 for each additional minute. If the total charge for the call was $4.78, how many minutes was the call?

_____

16. Seventeen less than four times a number is twenty-seven. Find the number.

_____

Problem Solving

The chart below describes three different long-distance calling plans. Jamie has budgeted $20 per month for long-distance calls. Write the correct answer.

1. How many minutes will Jamie be able to use per month with plan A? Round to the nearest minute.

   _____

Plan	Monthly Access Fee	Charge per minute
A	$3.95	$0.08
B	$8.95	$0.06
C	$0	$0.10

2. How many minutes will Jamie be able to use per month with plan B? Round to the nearest minute.

   _____

3. How many minutes will Jamie be able to use per month with plan C? Round to the nearest minute.

   _____

4. Which plan is the best deal for Jamie's budget?

   _____

5. Nolan has budgeted $50 per month for long distance. Which plan is the best deal for Nolan's budget?

   _____

The table describes three different car loans that Susana can get to finance her new car. The total column gives the amount she will end up paying for the car including the down payment and the payments with interest. Choose the letter for the best answer.

6. How much will Susana pay each month with loan A?

   A $252.04   C $330.35
   B $297.02   D $353.68

Loan	Down Payment	Number of Months	Total
A	$2000	60	$19,821.20
B	$1000	48	$19,390.72
C	$0	60	$20,197.20

7. How much will Susana pay each month with loan B?

   F $300.85   H $323.17
   G $306.50   J $383.14

8. How much will Susana pay each month with loan C?

   A $336.62   C $369.95
   B $352.28   D $420.78

9. Which loan will give Susana the smallest monthly payment?

   F Loan A   H Loan C
   G Loan B   J They are equal

© Houghton Mifflin Harcourt Publishing Company

CHAPTER 1

Problem Solving Connections

The Plot Thickens Taylor Middle School has a new school garden. Students can get a plot in the garden if they develop a plan for the plot and present a budget that shows the cost of setting up the plot. Amani and Jacob decide to work together on a plan. How much will it cost to set up their garden plot?

COMMON CORE

CC.8.NS.1
CC.8.EE.7
CC.8.EE.7b

1 Find the Cost of the Fence

Each plot in the school garden is a rectangle with the dimensions shown in the figure. Amani and Jacob decide that they would like to put a small fence around their plot.

$8\frac{3}{4}$ ft

$12\frac{1}{8}$ ft

A Write an expression that gives the perimeter of the plot. Then find the perimeter.

B Write the perimeter as a decimal.

C Is the decimal you wrote a repeating decimal or a terminating decimal? Is the perimeter a rational number or an irrational number? Explain.

D The fence that Amani and Jacob want to put around the plot costs $1.40 per foot. Explain how to find the cost of the fence.

2 Find the Cost of the Beds

Amani and Jacob decide to have four raised beds in their garden plot with paths between and around the beds. The figure shows the dimensions that Amani has already determined.

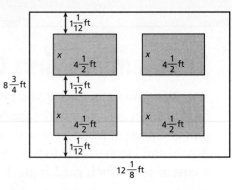

A The four beds are identical rectangles. Each bed is $4\frac{1}{2}$ feet long. Amani decides that the width of three of the paths should be 13 inches (or $1\frac{1}{12}$ feet), as shown. She still needs to determine the width x of each bed. Write and solve an equation to find the width of each bed.

B Amani will make the raised beds from wood boards. In order to know how much wood to buy, Amani wants to know the distance around each bed. Find the perimeter of each bed.

C What is the total length of the wood boards that will be needed to make the four raised beds?

D The boards are only available in 8-foot lengths. How many boards will Amani have to buy? Explain.

E The cost of the boards is $1.20 per foot. Explain how to find the total cost of the boards.

© Houghton Mifflin Harcourt Publishing Company

3 Find the Cost of the Soil

Next, Jacob wants to calculate the amount of soil that will be needed to fill the four raised beds and the total cost of the soil.

A Three times the height of each bed is 0.25 feet more than the width of the bed. Write and solve an equation to find the height h of each bed.

B Complete the figure of one of the raised beds by filling in the dimensions. Write all dimensions as decimals.

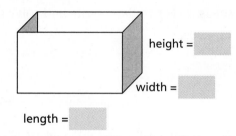

height =

width =

length =

C The volume of a rectangular prism is the product of the length times the width times the height. What is the volume of each raised bed?

D What is the total volume of the four raised beds?

E The soil is sold in bags that each contain 4.5 ft^3 of soil. Write and solve an equation to find out how many bags Jacob will have to buy in order to completely fill the four raised beds.

F The bags of soil each cost $7.45. What is the total cost of the soil for the four beds?

4 Find the Cost of the Seeds

Amani has a $10 gift card for a gardening store. She plans use her gift card to order some packets of seeds at the store's web site.

A The web site allows users to enter the number of packets of seeds they wish to purchase and find out the remaining balance on their gift card. Amani decides that she and Jacob need 9 packets of seeds. She enters this amount on the web site and sees the result at right. What does the negative card balance represent?

Value of gift card:	$10
Enter number of packets of seeds	9
Card balance:	–$11.15

B Suppose each packet of seeds costs p dollars. Write and solve an equation to find the cost of a packet of seeds.

C Amani decides she will use her gift card to buy the packets of seeds. She and Jacob will include the balance (the amount of money not covered by the gift card) in their budget. How much will they include in the budget?

5 Answer the Question

Amani and Jacob are ready to prepare their budget for their garden plot.

A Look back at your work to complete the table.

Amani and Jacob's Budget	
Item	**Total Cost**
Fence for perimeter of garden plot	
Wood boards for raised beds	
Soil for raised beds	
Seed packets	
TOTAL	

B Amani and Jacob learn that a community organization will pay for 20% of the total cost of each garden plot. This means Amani and Jacob only need to ask for 80% of their total cost when they present their budget. Multiply the total cost by 0.8 to find the final amount that will appear in their budget.

© Houghton Mifflin Harcourt Publishing Company

Performance Task

⭐ **1.** Kareem is driving home from work. The equation $24 = 30 - \frac{2}{3}m$ can be used to determine how many more minutes m he has left to drive.

   a. Solve the equation.

   b. Jen replaces the $\frac{2}{3}$ in the equation with 0.6. Will she get the same answer? Explain the difference between 0.6 and the decimal form of $\frac{2}{3}$.

⭐ **2.** Bill wants to have 2,000 songs on his mp3 player. He currently has 1,808 songs, and downloads about 2 new albums each week.

   a. Suppose an album typically has about 12 songs. Write an equation to determine how many weeks it will take for Bill to have 2,000 songs.

   b. Solve your equation from part **a**. Show your work.

⭐⭐ **3.** Jessica is going to type a manuscript that is written by hand. There are 206 pages, and the first 10 pages are already typed. She has 2 weeks (including weekends) to complete the project.

   a. Write an equation to determine how many pages per day Jessica must type to finish in 2 weeks.

b. Solve your equation from part **a**. Explain what the solution means.

c. Jessica can type 12 pages per day. Should she ask for an extension to complete the project? If so, how many days does she need? She cannot ask for a part of a day as an extension. Explain your answer.

★★★ **4.** Fred is taking an online test. To pass, he must answer $\frac{7}{10}$ of the questions correctly. There are 120 multiple-choice questions on the test. After answering 45 questions, Fred has gotten 21 correct.

a. Write and solve an equation to determine how many more questions Fred must answer correctly to pass the test.

b. What fraction of the questions has Fred gotten right so far? What fraction must he get right from now on to pass the test? Is it likely he will pass? Explain your reasoning.

© Houghton Mifflin Harcourt Publishing Company

Name _____ **Class** _____ **Date** _____

SELECTED RESPONSE

1. Solve $\frac{z}{9} + 5 = 10$.

    A. $z = 14$ **C.** $z = 135$

    B. $z = 85$ **D.** $z = 45$

2. Solve $3 + 5z = -12$.

    F. $z = -3$ **H.** $z = 1$

    G. $z = -15$ **J.** $z = -1.8$

3. Solve $y + \frac{4}{5} = -\frac{1}{10}$. Make sure your answer is in simplest form.

    A. $y = \frac{7}{10}$ **C.** $y = \frac{9}{10}$

    B. $y = -\frac{7}{10}$ **D.** $y = -\frac{9}{10}$

4. What is the value for m for this equation: $3m - 6.8 = 31$?

    F. 8.06   **H.** 37.8

    G. 12.6   **J.** 40.8

5. Solve $3.7a + 4.4 = -40$.

    A. $a = -11$ **C.** $a = -13$

    B. $a = -2$ **D.** $a = -12$

6. Solve $5 = \frac{1}{2}m + 3$.

    F. $m = 1\frac{1}{2}$ **H.** $m = 6$

    G. $m = 4$ **J.** $m = 10$

7. Solve $4b = -\frac{2}{3}$.

    A. $b = -\frac{1}{6}$ **C.** $b = \frac{8}{3}$

    B. $b = -\frac{8}{3}$ **D.** $b = \frac{1}{6}$

8. Solve $m - 13.5 = -16.5$.

    F. $m = 3$ **H.** $m = -29$

    G. $m = -3$ **J.** $m = 29$

9. Solve $-\frac{5}{6}w = -\frac{3}{5}$.

    A. $w = \frac{18}{25}$ **C.** $w = \frac{17}{60}$

    B. $w = \frac{50}{39}$ **D.** $w = \frac{7}{30}$

10. Solve $-1.7p = 3.4$.

    F. $p = -5.78$ **H.** $p = -8$

    G. $p = -0.5$ **J.** $p = -2$

11. Solve $7 = \frac{1}{2}m + 9$.

    A. $m = -1\frac{1}{2}$ **C.** $m = 46$

    B. $m = -4$ **D.** $m = -10$

12. Solve $\frac{1}{2}y + 10 = -25$.

    F. $y = -70$ **H.** $y = -30$

    G. $y = -35$ **J.** $y = 70$

13. Your class earned $110.00 Saturday afternoon by washing cars to raise money for a class trip. This is $\frac{1}{4}$ of the money needed for the trip. What is the total amount needed?

    A. $114.00

    B. $27.50

    C. $106.00

    D. $440.00

14. A group of friends share a large popcorn at the movies. It costs $3.15 to buy it and $0.85 for each refill. If they spent $7.40, how many times did the group of friends refill their popcorn? Show your work.

15. John has picked 40 apples, which is $\frac{1}{3}$ of the amount his grandmother uses to make applesauce. How many apples does she use to make applesauce? Show your work.

16. If you can find the number of bones the dog buried in the backyard this week as compared to last week by using the equation $b + 7 = 15$, then did the dog bury 22 bones, 8 bones, or 9 bones this week?

_____

_____

_____

17. By dividing the number of houses in Antonio's subdivision by 4 and adding 15, you can find the number of houses in Hector's subdivision. If Hector has 47 houses in his subdivision, how many houses are in Antonio's subdivision? Show your work.

Graphs and Functions

Chapter Focus

You will determine whether an ordered pair is a solution of an equation. You will locate and name points in the coordinate plane. You will also describe a relationship given a graph and sketch a graph given a description. A function is a rule that assigns exactly one output to each input. You will represent a function with a table or graph. Finally, you will use equations, tables, and graphs to represent relationships between two variables.

Chapter at a Glance

COMMON CORE

Lesson	Standards for Mathematical Content
2-1 Ordered Pairs	PREP FOR **CC.8.EE.8**
2-2 Graphing on a Coordinate Plane	PREP FOR **CC.8.SP.1**
2-3 Interpreting Graphs	**CC.8.F.5**
2-4 Functions	**CC.8.F.1**
2-5 Equations, Tables, and Graphs	**CC.8.F.4**
Problem Solving Connections	
Performance Task	
Assessment Readiness	

CHAPTER 2

Unpacking the Standards

Understanding the standards and the vocabulary terms in the standards will help you know exactly what you are expected to learn in this chapter.

Describe qualitatively the functional relationship between two quantities by analyzing a graph (e.g., where the function is increasing or decreasing, linear or nonlinear). Sketch a graph that exhibits the qualitative features of a function that has been described verbally.

Key Vocabulary

linear function *(función lineal)* A function whose graph is a straight line.

nonlinear function *(función no lineal)* A function whose graph is not a straight line.

What It Means to You

You will describe a function and sketch a graph that shows the features you described.

EXAMPLE

Create a graph for the situation. Tell whether the graph is continuous or discrete.

The table shows the altitude of an airplane over time.

Time (min)	Altitude (ft)
0	0
10	10,000
20	20,000
30	30,000
60	30,000
70	20,000
80	10,000
90	0

Graph points for the data in the table.

The graph is continuous.

CHAPTER 2

CC.8.F.1

Understand that a function is a rule that assigns to each input exactly one output. The graph of a function is the set of ordered pairs consisting of an input and the corresponding output.

Key Vocabulary

function *(función)* An input-output relationship that has exactly one output for each input.

input *(valor de entrada)* The value substituted into an expression or function.

output *(valor de salida)* The value that results from the substitution of a given input into an expression or function.

What It Means to You

You will generate ordered pairs of input and output values in order to graph an equation and determine if it is a function.

EXAMPLE

Make a table and a graph of $y = 2x + 1$. Then determine if the relation represents a function.

x	$2x + 1$	y
-2	$2(-2) + 1$	-3
-1	$2(-1) + 1$	-1
0	$2(0) + 1$	1
1	$2(1) + 1$	3
2	$2(2) + 1$	5

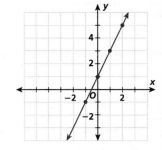

Each input x has only one output y and no vertical line will intersect the graph at more than one point. The relation is a function.

CC.8.F.4

Construct a function to model a linear relationship between two quantities. Determine the rate of change and initial value of the function from a description of a relationship or from two (x, y) values, including reading these from a table or from a graph. Interpret the rate of change and initial value of a linear function in terms of the situation it models, and in terms of its graph or a table of values.

Key Vocabulary

rate of change *(tasa de cambio)* A ratio that compares the amount of change in a dependent variable to the amount of change in an independent variable.

What It Means to You

You will learn to identify the slope of a line and the y-intercept using a table, graph, equation, or verbal description.

EXAMPLE

Use the table to make a graph and to write an equation.

x	0	1	2	3	4
y	0	6	12	18	24

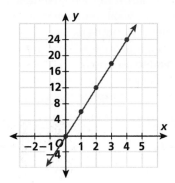

The equation is $y = 6x$

CHAPTER 2

Key Vocabulary

coordinate plane *(plano de coordenadas)* A plane formed by the intersection of a horizontal number line called the *x*-axis and a vertical number line called the *y*-axis.

function *(función)* An input-output relationship that has exactly one output for each input.

input *(valor de entrada)* The value substituted into an expression or function.

ordered pair *(par ordenado)* A pair of numbers that can be used to locate a point on a coordinate plane.

origin *(origen)* The point where the *x*-axis and *y*-axis intersect on the coordinate plane; (0, 0).

output *(valor de salida)* The value that results from the substitution of a given input into an expression or function.

quadrant *(cuadrante)* The *x*- and *y*-axes divide the coordinate plane into four regions. Each region is called a quadrant.

x-axis *(eje x)* The horizontal axis on a coordinate plane.

x-coordinate *(coordenada x)* The first number in an ordered pair; it tells the distance to move right or left from the origin (0, 0).

y-axis *(eje y)* The vertical axis on a coordinate plane.

y-coordinate *(coordenada y)* The second number in an ordered pair; it tells the distance to move up or down from the origin (0, 0).

MATHEMATICAL PRACTICE The Common Core Standards for Mathematical Practice describe varieties of expertise that mathematics educators at all levels should seek to develop in their students. Opportunities to develop these practices are integrated throughout this program.

1. **Make sense of problems and persevere in solving them.**
2. **Reason abstractly and quantitatively.**
3. **Construct viable arguments and critique the reasoning of others.**
4. **Model with mathematics.**
5. **Use appropriate tools strategically.**
6. **Attend to precision.**
7. **Look for and make use of structure.**
8. **Look for and express regularity in repeated reasoning.**

CHAPTER 2

Ordered Pairs
Going Deeper

Essential question: *How do you determine whether an ordered pair is a solution of an equation?*

An **ordered pair** (x, y) can be used to write a solution for a two-variable equation such as $y = 10x - 15$. The *order* in an *ordered* pair is important.

$(3, 15)$
↑ ↑
x-value y-value

video tutor

PREP FOR CC.8.EE.8

1 EXAMPLE Identifying an Ordered Pair as a Solution

A group of students is washing cars to raise money. They spend $15 on soap and charge $10 for each car *x*. The equation for the profit *y* is *y* = 10x − 15.

A Determine whether each ordered pair is a solution of $y = 10x - 15$.
Complete the following by substituting the correct values for each variable.

$(5, 35)$

$y = 10x - 15$
$35 \stackrel{?}{=} 10(5) - 15$
$35 \stackrel{?}{=} 50 - 15$
$35 = 35$

$(20, 195)$

$y = 10x - 15$
$195 \stackrel{?}{=} 10(\quad) - 15$
$195 \stackrel{?}{=} \quad - 15$
$195 \neq \quad$

$(50, 485)$

$y = 10x - 15$
$\quad \stackrel{?}{=} 10(\quad) - 15$
$\quad \stackrel{?}{=} \quad - 15$

Circle the correct answer.

$(5, 35)$ is / is not a solution of $y = 10x - 15$.

$(20, 195)$ is / is not a solution of $y = 10x - 15$.

$(50, 485)$ is / is not a solution of $y = 10x - 15$.

B What does the ordered pair $(50, 485)$ mean in this situation?

_____

_____

The ordered pair (x, y) represents (number of _____ , _____ in $).

TRY THIS!

Determine whether each ordered pair is a solution of $y = 10x - 15$.

1a. $(5, 25)$

1b. $(10, 75)$

1c. $(25, 235)$

_____   _____   _____

1d. **Error Analysis** A student claims that the ordered pair (10, 5) is a
solution of the equation $y = 21 - 2x$. Do you agree or disagree? Why?

_____

_____

PRACTICE

Complete each table of solutions.

1. The temperature y in Albany, NY, is 6°F
colder than the temperature x in New
York City. This situation is represented
by the equation $y = x - 6$.

x	$x - 6$	y	(x, y)
56			
48			
44			
41			

Is (60, 54) a solution to $y = x - 6$? What
does the ordered pair represent in this
situation?

_____

_____

_____

_____

2. Nate scored x number of 2-point baskets
and y number of 1-point free throws. He
scored 18 points in all. This situation is
represented by the equation $y = 18 - 2x$.

x	$18 - 2x$	y	(x, y)
3			
4			
5			
10			

Is (10, –2) a solution to $y = 18 - 2x$? What
does the ordered pair represent in this
situation and does it make sense?

_____

_____

_____

_____

3. Nina bought a frozen yogurt for $1.40. She paid with x quarters and y dimes.
Write an equation that represents the situation. Then find all ordered pair
solutions that make sense for the problem.

_____

4. Create an equation that has (3, 5) as a solution. Then give a possible
scenario for your equation.

_____

© Houghton Mifflin Harcourt Publishing Company

Additional Practice

Determine whether each ordered pair is a solution of $y = 4 + 2x$.

1. (1, 1)   2. (2, 8)   3. (0, 4)   4. (8, 2)

_____   _____   _____   _____

Determine whether each ordered pair is a solution of $y = 3x - 2$.

5. (1, 1)   6. (3, 7)   7. (5, 15)   8. (6, 16)

_____   _____   _____   _____

Use the given values to complete the table of solutions.

9. $y = x + 5$ for $x = 0, 1, 2, 3, 4$

x	$x + 5$	y	(x, y)
0			
1			
2			
3			
4			

10. $y = 3x + 1$ for $x = 1, 2, 3, 4, 5$

x	$3x + 1$	y	(x, y)
1			
2			
3			
4			
5			

11. $y = 2x + 6$ for $x = 0, 1, 2, 3, 4$

x	$2x + 6$	y	(x, y)
0			
1			
2			
3			
4			

12. $y = 4x - 2$ for $x = 2, 4, 6, 8, 10$

x	$4x - 2$	y	(x, y)
2			
4			
6			
8			
10			

13. Alexis opened a savings account with a $120 deposit. Each week she will put $20 into the account. The equation that gives the total amount t in her account is $t = 120 + 20w$, where w is the number of weeks since she opened the account. How much money will Alexis have in her savings account after 5 weeks?

_____

Problem Solving

Use the table at the right for Exercises 1–2.

1. Write the ordered pair that shows the average miles per gallon in 1990.

   _____

2. The data can be approximated by the equation $m = 0.30887x - 595$ where m is the average miles per gallon and x is the year. Use the equation to find an ordered pair (x, m) that shows the estimated miles per gallon in the year 2020.

   _____

Average Miles per Gallon

Year	Miles per Gallon
1970	13.5
1980	15.9
1990	20.2
1995	21.1
1996	21.2
1997	21.5

For Exercises 3–4 use the equation $F = 1.8C + 32$, which relates Fahrenheit temperatures F to Celsius temperatures C.

3. Write ordered pair (C, F) that shows the Celsius equivalent of 86 °F.

   _____

4. Write ordered pair (C, F) that shows the Fahrenheit equivalent of 22 °C.

   _____

Choose the letter for the best answer.

5. A taxi charges a $2.50 flat fee plus $0.30 per mile. Use an equation for taxi fare t in terms of miles m. Which ordered pair (m, t) shows the taxi fare for a 23-mile cab ride?

   A (23, 6.90) C (23, 9.40)

   B (23, 18.50) D (23, 64.40)

6. The perimeter p of a square is four times the length of a side s, or $p = 4s$. Which ordered pair (s, p) shows the perimeter for a square that has sides that are 5 in.?

   F (5, 1.25) H (5, 9)

   G (5, 20) J (5, 25)

7. Maria pays a monthly fee of $3.95 plus $0.10 per minute for long-distance calls. Use an equation for the phone bill p in terms of the number of minutes m. Which ordered pair (m, p) shows the phone bill for 120 minutes?

   A (120, 15.95) C (120, 28.30)

   B (120, 474.10) D (120, 486.00)

8. Tickets to a baseball game cost $12 each, plus $2 each for transportation. Use an equation for the cost c of going to the game in terms of the number of people p. Which ordered pair (p, c) shows the cost for 6 people?

   F (6, 74) H (6, 84)

   G (6, 96) J (6, 102)

2-2

Graphing on a Coordinate Plane
Going Deeper

Essential question: *How do you locate and name points in the coordinate plane?*

video tutor

The **coordinate plane** is formed by two number lines: the **x-axis**, which is a horizontal number line, and the **y-axis**, a vertical number line. These axes intersect at right angles to divide the plane into four **quadrants**.

The point where the two axes intersect is the **origin** and labeled by the ordered pair (0, 0). In an ordered pair (x, y), the first number is the **x-coordinate**. It tells how many units to move **right** or **left**. The **y-coordinate** tells how many units to move **up** or **down**.

Move **up** or **down**

(x, y)

Move **right** or **left**

PREP FOR **CC.8.SP.1**

1 EXAMPLE **Graphing Points in the Coordinate Plane**

An air traffic operator stationed at (0, 0) reports airplane *A* at (4, 3), which represents 4 miles east and 3 miles north of her location. She spots airplane *B* at (−3, −2), or 3 miles west and 2 miles south, and airplane *C* at (5.5, −2), or 5.5 miles east and 2 miles south. Graph the location of each airplane.

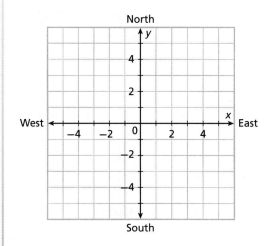

Airplane *A*: (4, 3)

    4 units right, 3 units up

Airplane *B*: (−3,   )

    3 units left, 2 units down

Airplane *C*: (5.5, −2)

    5.5 units _____, 2 units _____

TRY THIS!

1a. Using the same coordinate plane, graph the location of airplane *D* at $\left(-3, 3\frac{1}{2}\right)$ and airplane *E* at (0, −4).

1b. What does the location $\left(-3, 3\frac{1}{2}\right)$ represent?

_____

_____

1c. How far is airplane *B* from airplane *D*? How can you use the coordinate plane to determine this distance?

_____

_____

1d. What do you know when an ordered pair has the same *x*- and *y*-coordinate?

_____

_____

PRACTICE

Use the coordinate plane for 1–8.

Write an ordered pair to represent each location. Then graph ordered pairs not shown on the coordinate plane.

1. The public library is located at *M*.

$M(\quad , \quad)$

This coordinate plane represents a neighborhood measured in blocks.

2. The fire station is located at *N*.

$N(\quad , \quad)$

3. Ben, Carlos, and Deena live in a house located at the origin.

$O(\quad , \quad)$

4. From home, Ben walks 2 blocks east, turns and walks 4.5 blocks south, and stops.

$B(\quad , \quad)$

5. Carlos starts from home, walks 4.5 blocks north, walks west for 2.5 blocks, and then stops.

$C(\quad , \quad)$

6. Deena walks 4 blocks west from home, turns and walks 4.5 blocks south, and then stops.

$D(\quad , \quad)$

7. How far from Ben is Deena at the end of their walks?

8. There is a pizza restaurant halfway between Deena's location and Ben's location. What are the coordinates of the restaurant? How far will they each have to walk to meet there?

Additional Practice

Give the coordinates and quadrant of each point.

1. *F*

   _____

2. *X*

   _____

3. *T*

   _____

4. *B*

   _____

5. *D*

   _____

6. *R*

   _____

7. *H*

   _____

8. *Y*

   _____

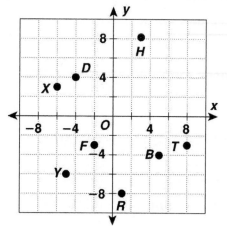

Graph each point on a coordinate plane.

9. $A(2\frac{1}{2}, 1)$

10. $B(0, 4)$

11. $C(2, -1.5)$

12. $D(-2, 3.5)$

13. $E(-2\frac{1}{3}, 0)$

14. $F(-1\frac{1}{2}, -3)$

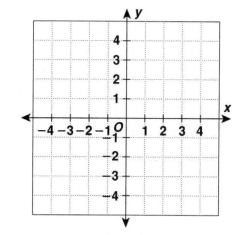

Find the distance between each pair of points.

15. *A* and *B*

    _____

16. *C* and *D*

    _____

17. *D* and *E*

    _____

18. *E* and *F*

    _____

Problem Solving

Graph the points to answer each question.

1. Graph the points (–4, 1), (–4, –2), (1, 1), and (1, –2).

2. What type of quadrilateral do the vertices form?

    _____

3. What is the perimeter of the figure?

    _____

4. What is the area of the figure?

    _____

5. Graph the points (–3, 1), (–3, –5), (3, 1), and (3, –5).

6. What type of polygon do the vertices form?

    _____

7. What is the perimeter of the figure?

    _____

8. What is the area of the figure?

    _____

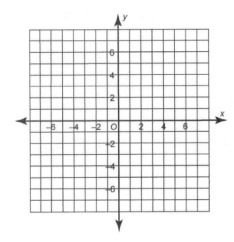

Solve each problem.

9. The point (4, –2) is in which quadrant?

    A I   C III

    B II   D IV

10. The point (–1, 7) is in which quadrant?

    A I   C III

    B II   D IV

11. Which of the following points is the same distance from (–2, 3) as (3, 3)?

    A (3, –2)   C (3, 8)

    B (–2, –2)   D (–1, 3)

12. A rectangle is formed with the vertices (0, 0), (6, 0), and (0, 5). Which point is the fourth vertex of the rectangle?

    A (–6, 5)   C (6, 5)

    B (5, 5)   D (0, –5)

Interpreting Graphs
Going Deeper

Essential question: *How can you describe a relationship given a graph and sketch a graph given a description?*

CC.8.F.5

1 **E X P L O R E** **Interpreting Graphs**

A roller coaster park is open from May to October each year. The graph shows the number of park visitors over its season.

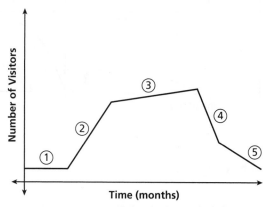

A Segment 1 shows that attendance during the opening days of the park's season stayed constant. Describe what Segment 2 shows.

_____

_____

B Based on the time frame, give a possible explanation for the change in attendance represented by Segment 2.

_____

_____

C Which segments of the graph show decreasing attendance? Give a possible explanation.

_____

_____

REFLECT

1. Explain how the slant of each segment of the graph is related to whether attendance increases or decreases.

_____

_____

2 EXPLORE   Matching Graphs to Situations

Grace, Jet, and Mike are studying 100 words for a spelling bee.

- **Grace started by learning many words each day, but then learned fewer and fewer words each day.**
- **Jet learned the same number of words each day.**
- **Mike started by learning only a few words each day, but then learned a greater number of words each day.**

Match each student's study progress with the correct graph.

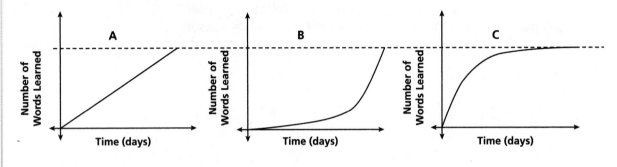

_____   _____   _____

A Describe the progress represented by Graph A.

_____

_____

_____

B Describe the progress represented by Graph B.

_____

_____

_____

C Describe the progress represented by Graph C.

_____

_____

_____

D Determine which graph represents each student's study progress and write the students' names under the appropriate graphs.

REFLECT

2. What would it mean if one of the graphs slanted downward from left to right?

_____

_____

3 EXPLORE   Sketching a Graph for a Situation

Mrs. Sutton provides free math tutoring to her students every day after school. No one comes to tutoring sessions during the first week of school. Over the next two weeks, use of the tutoring service gradually increases.

A Sketch a graph showing the number of students who use the tutoring service over the first three weeks of school.

B Mrs. Sutton's students are told that they will have a math test at the end of the fifth week of school. How do you think this will affect the number of students who come to tutoring?

_____

_____

C Considering your answer to **B**, sketch a graph showing the number of students who might use the tutoring service over the first six weeks of school.

REFLECT

3a. Suppose Mrs. Sutton offered bonus credit to students who came to tutoring sessions. How do you think this would affect the number of students who come to tutoring?

_____

_____

3b. How would your answer to **3a** affect the graph?

_____

_____

In a lab environment, colonies of bacteria follow a predictable pattern of growth. The graph shows this growth over time.

1. During which phase is growth slowest? During which phase is growth fastest? Explain.

_____

_____

_____

_____

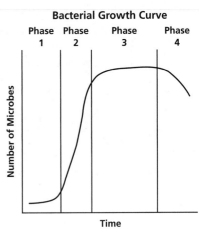

Bacterial Growth Curve

Phase 1 Phase 2 Phase 3 Phase 4

Number of Microbes

Time

2. What is happening to the population during Phase 3?

_____

_____

_____

3. What is happening to the population during Phase 4?

_____

_____

A woodland area on an island contains a population of foxes. The graph describes the changes in the fox population over time.

4. What is happening to the fox population before time *t*?

_____

_____

Fox Population

Population

Time

t

5. At time *t*, a conservation organization moves a large group of foxes to the island. Sketch a graph to show how this action might affect the population on the island after time *t*.

6. At some point after time *t*, a forest fire destroys part of the woodland area on the island. Describe how your graph from problem **5** might change.

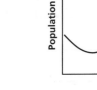

Fox Population

Population

Time

t

_____

_____

_____

Additional Practice

The table gives the speed of three dogs in mi/h at the given times.
Tell which dog corresponds to each situation described below.

Time	5:00	5:01	5:02	5:03	5:04
Dog 1	0	1	12	0	0
Dog 2	5	23	4	0	0
Dog 3	14	0	18	2	9

1. Leshaan walks his dog. Then he lets the dog off the leash
   and it runs around the yard. Then they go into the house
   and the dog stands eating from his dog dish and drinking
   from his water bowl. _____

2. Luke's dog is chasing its tail. Then it stops and pants. The
   dog then runs to the backyard fence and walks along the
   fence, barking at a neighbor. Then it runs to Luke at the
   back door. _____

Tell which graph corresponds to each situation in Exercises 1–2.

3.

4.

_____   _____

5. Create a graph that illustrates the temperature
   inside the car.

Location	Temperature on Arrival	Temperature on Departure
Home	—	74° at 8:30
Summer job	77° at 9:00	128° at 12:05
Pool	92° at 12:15	136° at 2:30
Library	95° at 2:40	77° at 5:10

Problem Solving

Sketch a graph that illustrates each situation.

1. Ryan walks for several blocks, and then he begins to run. After running for 10 minutes, he walks for several blocks and then stops.

2. Susanna starts running. After 10 minutes, she sees a friend and stops to talk. When she leaves her friend, she runs home and stops.

3. Mark stands on the porch and talks to a friend. Then he starts walking home. Part way home he decides to run the rest of the way, and he doesn't stop until he gets home.

The graph represents the height of water in a bathtub over time. Choose the correct letter.

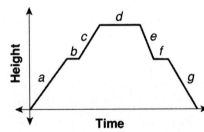

4. Which part of the graph best represents the tub being filled with water?

    A a   C c

    B d   D g

5. Which part of the graph shows the tub being drained of water?

    A c   C d

    B e   D g

6. Which part of the graph shows someone soaking in the tub?

    F b   H d

    G e   J f

7. Which part of the graph shows when someone gets into the tub?

    A a   C c

    B e   D f

8. Which parts of the graph show when the water level is not changing in the tub?

    F a, b, c   H b, d, g

    G b, d, f   J c, e, f

Functions
Going Deeper

Essential question: *How do you represent a function with a table or graph?*

CC.8.F.1

1 EXPLORE   **Understanding Relationships**

Carlos needs to buy some new pencils from the school supply cabinet at school. Carlos asks his classmates if they know how much pencils cost. Angela says she bought 2 pencils for $0.50. Paige bought 3 pencils for $0.75, and Spencer bought 4 pencils for $1.00.

Carlos thinks about the rule for the price of a pencil as a machine. When he puts the number of pencils he wants to buy into the machine, the machine applies a rule and tells him the total cost of that number of pencils.

	Number of pencils	Rule	Cost of pencils
i.	2	?	
ii.	3	?	
iii.	4	?	
iv.	x		
v.	12		

A   Use the prices in the problem to fill in rows **i–iii** of the table.

B   Describe any patterns you see. Use your pattern to determine the cost of 1 pencil.

_____

_____

C   Use the pattern you identified to write the rule applied by the machine. Write the rule as an algebraic expression and fill in row **iv** of the table.

D   Carlos wants to buy 12 pencils. Use your rule to fill in row **v** of the table to show how much Carlos will pay for 12 pencils.

There are 6 pencil-top erasers in 2 packages of erasers. There are 9 erasers in 3 packages.

1a. Write a rule in words for the number of packages Carlos needs to buy to get *x* erasers. Then write the rule as an algebraic expression.

_____

1b. How many packages does Carlos need to buy to get 18 erasers?

_____

REFLECT

1c. How can you decide what operation to use in your rule?

_____

_____

_____

The rules in ① are functions, and the machines are function machines. The value that is put into a function machine is the **input**. The result after applying the function machine's rule is the **output**. A **function** is a rule that assigns exactly one output to each input.

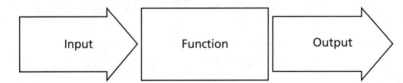

A table of values can represent a function if each input value is paired with only one output value.

CC.8.F.1
2 EXAMPLE Recognizing Functions

Tell whether each relationship is a function.

A
Input	Output
15	70
60	88
75	95
45	80

Each input has only one _____.

This relationship _____ a function.

B

Input	Output
14	60
13	55
14	57
15	52

The input _____ has more than one output.

This relationship _____ a function.

The input values (x) and output values (y) of a function can be displayed in a table or written as ordered pairs (x, y). These ordered pairs can be graphed in the coordinate plane to show a graph of the function.

Some function rules can be written as equations such as $y = 2x$. By substituting values for x, you can generate corresponding y-values. The ordered pairs (x, y) are solutions of the equation.

CC.8.F.1

3 EXAMPLE   **Graphing a Function**

Graph the function $y = 2x + 3$.

Create a table of values.

x	$2x + 3$	y
−4	$2(-4) + 3$	
−1	$2(\quad) + 3$	
0		
2		
3		

Write ordered pairs.

(x, y)
$\left(-4, \quad\right)$
$\left(-1, \quad\right)$
$\left(0, \quad\right)$
$\left(\quad, \quad\right)$
$\left(\quad, \quad\right)$

Graph the ordered pairs.

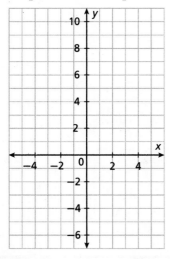

Draw a line through the points to represent all the possible x-values and their corresponding y-values.

Fill in each table. In the row with *x* as the input, write a rule as an algebraic expression for the output. Then complete the last row of the table using the rule.

1.

Input	Output
Tickets	Cost ($)
2	40
5	100
7	140
8	160
x	
10	

2.

Input	Output
Minutes	Pages Read
2	1
10	5
20	10
30	15
x	
60	

3.

Input	Output
Muffins	Cost ($)
1	2.25
3	6.75
6	13.50
12	27.00
x	
18	

Tell whether each relationship is a function.

4.

Input	6	7	8	7	9
Output	75	80	87	88	95

5.

Input	1	2	3	4	5
Output	4	8	12	16	20

_____

_____

6. (1, 3), (2, 5), (3, 0), (4, −1), (5, 5)

7. (2, 7), (6, 4), (0, 3), (2, 6), (1, 5)

_____

_____

Graph each function on the coordinate plane.

8. $y = -2x$

9. $y = x - 3$

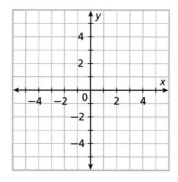

Additional Practice

Complete the table and graph each function.

1. $y = -2x + 5$

x	−2x + 5	y
−2		
−1		
0		
1		
2		

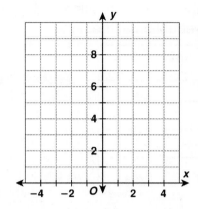

2. $y = x - 2$

x	x − 2	y
−2		
−1		
0		
1		
2		

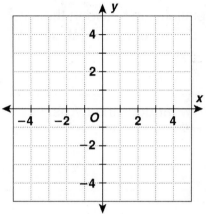

Determine if each relation represents a function.

3. (−2, 1), (−1, 2), (0, 3), (1, 4)

_____

4.

x	1	2	1	2
y	6	5	−6	−5

_____

5.

x	y
0	0
1	−1
2	−8
3	−27
4	−64

_____

6. (7, −1), (9, −7), (7, 0), (12, −1), (15, 0)

_____

Problem Solving

A cyclist rides at an average speed of 20 miles per hour. The equation $y = 20x$ shows the distance, y, the cyclist travels in x hours.

1. Make a table for the equation and graph the equation at the right.

x	20x	y
0		
1		
2		
3		

2. Is the relationship between the time and the distance the cyclist rides a function?

_____

3. If the cyclist continues to ride at the same rate, about how far will the cyclist ride in 4 hours?

_____

4. About how far does the cyclist ride in 1.5 hours?

_____

5. If the cyclist has ridden 50 miles, about how long has the cyclist been riding?

_____

The cost of renting a jet-ski at a lake is represented by the equation $f(x) = 25x + 100$ where x is the number of hours and $f(x)$ is the cost including an hourly rate and a deposit. Choose the letter for the best answer.

6. How much does it cost to rent the jet-ski for 5 hours?

   A $125
   B $225
   C $385
   D $525

7. If the cost to rent the jet-ski is $300, for how many hours is the jet-ski rented?

   F 6 hours
   G 8 hours
   H 12 hours
   J 16 hours

© Houghton Mifflin Harcourt Publishing Company

2-5

Equations, Tables, and Graphs
Going Deeper

Essential question: *How can you use equations, tables, and graphs to represent relationships between two variables?*

video tutor

CC.8.F.4

1 E X A M P L E Generating Different Representations of Data

Lisa and Leon work after school at their uncle's store. The table shows the hours Lisa worked x and the hours Leon worked y each week for a month.

Lisa, x	3	4	6	8
Leon, y	5	6	8	10

A Write an equation from the data in the table.

Compare each output value with its corresponding input value.

Lisa, x	3	4	6	8	← input values
Leon, y	5	6	8	10	← output values

$5 - 3 = \blacksquare$ $6 - \blacksquare = \blacksquare$ $\blacksquare - \blacksquare = \blacksquare$ $\blacksquare - \blacksquare = \blacksquare$

For each hour Lisa worked, Leon worked _____ more hours.

The equation is Leon = Lisa + $\blacksquare$.

$$y = \blacksquare + \blacksquare$$

B Make a graph of the data.

Write the input and output values as ordered pairs.

x	y	(x, y)
3	5	(3, 5)
4	6	(4, $\blacksquare$)
6	8	($\blacksquare$, $\blacksquare$)
8	10	($\blacksquare$, $\blacksquare$)

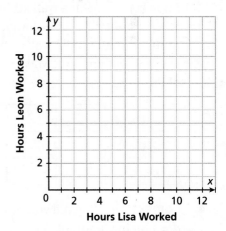

Then plot the ordered pairs and connect the points with a line.

TRY THIS!

1a. Write an equation from the data in the table. Then write the input and output values as ordered pairs.

_____

x	0	1	2	3
y	0	3	6	9
(x, y)				

1b. How can you use the graph to predict the number of hours Leon will work when Lisa works 10 hours?

_____

_____

_____

PRACTICE

Complete each table to write an equation. Use the same grid to graph each equation.

1.

x	0	1	3	5
y	4	5	7	9
(x, y)				

_____

2.

x	0	−1	−2	−3
y	0	2	4	6
(x, y)				

_____

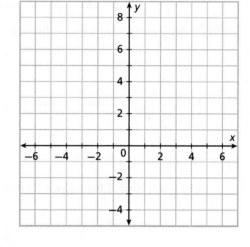

3. Lupe is walking in a walkathon. The distance she walks is represented by the equation $d = 1.5h$, where h is the number of hours she walks and 1.5 is how many miles she walks in an hour. Make a table and sketch a graph of the data.

h	0	2	4	6
d				
(h, d)				

4. Conjecture Why did you not graph the equation $d = 1.5h$ in Quadrant IV?

_____

5. Over 5 days, the temperatures in Chicago, in °F, were 0, −2, −3, −1, and 2. On those same days, the temperatures in Detroit were three degrees warmer. Write an equation and sketch a graph of the data.

_____

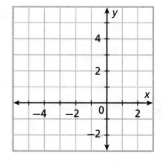

Additional Practice

1. The amount of water in a tank being filled is represented by the equation $g = 20m$, where g is the number of gallons in the tank after m minutes. Complete the table and sketch a graph of the equation.

m	20m	g
0		
1		
2		
3		
4		

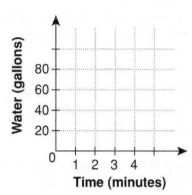

2. Use the table to make a graph and to write an equation.

x	0	2	5	8	12
y	4	6	9	12	16

_____

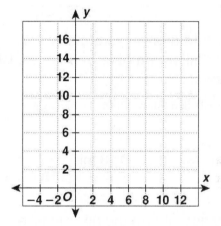

3. Use the graph to make a table and to write an equation.

x					
y					

_____

Problem Solving

Use the graph to answer Exercises 1–4. An aquarium tank is being drained. The graph shows the number of gallons of water, *q*, in the tank after *m* minutes. Write the correct answer.

1. How many gallons of water are in the tank before it is drained?

   _____

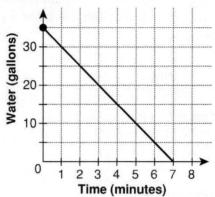

2. How many gallons of water are left in the tank after 2 minutes?

   _____

3. How long does it take until there are 10 gallons of water left in the tank?

   _____

4. How long does it take to drain the tank?

   _____

Use the graph to answer Exercises 5–7. The graph shows the distance, *d*, a hiker can hike in *h* hours. Choose the letter of the best answer.

5. How far can the hiker hike in 4 hours?

   A $1\frac{1}{3}$ mi   C 8 mi

   B 4 mi   D 12 mi

6. How long does it take the hiker to hike 6 miles?

   F 2 *h*   H 4 *h*

   G 3 *h*   J 18 *h*

7. Which equation represents the graph?

   A $d = 3h$ C $d = h + 3$

   B $d = \frac{1}{3}h$ D $d = h - 3$

Problem Solving Connections

Which Is Which? Sonia is writing an article about places to rent inline skates in her town. She collected data about Wheel World, Super Skates, and Roller Rentals. Unfortunately, the names of the skate shops got separated from the data. How can Sonia use her notes to match the names to the data?

1 Compare Rental Data

Sonia calls the skate shops A, B, and C until she figures out which is which. She starts by looking at graphs that show the number of daily rentals over the course of a year (January through December).

A   Describe what each segment shows in the graph for Shop A.

B   What does the graph for Shop B tell you about rentals at that shop?

C   Shop C is closed for the first 3 months of the year. Then the number of daily rentals increases quickly. It remains constant throughout the summer. Toward the end of the year, the number of daily rentals increases very slowly. Use the above axes to sketch a graph that shows this information.

2 Analyze Pricing at Shop A

Sonia looks through her notes and finds a table that gives information about the cost of inline skate rentals at Shop A.

A Look for patterns to complete the table.

Number of Hours, x	2	3	4	5	6
Cost of Rental, y	$5.00	$7.50		$12.50	

B What is the cost of renting inline skates for 1 hour?

C Write an equation that gives the cost y of renting skates for x hours.

D Is the ordered pair (8, 20) a solution of the equation? Why or why not?

E What does the ordered pair (8, 20) represent in this situation?

F Write the values from the above table as ordered pairs.

G Plot the ordered pairs on the coordinate plane to help you graph the equation. Then describe the graph.

3 Analyze Pricing at Shop B

Sonia's notes also include some information about pricing at Shop B. At this shop, the cost y of renting inline skates for x hours is given by $y = 1.50x + 3$.

A Is the ordered pair $(2, 8)$ a solution of the equation? Why or why not?

B Complete the table of values.

Number of Hours, x	1	2	3	4	5
Cost of Rental, y					

C Write the values from the table as ordered pairs.

D Plot the ordered pairs on the coordinate plane to help you graph the equation. Then describe the graph.

E Explain how to use the graph to find the cost of renting inline skates for 6 hours from Shop B.

4 Analyze Pricing at Shop C

Sonia's notes include this table that gives the price of renting inline skates at Shop C.

Number of Hours, x	Cost of Rental, y
1	$7.50
2	$7.50
3	$7.50
4	$7.50
5	$7.50

A Is the relationship shown in the table a function? Why or why not?

B Make a graph that shows the cost of renting inline skates at Shop C. Then describe the graph.

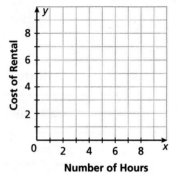

C What do the table and graph tell you about the cost of renting skates at Shop C?

5 Answer the Question

Sonia discovers that her notes include a scrap of paper with some information she jotted down.

A Use the information on the scrap of paper to determine which shop is which. Write the names of the shops in the table.

- At Wheel World, it costs $7.50 to rent inline skates for 3 hours.
- Super Skates has their busiest time of the year at the end of the year.
- At Roller Rentals, a 7-hour rental costs $13.50.

Skate Shop	Name of Shop
Shop A	
Shop B	
Shop C	

CHAPTER 2

Performance Task

COMMON
CORE

CC.8.F.1
CC.8.F.2
CC.8.F.4
CC.8.F.5

⭐ **1.** Tericho earns $8.80 per hour working at an ice cream shop. Janelle's earnings at a drugstore follow the pattern in the table.

Number of Hours	3	7	12	20
Earnings	$25.50	$59.50	$102	$170

Who makes more money per hour? By how much?

⭐ **2.** Members of the Band Boosters Club pay yearly dues of $25 and $8.95 to attend each monthly luncheon. Write a function that describes this situation. Then find the total that a Band Booster would spend in a year if he attends 10 of the monthly luncheons.

⭐ **3.** Aimee dove off the pier and swam out into the lake. The given set of
⭐ ordered pairs represent the number of seconds since she left the pier and the distance in feet she is from the pier.

(2, 10), (5, 15), (12, 43), (15, 49), (18, 49), (20, 46), (22, 36)

a. Is this relation a function? Explain.

b. Graph the ordered pairs and connect them with line segments. Where is the graph increasing? Where is it decreasing?

c. What might Aimee be doing between 15 and 18 seconds after she leaves the pier?

4. A train travels at an average speed of 60 miles per hour from Portland to Los Angeles, a distance of 963 miles. Susanna is taking the train to Los Angeles to see a football game. The game is at 8 PM and it takes her 30 minutes to get from the train station to her seat in the stadium.

a. By what time does the train need to leave Portland for Susanna to arrive in time? As part of your answer, write a function that describes the situation.

b. Susanna does not want to leave Portland later than 10 PM or earlier than 6 AM. Does the train in part **a** meet her requirements? If not, give a new departure time that would allow her to still get to the game on time, and find the arrival time of that train.

© Houghton Mifflin Harcourt Publishing Company

Name _____ Class _____ Date _____

SELECTED RESPONSE

1. Gloria drives her daughter to school in the morning and then comes back home. She stays home until she has to go to pick up her daughter from school, and then they both return home again. Which graph best shows the situation?

   A.

   C.

   B.

   D.

2. Which situation is best represented by the graph?

   F. A swimmer starts at a steady pace, slows down to a stop, and then starts up swimming again, but at a slower pace than when she first started.

   G. After a ball is thrown into the air, it falls back to the ground and bounces.

   H. An airplane starts slowly on the runway, and then quickly takes off before finding a nice cruising speed.

   J. A car starts on flat ground and drives quickly up a hill, and then it keeps driving.

3. Determine if the relation represents a function.

x	y
0	−5
1	−1
2	3
3	6

   A. The relation is a function.

   B. The relation is not a function.

4. The data in the table below form a function. What values in the table would change the relation to NOT be a function?

x	y
4	9
6	1
0	2
−2	7
−8	10

   F. $(1, 9)$

   G. $(−3, 7)$

   H. $(9, 4)$

   J. $(6, 5)$

5. Choose the equation that is represented by the data in the table.

b	c
−1	5
0	6
1	7
2	8

   A. $b = c + 4$ **C.** $c = b − 4$

   B. $c = b − 6$ **D.** $c = b + 6$

6. Which table is a function table for $y = -3x + 3$?

F.

x	−3	0	3	6	9
y	−2	−1	0	1	2

G.

x	−2	−1	0	1	2
y	9	6	3	0	−3

H.

x	−2	−1	0	1	2
y	−3	0	3	6	9

J.

x	9	6	3	0	−3
y	−2	−1	0	1	2

CONSTRUCTED RESPONSE

7. Robert starts walking on a flat surface. He goes up a gradual incline until he reaches its peak, and then he immediately starts down a gradual decline. After reaching the bottom of the decline, he continues walking on a flat surface. Make a graph of elevation versus time to demonstrate this situation. Explain your graph.

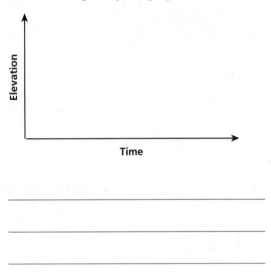

_____

_____

_____

_____

_____

_____

_____

8. Write a statement that best tells the story of the graph.

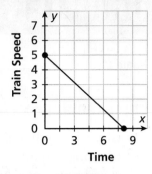

_____

_____

_____

9. Find the output for each input.

Input	Rule	Output
x	$-9x + 15$	y
−5		
1		
3		

10. Gasoline is pumped at a rate of 3 gallons per minute into a container that already has 4 gallons inside it. Write a linear function that describes the amount of gas in the container over time. Then make a graph to show the amount of gas in the container over the first 5 minutes.

_____

Exponents and Roots

Chapter Focus

You will evaluate expressions with negative exponents and develop and use the properties of integer exponents. You will use scientific notation to express very large and very small quantities. You will also add, subtract, multiply, and divide using scientific notation. The square root of a positive number p is x if $x^2 = p$. The cube root of a positive number p is x if $x^3 = p$ You will evaluate square roots of perfect squares and cube roots of perfect cubes. You will estimate the square root of numbers that are not perfect squares and compare and order irrational numbers. You will determine whether a number is rational or irrational. Finally, you will prove the Pythagorean Theorem and its converse and use the Pythagorean Theorem to solve problems.

Chapter at a Glance

COMMON CORE

Lesson	Standards for Mathematical Content
3-1 Integer Exponents	CC.8.EE.1
3-2 Properties of Exponents	CC.8.EE.1
3-3 Scientific Notation	CC.8.EE.3
3-4 Operating with Scientific Notation	CC.8.EE.4
3-5 Squares and Square Roots	CC.8.EE.2
3-6 Estimating Square Roots	CC.8.NS.2
3-7 The Real Numbers	CC.8.NS.1
3-8 The Pythagorean Theorem	CC.8.G.7, CC.8.G.8
3-9 Applying the Pythagorean Theorem and Its Converse	CC.8.G.6
Problem Solving Connections	
Performance Task	
Assessment Readiness	

CHAPTER 3

Unpacking the Standards

Understanding the standards and the vocabulary terms in the standards will help you know exactly what you are expected to learn in this chapter.

COMMON CORE CC.8.EE.1

Know and apply the properties of integer exponents to generate equivalent numerical expressions.

Key Vocabulary

integers *(enteros)* The set of whole numbers and their opposites.

exponent *(exponente)* The number that indicates how many times the base is used as a factor.

What It Means to You

You will simplify expressions involving positive and negative exponents.

EXAMPLE
Simplify.

$$5^4 \cdot 5^3 \qquad \frac{10^8}{10^5} \qquad (2^{-7})^{-2}$$

$$= 5^{4+3} \qquad = 10^{8-5} \qquad = 2^{-7\cdot(-2)}$$

$$= 5^7 \qquad = 10^3 \qquad = 2^{14}$$

COMMON CORE CC.8.EE.4

Perform operations with numbers expressed in scientific notation, including problems where both decimal and scientific notation are used. Use scientific notation and choose units of appropriate size for measurements of very large or very small quantities (e.g., use millimeters per year for seafloor spreading). Interpret scientific notation that has been generated by technology.

Key Vocabulary

scientific notation *(notación científica)* A method of writing very large or very small numbers by using powers of 10.

What It Means to You

You will perform operations with numbers written in scientific notation.

EXAMPLE
The mass of Jupiter is 1.89×10^{27} kg, and the mass of Earth is 5.97×10^{24} kg. About how many times greater is the mass of Jupiter than the mass of Earth? Write your answer is scientific notation.

$$\frac{1.89 \times 10^{27} \text{ kg}}{5.97 \times 10^{24} \text{ kg}}$$

$$= \frac{1.89}{5.97} \times \frac{10^{27}}{10^{24}}$$

$$= 0.3166 \times 10^3$$

$$= 3.166 \times 10^2$$

Jupiter's mass is about 3.166×10^2 times the mass of Earth.

COMMON CORE **CC.8.EE.2**

Use square root and cube root symbols to represent solutions to equations of the form $x^2 = p$ and $x^3 = p$, where p is a positive rational number. Evaluate square roots of small perfect squares and cube roots of small perfect cubes. Know that $\sqrt{2}$ is irrational.

Key Vocabulary

square root *(raíz quadrada)* A number that is multiplied by itself to form a product is called a square root of that product.

cube root *(raíz cúbica)* A number that is raised to the third power to form a product is called a cube root of that product.

perfect square *(cuadrado perfecto)* A square of a whole number.

perfect cube *(cubo perfecto)* A cube of a whole number.

What It Means to You

You will find square roots and cube roots.

EXAMPLE

A square window has an area of 169 square inches. How wide is the window?

$$S^2 = 169$$

$$S^2 = \pm\sqrt{169}$$

$$S = \pm 13$$

The window is 13 inches wide.

COMMON CORE **CC.8.G.7**

Apply the Pythagorean Theorem to determine unknown side lengths in right triangles in real-world and mathematical problems in two and three dimensions.

Key Vocabulary

Pythagorean Theorem *(Teorema de Pitágoras)* In a right triangle, the square of the length of the hypotenuse is equal to the sum of the squares of the lengths of the legs.

What It Means to You

You will use the Pythagorean Theorem to find the lengths of sides in a right triangle.

EXAMPLE

Mark and Sarah start walking at the same point, but Mark walks 50 feet north while Sarah walks 75 feet east. How far apart are Mark and Sarah when they stop?

$$a^2 + b^2 = c^2$$

$$50^2 + 75^2 = c^2$$

$$2500 + 5625 = c^2$$

$$8125 = c^2$$

$$90.1 \approx c$$

Mark and Sarah are approximately 90.1 feet apart.

CHAPTER 3

Key Vocabulary

cube root *(raíz cúbica)* A number that is multiplied 3 times to form a product is called a cube root of that product.

hypotenuse *(hipotenusa)* In a right triangle, the side opposite the right angle.

irrational number *(número irracional)* A number that cannot be expressed as a ratio of two integers or as a repeating or terminating decimal.

legs *(catetos)* In a right triangle, the sides that include the right angle; in an isosceles triangle, the pair of congruent sides.

perfect cube *(cubo perfecto)* A cube of a whole number.

perfect square *(cuadrado perfecto)* A square of a whole number.

principal square root *(raíz cuadrada principal)* The nonnegative square root of a number.

real numbers *(número real)* A rational or irrational number.

scientific notation *(notación científica)* A method of writing very large or very small numbers by using powers of 10.

square root *(raíz quadrada)* A number that is multiplied by itself to form a product is called a square root of that product.

MATHEMATICAL PRACTICE

The Common Core Standards for Mathematical Practice describe varieties of expertise that mathematics educators at all levels should seek to develop in their students. Opportunities to develop these practices are integrated throughout this program.

1. **Make sense of problems and persevere in solving them.**
2. **Reason abstractly and quantitatively.**
3. **Construct viable arguments and critique the reasoning of others.**
4. **Model with mathematics.**
5. **Use appropriate tools strategically.**
6. **Attend to precision.**
7. **Look for and make use of structure.**
8. **Look for and express regularity in repeated reasoning.**

Integer Exponents
Reasoning

Essential question: *How can you evaluate negative exponents?*

CC.8.EE.1

1 **E X P L O R E**   **Using Patterns of Integer Exponents**

The table below shows powers of 5, 4, and 3.

$5^4 = 625$	$5^3 = 125$	$5^2 = 25$	$5^1 = 5$	$5^0 =$	$5^{-1} =$	$5^{-2} =$
$4^4 = 256$	$4^3 = 64$	$4^2 = 16$	$4^1 = 4$	$4^0 =$	$4^{-1} =$	$4^{-2} =$
$3^4 = 81$	$3^3 = 27$	$3^2 = 9$	$3^1 = 3$	$3^0 =$	$3^{-1} =$	$3^{-2} =$

A   What pattern do you see in the powers of 5?

_____

_____

B   What pattern do you see in the powers of 4?

_____

_____

C   Complete the table for the values of $5^0, 5^{-1}, 5^{-2}$.

D   Complete the table for the values of $4^0, 4^{-1}, 4^{-2}$.

E   Complete the table for the values of $3^0, 3^{-1}, 3^{-2}$.

F   **Conjecture** Write a general rule for the values of a^0 and a^{-n} based on the patterns in the table.

_____

TRY THIS!

Find the value of each power.

1a. 6^{-4} **1b.** 12^0 **1c.** 8^{-1} **1d.** 7^{-3}

_____   _____   _____   _____

1e. 347^0 **1f.** 15^{-2} **1g.** 20^2 **1h.** 6^{-5}

_____   _____   _____   _____

Find the value of each power.

1. 10^{-4}

2. 2^{-5}

3. n^{-2}

_____

_____

_____

Simplify each expression. Write in decimal form.

4. $(10 \cdot 10)^{-1}$

5. $10 + (10 \cdot 10)^{-3}$

_____

_____

Simplify each expression.

6. $(9 - 5)^{-1}$

7. $(3 \cdot 3)^{-2}$

_____

_____

8. $12 + (4 \cdot 10^0)$

9. $25 - \left(\frac{9}{10} + 10^{-1}\right)$

_____

_____

10. $(5^2 - 3^2) \cdot 8^0$

11. $3^{-2} + 4^{-1} \cdot 3^0$

_____

_____

Solve.

12. An *ohm* is a unit of electrical resistance. Erin measures the resistance of a resistor. She finds it to be $\frac{1}{10^4}$ ohms. How can you write this resistance using negative exponents?

13. An *amp* is a unit for measuring electrical current. Luis orders a 10^{-3} amp fuse to replace one that has blown. How can you write this number of amps in decimal *and* fraction form?

_____

_____

Polonium is a highly radioactive chemical element that has a half-life of about 140 days. This means that one half of a given amount of the element decays in that time. Write each amount as a negative exponent and as a fraction.

14. How much polonium remains after 140 days? _____

15. How much polonium remains after 560 days? _____

16. **Conjecture** Examine some positive numbers and their reciprocals, such as 3 and $\frac{1}{3}$. As numbers increase, what happens to their reciprocals?

_____

_____

Additional Practice

Simplify. Write in decimal form.

1. 10^{-3} 2. 10^3 3. 10^{-5} 4. 10^{-2}

_____   _____   _____   _____

5. 10^0 6. 10^4 7. 10^1 8. 10^5

_____   _____   _____   _____

Simplify.

9. 6^{-2} 10. 9^{-3} 11. 2^{-5}

_____   _____   _____

12. 3^{-4} 13. 12^{-1} 14. 6^{-3}

_____   _____   _____

15. $10 - (3 + 2)^0 + 2^{-1}$ 16. $15 + 6^0 + 3^{-2}$

_____   _____

17. $6(8 - 2)^0 + 4^{-2}$ 18. $2^{-2} + 4^{-1}$

_____   _____

19. $3(1 + 2)^{-2} + 9^{-1} + 12^0$ 20. $9^0 + 64(3 + 5)^{-2}$

_____   _____

21. One milliliter equals 10^{-3} liter. Simplify 10^{-3}.

_____

22. The volume of a cube is 10^6 cubic feet. Simplify 10^6.

_____

Problem Solving

Write the correct answer.

1. The weight of 10^7 dust particles is 1 gram. Simplify 10^7.

   _____

2. The weight of one dust particle is 10^{-7} gram. Simplify 10^{-7}.

   _____

3. As of 2001, only 10^6 rural homes in the United States had broadband Internet access. Simplify 10^6.

   _____

4. Atomic clocks measure time in microseconds. A microsecond is 10^{-6} second. Simplify 10^{-6}.

   _____

Choose the letter for the best answer.

5. The diameter of the nucleus of an atom is about 10^{-15} meter. Simplify 10^{-15}.

   A   0.0000000000001

   B   0.00000000000001

   C   0.0000000000000001

   D   0.000000000000001

6. The diameter of the nucleus of an atom is 0.000001 nanometer. How many nanometers is the diameter of the nucleus of an atom?

   F $(-10)^5$

   G $(-10)^6$

   H 10^{-6}

   J 10^{-5}

7. A ruby-throated hummingbird weighs about 3^{-2} ounce. Simplify 3^{-2}.

   A -9

   B -6

   C $\dfrac{1}{9}$

   D $\dfrac{1}{6}$

8. A ruby-throated hummingbird breathes 2×5^3 times per minute while at rest. Simplify this amount.

   F   1,000

   G   250

   H   125

   J   30

Properties of Exponents
Reasoning

Essential question: *How can you develop and use the properties of integer exponents?*

CC.8.EE.1

1 EXPLORE Applying Properties of Integer Exponents

A Complete the following equations.

$$3 \cdot 3 \cdot 3 \cdot 3 \cdot 3 = 3^{\boxed{}}$$

$$(3 \cdot 3 \cdot 3 \cdot 3) \cdot 3 = 3^{\boxed{}} \cdot 3^{\boxed{}} = 3^{\boxed{}}$$

$$(3 \cdot 3 \cdot 3) \cdot (3 \cdot 3) = 3^{\boxed{}} \cdot 3^{\boxed{}} = 3^{\boxed{}}$$

What pattern do you see when multiplying two powers with the same base?

_____

_____

Use your pattern to complete this equation: $5^2 \cdot 5^5 = 5^{\boxed{}}$.

Conjecture Write a general rule for the result of $a^m \cdot a^n$. _____

B Complete the following equation: $\dfrac{4^5}{4^3} = \dfrac{4 \cdot 4 \cdot 4 \cdot 4 \cdot 4}{4 \cdot 4 \cdot 4} = \dfrac{\overset{1}{\cancel{4}} \cdot \overset{1}{\cancel{4}} \cdot \overset{1}{\cancel{4}} \cdot 4 \cdot 4}{\underset{1}{\cancel{4}} \cdot \underset{1}{\cancel{4}} \cdot \underset{1}{\cancel{4}}} = 4 \cdot 4 = 4^{\boxed{}}$

What pattern do you see when dividing two powers with the same base?

_____

_____

Use your pattern to complete this equation: $\dfrac{6^8}{6^3} = 6^{\boxed{}}$.

Conjecture Write a general rule for the result of $\dfrac{a^m}{a^n}$. _____

C Complete the following equations:

$$\left(5^3\right)^2 = (5 \cdot 5 \cdot 5)^{\boxed{}}$$

$$= (5 \cdot 5 \cdot 5) \cdot (5 \cdot 5 \cdot 5)$$

$$= 5^{\boxed{}}$$

What pattern do you see when raising a power to a power?

_____

_____

Use your pattern to complete this equation: $\left(7^2\right)^4 = 7^{\boxed{}}$.

Conjecture Write a general rule for the result of $\left(a^m\right)^n$. _____

Use properties of exponents to write an equivalent expression.

1a. $9^2 \cdot 9^4$ **1b.** $\dfrac{12^{22}}{12^4}$ **1c.** $\left(4^{10}\right)^5$ **1d.** $\dfrac{6^9}{6^{12}}$

_____   _____   _____   _____

CC.8.EE.1

2 EXAMPLE   **Applying Properties of Integer Exponents**

Simplify each expression.

A $(5-2)^5 \cdot 3^{-8} + (5+2)^0$

$(5-2)^5 \cdot 3^{-8} + (5+2)^0$ *Follow the order of operations.*

$\left(\boxed{}\right)^5 \cdot 3^{-8} + \left(\boxed{}\right)^0$ *Simplify within parentheses.*

$3^{\boxed{}} + \boxed{}$ *Use properties of exponents.*

$3^{\boxed{}} + \boxed{}$ *Simplify.*

$\dfrac{1}{\boxed{}} + \boxed{}$ *Add.*

$1\dfrac{1}{\boxed{}}$

B $(10-6)^3 \cdot 4^2 + (10+2)^2$

$(10-6)^3 \cdot 4^2 + (10+2)^2$ *Follow the order of operations.*

$\left(\boxed{}\right)^3 \cdot 4^2 + \left(\boxed{}\right)^2$ *Simplify within parentheses.*

$4^{\boxed{}} + \boxed{}$ *Use properties of exponents.*

$4^{\boxed{}} + \boxed{}$ *Simplify.*

$\boxed{} + \boxed{}$ *Add.*

$\boxed{}$

Simplify each expression.

2a. $\dfrac{\left[(6-1)^2\right]^2}{(3+2)^3}$ _____

2b. $(2^2)^3 - (10-6)^3 \cdot 4^{-5}$ _____

P R A C T I C E

Complete each table.

1.

Product of Powers	Write the Factors	Write as a Single Power
$2^2 \cdot 2^4$	$(2 \cdot 2)(2 \cdot 2 \cdot 2 \cdot 2) = 2 \cdot 2 \cdot 2 \cdot 2 \cdot 2 \cdot 2$	
$4^4 \cdot 4^3$		
	$(5)(5 \cdot 5 \cdot 5 \cdot 5) = 5 \cdot 5 \cdot 5 \cdot 5 \cdot 5$	

2.

Quotient of Powers	Write the Factors	Write as a Single Power
$\dfrac{3^5}{3^2}$	$\dfrac{3 \cdot 3 \cdot 3 \cdot \cancel{3} \cdot \cancel{3}}{\cancel{3} \cdot \cancel{3}}$	
$\dfrac{5^4}{5^1}$		
$\dfrac{4^4}{4^6}$		

Use properties of integers to write an equivalent expression.

3. $15^2 \cdot 15^{-5}$

_____

4. $\dfrac{20^{10}}{20^7}$

_____

5. $\dfrac{14^4}{14^9}$

_____

6. $(8^4)^{12}$

_____

7. $(12^{-5})^3$

_____

8. $4^{-3} \cdot 4^{-21}$

_____

9. $m \cdot m^4$

_____

10. $\dfrac{r^5}{r^2}$

_____

11. $(a^3)^{-3}$

_____

Find the missing exponent.

12. $b^{\boxed{}} \cdot b^2 = b^8$

13. $\dfrac{x^5}{x^{\boxed{}}} = x^{-2}$

14. $\left(n^{\boxed{}}\right)^4 = n^0$

Simplify each expression.

15. $3 \cdot \left(3^2\right)^2 + (8 - 4)^{-3}$ _____

16. $\left[(5 + 1)^2 \div 3\right] - 9^0$ _____

17. $\dfrac{\left(6 - 2^2\right)^1}{(5 - 4)^6}$ _____

18. $\dfrac{\left[(4 - 1)^2\right]^0}{(2 + 1)^2}$ _____

19. $(2 + 4)^2 + 8^{-6} \times (12 - 4)^{10}$ _____

20. $\left(3^3\right)^2 \times \left(\dfrac{(5 - 2)^3}{3^4}\right) + (10 - 4)^2 \times 6^{10}$ _____

21. There are $2^5 + 3^2$ games in half a full NBA season. How many games are in a full NBA season?

_____

22. From Earth, it is about 22^4 miles to the moon and about 9.3×10^7 to the sun. About how much farther is it to the sun than to the moon?

_____

23. **Error Analysis** A student simplified the expression $\dfrac{4^3}{16^3}$ as $\dfrac{1}{4}$. Do you agree with the student? Justify your answer.

_____

_____

24. Find the values of $x^5 \cdot x^{-3}$ and $\dfrac{x^5}{x^3}$. What do you notice about the two values? Explain why your results make sense based on the properties you learned in this lesson.

_____

_____

25. **Reasoning** Eric says that you can find the product of $2^4 \cdot 3^3$ by combining the exponents and then multiplying. Is he right? Explain.

_____

_____

Additional Practice

Multiply. Write the product as one power.

1. $10^5 \cdot 10^7$ 2. $x^9 \cdot x^8$ 3. $14^7 \cdot 14^9$ 4. $12^6 \cdot 12^8$

_____   _____   _____   _____

5. $y^{12} \cdot y^{10}$ 6. $15^9 \cdot 15^{14}$ 7. $11^{20} \cdot 11^{10}$ 8. $a^6 \cdot a^7$

_____   _____   _____   _____

Divide. Write the quotient as one power.

9. $\dfrac{12^9}{12^2}$ 10. $\dfrac{11^{12}}{11^8}$ 11. $\dfrac{x^5}{x^{10}}$ 12. $\dfrac{16^{10}}{16^2}$

_____   _____   _____   _____

13. $\dfrac{17^{19}}{17^2}$ 14. $\dfrac{14^{13}}{14^{15}}$ 15. $\dfrac{23^{17}}{23^9}$ 16. $\dfrac{a^{12}}{a^7}$

_____   _____   _____   _____

Simplify.

17. $(6^2)^4$ 18. $(2^4)^{-3}$ 19. $(3^5)^{-1}$ 20. $(y^5)^2$

_____   _____   _____   _____

21. $(9^{-2})^3$ 22. $(10^0)^3$ 23. $(x^4)^{-2}$ 24. $(5^{-2})^0$

_____   _____   _____   _____

Write the product or quotient as one power.

25. $\dfrac{w^{12}}{w^3}$ 26. $d^8 \cdot d^5$ 27. $15^5 \cdot 15^{10}$

_____   _____   _____

28. Jefferson High School has a student body of 6^4 students. Each class has approximately 6^2 students. How many classes does the school have? Write the answer as one power.

_____

29. Write the expression for a number used as a factor fifteen times being multiplied by a number used as a factor ten times. Then, write the product as one power.

_____

Problem Solving

Write each answer as a power.

1. Cindy separated her fruit flies into equal groups. She estimates that there are 2^{10} fruit flies in each of 2^2 jars. How many fruit flies does Cindy have in all?

   _____

2. Suppose a researcher tests a new method of pasteurization on a strain of bacteria in his laboratory. If the bacteria are killed at a rate of 8^9 per sec, how many bacteria would be killed after 8^2 sec?

   _____

3. A satellite orbits the earth at about 13^4 km per hour. How long would it take to complete 24 orbits, which is a distance of about 13^5 km?

   _____

4. The side of a cube is 3^4 centimeters long. What is the volume of the cube? (Hint: $V = s^3$.)

   _____

Use the table to answer Exercises 5–6. The table describes the number of people involved at each level of a pyramid scheme. In a pyramid scheme each individual recruits so many others to participate who in turn recruit others, and so on. Choose the letter of the best answer.

5. Using exponents, how many people will be involved at level 6?

   A 6^6 C 5^5

   B 6^5 D 5^6

6. How many times as many people will be involved at level 6 than at level 2?

   F 5^4 H 5^5

   G 5^3 J 5^6

Pyramid Scheme
Each person recruits 5 others.

Level	Total Number of People
1	5
2	5^2
3	5^3
4	5^4

7. There are 10^3 ways to make a 3-digit combination, but there are 10^6 ways to make a 6-digit combination. How many times more ways are there to make a 6-digit combination than a 3-digit combination?

   A 5^{10} C 2^5

   B 2^{10} D 10^3

8. After 3 hours, a bacteria colony has $(25^3)^3$ bacteria present. How many bacteria are in the colony?

   F 25^1 H 25^9

   G 25^6 J 25^{33}

Scientific Notation
Going Deeper

Essential question: *How can you use scientific notation to express very large and very small quantities?*

Scientific notation is a method of expressing very large and very small numbers as a product of a number greater than or equal to 1 and less than 10, and a power of 10.

video tutor

CC.8.EE.3

1 EXPLORE Using Scientific Notation

The weights of various sea creatures are shown in the table. You can write the weights in scientific notation.

Sea Creature	Blue Whale	Whale Shark	Eel	Minnow
Weight (lb)	250,000	41,200	133.25	0.95

Write the weight of the blue whale in scientific notation.

A Move the decimal point in 250,000 to the left as many places as necessary to find a number that is greater than or equal to 1 and less than 10.

What number did you find? _____

B Divide 250,000 by your answer to **A**. Write your answer as a power of 10.

_____

C Combine your answers to **A** and **B** to represent 250,000.

$250{,}000 = \boxed{} \times 10^{\boxed{}}$

Write the weight of the minnow in scientific notation.

D Move the decimal point in 0.95 to the right as many places as necessary to find a number that is greater than or equal to 1 and less than 10.

What number did you find? _____

E Divide 0.95 by your answer to **D**. Write your answer as a power of 10.

_____

F Combine your answers to **D** and **E** to represent 0.95.

$0.95 = \boxed{} \times 10^{\boxed{}}$

1a. What do you notice about the sign of the exponent for weights greater than one pound?

_____

1b. What do you notice about the sign of the exponent for weights less than one pound?

_____

To translate between standard notation and scientific notation, you can count the number of places the decimal point moves.

Writing Numbers in Scientific Notation

When the number is greater than or equal to 1, use a positive exponent.	$84,000 = 8.4 \times 10^4$	*The decimal point moves 4 places.*
When the number is less than 1, use a negative exponent.	$0.0783 = 7.83 \times 10^{-2}$	*The decimal point moves 2 places.*

CC.8.EE.3

2 EXAMPLE Writing a Number in Scientific Notation

An estimate of the world population in 2010 was 6,880,000,000. Write the world's population in scientific notation.

To write 6,880,000,000 in scientific notation, move the decimal point as many places as necessary to find a number that is greater than or equal to 1 and less than 10.

Place the decimal point: 6 8 8 0 0 0 0 0 0 0

Which direction did you move the decimal point? _____

What number did you find? _____

How many places did you move the decimal point? _____

When 6,880,000,000 is written in scientific notation, should the exponent of the power of 10 be positive or negative? Explain.

_____

_____

The world's population, 6,880,000,000, written in scientific notation is

[   ] $\times 10^{[\ ]}$.

To translate between scientific notation and standard notation, you can move the decimal point the number of places indicated by the exponent in the power of 10. When the exponent is positive, move the decimal point to the right. When the exponent is negative, move the decimal point to the left.

© Houghton Mifflin Harcourt Publishing Company

3 EXAMPLE Writing a Number in Standard Notation

Write each number in standard notation.

A 4.18549×10^{12}

What is the exponent of the power of 10? _____

Which direction should you move the decimal point? _____

Place the decimal point. Add placeholder zeros if necessary.

__ __ __ __ __ __ 4 1 8 5 4 9 __ __ __ __ __ __ __ __ __

The number 4.18549×10^{12} written in standard notation is _____.

B 2.568×10^{-6}

What is the exponent of the power of 10? _____

Which direction should you move the decimal point? _____

Place the decimal point. Add placeholder zeros if necessary.

__ __ __ __ __ __ __ __ __ 2 5 6 8 __ __ __ __ __

The number 2.568×10^{-6} written in standard notation is _____.

4 EXAMPLE Comparing Numbers in Scientific Notation

The approximate weight of a whale shark is 4×10^4 pounds. The approximate weight of a common dolphin is 2×10^2 pounds. How many times as great as the weight of the whale shark is the weight of the dolphin?

First compare the values between 1 and 10.

The 4 in 4×10^4 is _____ times as great as the 2 in 2×10^2.

Next compare the powers of 10.

10^4 is _____ times as great as 10^2.

Circle the most reasonable answer.

The weight of the whale shark is $2 / 20 / 200 / 2000$ times as great as the weight of the dolphin.

REFLECT

4a. Scientists captured and released a whale shark that weighed about 6×10^5 units. Circle the best choice for the units this measurement is given in: ounces / pounds / tons.

4b. Explain how you chose a unit of measurement in **4a.**

_____

_____

_____

Write each number in scientific notation.

1. 58,927

_____

2. 1,304,000,000

_____

3. 0.000487

_____

4. 0.000028

_____

5. 0.000059

_____

6. 6,730,000

_____

7. 13,300

_____

8. 0.0417

_____

Write each number in standard notation.

9. 4×10^5

_____

10. 1.8499×10^9

_____

11. 8.3×10^{-4}

_____

12. 3.582×10^{-6}

_____

13. 2.97×10^{-2}

_____

14. 6.41×10^3

_____

15. 8.456×10^7

_____

16. 9.06×10^{-5}

_____

Circle the correct answer.

17. 8×10^5 is 2/20/200/ 2,000 times as great as 4×10^2.

18. 9×10^{10} is 30 / 300 / 3,000 / 30,000 times as great as 3×10^7.

19. 4×10^{-5} is 0.02/0.2/2/20 times as great as 2×10^{-4}.

20. 4×10^{-12} is 0.00001 / 0.0001 / 10 / 1000 times as great as 4×10^{-8}.

21. The mass of a proton is about 1.7×10^{-24} g. The mass of a neutron is about the same as a proton. The nucleus of an atom of carbon has 6 protons and 6 neutrons. The mass of the nucleus is about 2×10^{-26} units. Circle the best choice for the units this measurement is given in: g/ kg /tons

22. The air distance between Los Angeles, California, and New York City, New York, is about 3.9×10^3 units. Circle the best choice for the units this measurement is given in: cm / m / km

Additional Practice

Write each number in standard notation.

1. 2.54×10^2

2. 6.7×10^{-2}

3. 1.14×10^3

4. 3.8×10^{-1}

_____   _____   _____   _____

5. 7.53×10^{-3}

6. 5.6×10^4

7. 9.1×10^5

8. 6.08×10^{-4}

_____   _____   _____   _____

9. 8.59×10^5

10. 3.331×10^6

11. 7.21×10^{-3}

12. 5.88×10^{-4}

_____   _____   _____   _____

Write each number in scientific notation.

13. 75,000,000

14. 208

15. 907,100

_____   _____   _____

16. 56

17. 0.093

18. 0.00006

_____   _____   _____

19. 0.00852

20. 0.0505

21. 0.003007

_____   _____   _____

22. 5226

23. 0.04

24. 98,856

_____   _____   _____

25. Jupiter is about 778,120,000 kilometers from the Sun. Write this number in scientific notation.

_____

26. The *E. coli* bacterium is about 5×10^{-7} meters wide. A hair is about 1.7×10^{-5} meters wide. Which is wider, the bacterium or the hair?

_____

Problem Solving

Write the correct answer.

1. In June 2001, the Intel Corporation announced that they could produce a silicon transistor that could switch on and off 1.5 trillion times a second. Express the speed of the transistor in scientific notation.

_____

2. With this transistor, computers will be able to do 1×10^9 calculations in the time it takes to blink your eye. Express the number of calculations using standard notation.

_____

3. The elements in this fast transistor are 20 nanometers long. A nanometer is one-billionth of a meter. Express the length of an element in the transistor in meters using scientific notation.

_____

4. The length of the elements in the transistor can also be compared to the width of a human hair. The length of an element is 2×10^{-3} times smaller than the width of a human hair. Express 2×10^{-3} in standard notation.

_____

Use the table to answer Exercises 5–9. Choose the best answer.

5. Express a light-year in miles using scientific notation.

   A 58.8×10^{11} C 588×10^{10}

   B 5.88×10^{12} D 5.88×10^{-13}

6. How many miles is it from Earth to the star Sirius?

   F 4.705×10^{12} H 7.35×10^{12}

   G 4.704×10^{13} J 7.35×10^{11}

7. How many miles is it from Earth to the star Canopus?

   A 3.822×10^{15} C 3.822×10^{14}

   B 1.230×10^{15} D 1.230×10^{14}

8. How many miles is it from Earth to the star Alpha Centauri?

   F 2.352×10^{13} H 2.352×10^{14}

   G 5.92×10^{13} J 5.92×10^{14}

Distance From Earth To Stars
Light-Year = 5,880,000,000,000 mi.

Star	Constellation	Distance (light-years)
Sirius	Canis Major	8
Canopus	Carina	650
Alpha Centauri	Centaurus	4
Vega	Lyra	23

9. How many miles is it from Earth to the star Vega?

   A 6.11×10^{13} C 6.11×10^{14}

   B 1.3524×10^{13} D 1.3524×10^{14}

Operating with Scientific Notation
Going Deeper

Essential question: *How do you add, subtract, multiply, and divide using scientific notation?*

3-4

video tutor

CC.8.EE.4

1 EXPLORE Adding and Subtracting with Scientific Notation

The table below shows the population of the three largest countries in North America. Find the total population of the three countries.

Country	United States	Canada	Mexico
Population	3.1×10^8	3.38×10^7	1.1×10^8

Method 1:

A First write each population with the same power of 10.

United States: ☐ × 10☐

Canada: ☐ × 10☐

Mexico: ☐ × 10☐

B Add the multipliers for each population. $3.1 +$ ☐ $+ 1.1 =$ ☐

C Write the final answer in scientific notation. _____

Method 2:

D First write each number in standard notation.

United States: _____

Canada: _____

Mexico: _____

E Find the sum of the numbers in standard notation.

$310,000,000 +$ ☐ $+$ ☐ $=$ ☐

F Write the answer in scientific notation. _____

TRY THIS!

1a. Using the population table above, how many more people live in Mexico than in Canada?

When the sun makes an orbit around the center of the Milky Way, it travels 2.025×10^{14} kilometers. The orbit takes 225 million years. At what rate does the Sun travel around the Milky Way? Write your answer in scientific notation.

A Set up a division problem to represent the situation.

$$\text{Rate} = \frac{\text{Distance}}{\text{Time}}$$

$$\text{Rate} = \frac{\text{kilometers}}{\text{years}}$$

B Write 225 million years in scientific notation. _____

C Write the expression for rate with years in scientific notation.

$$\text{Rate} = \frac{\text{kilometers}}{\text{years}}$$

D Find the quotient by dividing the multipliers.

$2.025 \div \boxed{} = \boxed{}$

E Use the laws of exponents to divide the powers of 10.

$$\frac{10^{14}}{10^{8}} = 10^{\boxed{}} = 10^{\boxed{}}$$

F Combine the answers from **D** and **E** to write the rate in scientific notation.

_____

TRY THIS!

2a. Light from the Sun travels at a speed of 1.86×10^{5} miles per second. It takes sunlight about 4.8×10^{3} seconds to reach Saturn. Find the approximate distance from the Sun to Saturn. Write your answer in scientific notation.

$$d = rt$$

$$= \left(\boxed{} \times 10^{5} \right)\left(\boxed{} \times 10^{3} \right)$$

$$= \left(\boxed{} \right)(4.8) \times \left(\boxed{} \right)(10^{3})$$

$$= \boxed{} \times 10^{\boxed{}}$$

$$= \boxed{} \times 10^{\boxed{}} \text{ miles}$$

On many scientific calculators, you can enter numbers in scientific notation by using a function labeled "ee" or "EE". Usually, the letter "E" takes the place of "×10". So, the number 4.1×10^9 would appear as 4.1E9 on the calculator.

3 EXAMPLE Scientific Notation on a Calculator

The table below shows the approximate populations for the three continents with the greatest populations. What is the total population of these three continents? Use your calculator to find the answer.

Continent	Asia	Africa	Europe
Population	4.1×10^9	1.0×10^9	7.28×10^8

Find $4.1 \times 10^9 + 1.0 \times 10^9 + 7.28 \times 10^8$.

Enter 4.1E9 + 1E _____ + _____ E _____ on your calculator.

Write the results from your calculator. _____

Write this number in scientific notation. _____

The total population of the three continents is _____ people.

TRY THIS!

Write each number using calculator notation.

3a. 7.5×10^5

3b. 3×10^{-7}

3c. 2.7×10^{13}

Write each number using scientific notation.

3d. 4.5E−1

3e. 5.6E12

3f. 6.98E−8

PRACTICE

Add or subtract. Write your answer in scientific notation.

1. $3.2 \times 10^5 + 4.9 \times 10^8$

2. $4.378 \times 10^{12} + 7.701 \times 10^7$

3. $2.3 \times 10^8 - 2.12 \times 10^3$

4. $4.55 \times 10^{15} - 7.4 \times 10^{11}$

5. $6.35 \times 10^3 + 1.65 \times 10^6$

6. $5 \times 10^3 - 1.23 \times 10^2$

Multiply or divide. Write your answer in scientific notation.

7. $(1.8 \times 10^9)(6.78 \times 10^{12})$

8. $(5.092 \times 10^{21})(3.38 \times 10^6)$

9. $\dfrac{8.4 \times 10^{21}}{4.2 \times 10^{14}}$

10. $\dfrac{3.46 \times 10^{17}}{2 \times 10^9}$

11. A newborn baby has about 26,000,000,000 cells. An adult has about 1.9×10^3 times as many cells as a newborn. About how many cells does an adult have? Write your answer in scientific notation.

12. The edge of a cube measures 3.5×10^{-2} meters. What is the volume of the cube in cubic meters? Write your answer in scientific notation.

13. The smallest state in the United States is Rhode Island with a land area of about 2.9×10^{10} square feet. The largest state is Alaska whose land area is about 5.5×10^2 as great as the land area of Rhode Island. What is the land area of Alaska in square feet? Write your answer in scientific notation.

14. Astronomers estimate that the diameter of the Andromeda galaxy is approximately 2.2×10^5 light-years. A light-year is the distance light travels in a vacuum in 1 year. One light-year is approximately 5.9×10^{12} miles. What is the diameter of the Andromeda galaxy in miles? Write your answer in scientific notation.

The table below shows the approximate populations of three countries.

Country	China	France	Australia
Population	1.33×10^9	6.48×10^7	2.15×10^7

15. How many more people live in France than in Australia? Write your answer in scientific notation.

16. The area of Australia is about 2.95×10^6 square miles. What is the approximate average number of people per square mile in Australia?

17. What is the ratio of the population of China to the population of France? What does this mean?

© Houghton Mifflin Harcourt Publishing Company

Additional Practice

Write your answer in scientific notation.

1. Rhode Island is the smallest state. It has an area of
   approximately 1.55×10^3 square miles. Alaska is the largest
   state. The area of Alaska is 4.28×10^2 times greater than the
   area of Rhode Island.

   What is the approximate area of Alaska in square miles?

   _____

2. In 2008, the total trade between the United States and Japan
   was $\$2.04 \times 10^{11}$. The total trade between the U.S. and Australia
   was $\$3.28 \times 10^{10}$.

   How many times greater was the trade with Japan than the trade
   with Australia? _____

3. Between 2008 and 2009, Americans spent $\$8.48 \times 10^8$ on baby
   food. During the same period, Americans spent $\$4.52 \times 10^9$ on
   ice cream.

   How much did Americans spend altogether on ice cream and
   baby food between 2008 and 2009? _____

4. Wrangell-St. Elias National Park in Alaska is the largest national
   park. It includes approximately 1.32×10^7 acres. Thaddeus
   Kosciuszcko National Memorial in Pennsylvania is the smallest
   national park. It is located on approximately 2.0×10^{-2} acres.

   How many times greater is the area of Wrangell-St. Alias
   National Park than Thaddeus Kosciuszcko National Memorial?

   _____

5. Approximately 3.25×10^6 cubic yards of material were used to
   build Boulder Dam on the Arizona-Nevada border. The New
   Cornelia Tailings Dam in Arizona used 2.74×10^8 cubic yards of
   material.

   How many more cubic yards of material were used to build the
   Cornelia Tailings Dam than Boulder Dam? _____

Problem Solving

Write your answer in scientific notation.

1. The top speed of a garden snail is 3.0×10^{-2} miles per hour. The top speed of a cheetah is 7.0×10^{1}. How many times greater is the speed of the cheetah than the garden snail?

_____

2. The speed of light is approximately 1.86×10^{5} miles per second. How many miles will light travel in a 24-hour day?

_____

3. The total area for the 50 U.S. states and Washington, D.C. is 3.79×10^{6} square miles. Of that, 2.57×10^{5} square miles are water. The rest of the area is land. How many square miles is the land area?

_____

4. In 2008, Americans spent $\$3.8 \times 10^{9}$ on bottled water and $\$2.7 \times 10^{8}$ on coffee. How much did Americans spend altogether on bottled water and coffee?

_____

Choose the letter for the best answer.

5. The all-time top grossing U.S. movie, *Titanic*, made $\$6.008 \times 10^{8}$. In 2008, *Dark Knight* was the top grossing movie at $\$5.309 \times 10^{8}$. How much did Titanic and Dark Knight gross in all?

   A $\$1.13 \times 10^{9}$

   B $\$3.19 \times 10^{8}$

   C $\$6.99 \times 10^{8}$

   D $\$8.84 \times 10^{9}$

6. A large department store chain employs 1.8×10^{6} people. The average annual wage for the employees is $\$2.1 \times 10^{4}$. How much does the chain pay in employee wages each year?

   F $\$3.00 \times 10^{2}$

   G $\$3.78 \times 10^{10}$

   H $\$3.90 \times 10^{24}$

   J $\$8.57 \times 10^{10}$

7. Gary measures a paramecium and an ant. The paramecium is 4.2×10^{-4} meter long, and the ant is 3.8×10^{-3} meter long. How much longer, in meters, is the ant than the paramecium?

   A 4.00×10^{-2} C 3.82×10^{-3}

   B 3.38×10^{-3} D 4.22×10^{-3}

8. The average radius of Jupiter is 4.34×10^{4} miles. The average radius of the Sun is 4.32×10^{5}. How many times greater is the average radius of the sun?

   F 1.00×10^{1}

   G 2.00×10^{3}

   H 4.75×10^{1}

   J 9.95×10^{0}

Squares and Square Roots
Extension: Cube Roots

Essential question: *How do you evaluate square roots and cube roots?*

CC.8.EE.2

1 EXPLORE Finding the Square Root of Perfect Squares

video tutor

There are 9 square tiles used to make a square mosaic. There are 3 tiles along each side of the mosaic.

Another square mosaic is made using 64 square tiles. How many tiles are on each side of this mosaic?

A Use what you know about the mosaic made with 9 tiles to find the relationship between number of tiles on each side and the total number of square tiles.

_____

_____

B Use this relationship to find the number of tiles along the side of a square mosaic made of 64 square tiles.

_____

C In this context, the total number of tiles is the number of tiles along each side of the mosaic squared. When the total number of tiles is 9, the number of tiles along a side is 3. Because $3^2 = 9$, we call 3 a *square root* of 9. This is written as $3 = \sqrt{9}$.

Use this notation to write the square root of 64: $\sqrt{64} =$ [   ]

TRY THIS!

Evaluate each square root.

1a. $\sqrt{169}$ **1b.** $\sqrt{\frac{1}{16}}$ **1c.** $\sqrt{81}$ **1d.** $\sqrt{\frac{1}{400}}$

_____   _____   _____   _____

The **square root** of a positive number p is x if $x^2 = p$. There are two square roots for every positive number. For example, the square roots of 36 are 6 and -6 because $6^2 = 36$ and $(-6)^2 = 36$. The square roots of $\frac{1}{25}$ are $\frac{1}{5}$ and $-\frac{1}{5}$. You can write the square roots of $\frac{1}{25}$ as $\pm \frac{1}{5}$. The symbol $\sqrt{}$ indicates the positive, or **principal square root**.

A number that is a **perfect square** has square roots that are integers. The number 81 is a perfect square because its square roots are 9 and -9.

2 E X P L O R E   Finding the Cube Root

A cube shaped toy is made of 27 small cubes.
There are 3 cubes along each edge of the toy.

Another cube shaped toy is made using 8 small cubes.
How many small cubes are on each edge of this toy?

A Use what you know about the toy made with 27 small cubes to find the relationship between number of cubes on each edge and the total number of cubes.

_____

_____

_____

B Use this relationship to find the number of small cubes along each edge of a toy made of 8 small cubes.

_____

C In this situation, the total number of small cubes is the number of small cubes along each edge of the toy cube. When the total number of small cubes is 27, the number of small cubes along each edge is 3. Because $3^3 = 27$, we call 3 a *cube root* of 27. This is written as $\sqrt[3]{27} = 3$.

Use this notation to write the cube root of 8: $\sqrt[3]{8} = $ [   ]

REFLECT

2a. The product of 3 equal positive factors is positive / negative.

2b. The product of 3 equal negative factors is positive / negative.

2c. Use your answers to **2a** and **2b** to explain when there is only one cube root of a positive number.

_____

_____

_____

TRY THIS!

Evaluate each cube root.

2d. $\sqrt[3]{125}$ **2e.** $\sqrt[3]{\dfrac{1}{8}}$ **2f.** $\sqrt[3]{1000}$ **2g.** $\sqrt[3]{\dfrac{1}{343}}$

_____   _____   _____   _____

The **cube root** of a positive number p is x if $x^3 = p$. There is one cube root for every positive number. For example, the cube root of 8 is 2 because $2^3 = 8$. The cube root of $\frac{1}{27}$ is $\frac{1}{3}$ because $\left(\frac{1}{3}\right)^3 = \frac{1}{27}$. The symbol $\sqrt[3]{}$ indicates the cube root. A number that is a **perfect cube** has a cube root that is an integer. The number 125 is a perfect cube because its cube root is 5.

CC.8.EE.2
3 EXAMPLE Solving Equations Using Square Roots and Cube Roots

Solve each equation for x.

A $x^2 = 121$

$\sqrt{x^2} = \sqrt{121}$ *Solve for x by taking the square root of both sides.*

$x = \sqrt{121}$ *Think: What number squared equals 121?*

$x = \pm \boxed{}$ *Use $\pm$ to show both square roots.*

The solutions are _____ and _____.

B $x^2 = \frac{16}{169}$

$\sqrt{x^2} = \sqrt{\frac{16}{169}}$ *Solve for x by taking the square root of both sides.*

$x = \sqrt{\frac{16}{169}}$ *Think: What number squared equals $\frac{16}{169}$?*

$x = \pm \dfrac{4}{\boxed{}}$ *Use $\pm$ to show both square roots.*

The solutions are _____ and _____.

C $729 = x^3$

$\sqrt[3]{729} = \sqrt[3]{x^3}$ *Solve for x by taking the cube root of both sides.*

$\sqrt[3]{729} = x$ *Think: What number cubed equals 729?*

$\boxed{} = x$

The solution is _____.

D $x^3 = \frac{8}{125}$

$\sqrt[3]{x^3} = \sqrt[3]{\frac{8}{125}}$ *Solve for x by taking the cube root of both sides.*

$x = \sqrt[3]{\frac{8}{125}}$ *Think: What number cubed equals $\frac{8}{125}$?*

$x = \dfrac{2}{\boxed{}}$

The solution is _____.

Find the square roots of each number.

1. 144 _____

2. 256 _____

3. $\frac{1}{81}$ _____

4. $\frac{49}{900}$ _____

5. 400 _____

6. $\frac{1}{100}$ _____

Find the cube root of each number.

7. 216 _____

8. 8000 _____

9. $\frac{27}{125}$ _____

10. $\frac{1}{27}$ _____

11. $\frac{27}{64}$ _____

12. 512 _____

Simplify each expression.

13. $\sqrt{16} + \sqrt{25}$ _____

14. $\sqrt[3]{125} + 10$ _____

15. $\sqrt{25} + 10$ _____

16. $8 - \sqrt{64}$ _____

17. $\sqrt[3]{\frac{16}{2}} + 1$ _____

18. $\sqrt{\frac{16}{4}} + \sqrt{4}$ _____

19. The foyer of Ann's house is a square with an area of 36 square feet. What is the length of each side of the foyer?

_____

20. A chessboard has 32 black squares and 32 white squares arranged in a square. How many squares are along each side of the chessboard?

_____

21. A cubic aquarium holds 27 cubic feet of water. What is the length of each edge of the cube?

_____

22. Reasoning How can you check your answer when you find the square root(s) of a number?

_____

_____

23. Reasoning Can you arrange 12 small squares to make a larger square? Can you arrange 20 small cubes to make a larger cube? Explain how this relates to perfect squares and perfect cubes.

_____

_____

Additional Practice

Find the square roots of each number.

1. 36 _____

2. 81 _____

3. 49 _____

4. 100 _____

5. 64 _____

6. 121 _____

7. 25 _____

8. 144 _____

Find the cube root of each number.

9. 729 _____

10. $\dfrac{1}{512}$ _____

11. 8 _____

12. 343 _____

13. $\dfrac{8}{27}$ _____

14. $\dfrac{1}{1331}$ _____

15. 64 _____

16. $\dfrac{27}{1000}$ _____

Simplify each expression.

17. $\sqrt{100-19}$ _____

18. $36 - \sqrt{36}$ _____

19. $\sqrt{100} - \sqrt{25}$ _____

20. $\sqrt{\dfrac{25}{4}} + \dfrac{1}{2}$ _____

The Pyramids of Egypt are often called the first wonder of the world. This group of pyramids consists of Menkaura, Khufu, and Khafra. The largest of these is Khufu, sometimes called Cheops. During this time in history, each monarch had his own pyramid built to bury his mummified body. Cheops was a king of Egypt in the early 26th century B.C. His pyramid's original height is estimated to have been 482 ft. It is now approximately 450 ft. The estimated completion date of this structure was 2660 B.C.

21. If the area of the square base of Cheops' pyramid is 570,025 ft², what is the length of one of the sides of the ancient structure? (Hint: $A = s^2$)

_____

22. If a replica of the pyramid were built with a base area of 625 in², what would be the length of each side?

_____

Problem Solving

Write the correct answer.

1. For college wrestling competitions, the NCAA requires that the wrestling mat be a square with an area of 1764 square feet. What is the length of each side of the wrestling mat?

2. For high school wrestling competitions, the wrestling mat must be a square with an area of 1444 square feet. What is the length of each side of the wrestling mat?

3. The Japanese art of origami requires folding square pieces of paper. Elena begins with a large sheet of square paper that is 169 square inches. How many squares can she cut out of the paper that are 4 inches on each side?

4. When the James family moved into a new house they had a square area rug that was 132 square feet. In their new house, there are three bedrooms. Bedroom one is 11 feet by 11 feet. Bedroom two is 10 feet by 12 feet and bedroom three is 13 feet by 13 feet. In which bedroom will the rug fit?

Choose the letter for the best answer.

5. A square picture frame measures 36 inches on each side. The actual wood trim is 2 inches wide. The photograph in the frame is surrounded by a bronze mat that measures 5 inches. What is the maximum area of the photograph?

   A 841 sq. inches

   B 900 sq. inches

   C 1156 sq. inches

   D 484 sq. inches

6. To create a square patchwork quilt wall hanging, square pieces of material are sewn together to form a larger square. Which number of smaller squares can be used to create a square patchwork quilt wall hanging?

   F 35 squares   H 84 squares

   G 64 squares   J 125 squares

7. A can of paint claims that one can will cover 400 square feet. If you painted a square with the can of paint, how long would it be on each side?

   A 200 feet   C 25 feet

   B 65 feet   D 20 feet

8. A box of tile contains 12 square tiles. If you tile the largest possible square area using whole tiles, how many tiles will you have left from the box?

   F 9   H 3

   G 6   J 0

Practice and Problem Solving

Estimating Square Roots
Connect: Irrational Numbers

3-6

video tutor

Essential question: *How do you estimate and compare irrational numbers?*

Irrational numbers are numbers that are not rational. In other words, they cannot be written in the form $\frac{a}{b}$, where a and b are integers and $b \neq 0$. Square roots of integers that are not perfect squares are irrational. Other special numbers, like π, are also irrational.

CC.8.NS.2

1 EXPLORE Estimating Irrational Numbers

Estimate the value of $\sqrt{2}$.

A Since 2 is not a perfect square, $\sqrt{2}$ is irrational.

To estimate $\sqrt{2}$, first find two consecutive perfect squares that 2 is between. Complete the inequality by writing these perfect squares in the boxes.

Now take the square root of each number.

Simplify the square roots of perfect squares.

$\sqrt{2}$ is between _____ and _____.

Estimate that $\sqrt{2} \approx 1.5$.

$\sqrt{2} \approx 1.5$

```
+--+--+--+--+--+
0  1  2  3  4
```

B To find a better estimate, first choose some numbers between 1 and 2 and square them. For example, choose 1.3, 1.4, and 1.5.

$1.3^2 = $ _____ $1.4^2 = $ _____ $1.5^2 = $ _____

Is $\sqrt{2}$ between 1.3 and 1.4? How do you know?

_____

Is $\sqrt{2}$ between 1.4 and 1.5? How do you know?

_____

$\sqrt{2}$ is between _____ and _____, so $\sqrt{2} \approx$ _____.

Locate and label this value on the number line.

```
+--+--+--+--+--+
1.1 1.2 1.3 1.4 1.5
```

REFLECT

1a. How could you find an even better estimate of $\sqrt{2}$?

_____

1b. Use your method from **1a** to find a better estimate of $\sqrt{2}$. Draw a number line and locate and label your estimate.

$\sqrt{2}$ is between _____ and _____, so $\sqrt{2} \approx$ _____.

© Houghton Mifflin Harcourt Publishing Company

1c. Estimate the value of $\sqrt{7}$ to the nearest hundredth.
Draw a number line and locate and label your estimate.

$\sqrt{7}$ is between _____ and _____, so $\sqrt{7} \approx$ _____.

CC.8.NS.2

2 EXAMPLE Comparing Irrational Numbers

Compare. Write <, >, or =.

A $\sqrt{3} + 5$ ⬤ $3 + \sqrt{5}$

First approximate $\sqrt{3}$ to the nearest tenth.

$\sqrt{3}$ is between _____ and _____, so $\sqrt{3} \approx$ _____.

Next approximate $\sqrt{5}$ to the nearest tenth.

$\sqrt{5}$ is between _____ and _____, so $\sqrt{5} \approx$ _____.

Then use your approximations to simplify the expressions.

$\sqrt{3} + 5$ ⬤ $3 + \sqrt{5}$

[ ] $+ 5$ ⬤ $3 +$ [ ]   *Substitute your approximations.*

[ ] ⬤ [ ]   *Simplify, then compare.*

So, $\sqrt{3} + 5$ ◯ $3 + \sqrt{5}$

B $\sqrt{10} + 2$ ⬤ $10 + \sqrt{2}$

First approximate $\sqrt{10}$ to the nearest tenth.

$\sqrt{10}$ is between _____ and _____, so $\sqrt{10} \approx$ _____.

Next approximate $\sqrt{2}$ to the nearest tenth.

$\sqrt{2}$ is between _____ and _____, so $\sqrt{2} \approx$ _____.

Then use your approximations to simplify the expressions.

$\sqrt{10} + 2$ ⬤ $10 + \sqrt{2}$

[ ] $+ 2$ ⬤ $10 +$ [ ]   *Substitute your approximations.*

[ ] ⬤ [ ]   *Simplify, then compare.*

So, $\sqrt{10} + 2$ ◯ $10 + \sqrt{2}$

Compare. Write <, >, or =.

2a. $\sqrt{2} + 4$ ◯ $2 + \sqrt{4}$ **2b.** $\sqrt{12} + 6$ ◯ $12 + \sqrt{6}$

CC.8.NS.2

3 EXAMPLE   **Ordering Irrational Numbers**

Order $\sqrt{3}$, π, and 1.5 from least to greatest.

First approximate $\sqrt{3}$ to the nearest tenth.

    $\sqrt{3}$ is between _____ and _____, so $\sqrt{3} \approx$ _____.

You need to find a better estimate for $\sqrt{3}$ so you can compare it to 1.5.
Approximate $\sqrt{3}$ to the nearest hundredth.

    $\sqrt{3}$ is between _____ and _____, so $\sqrt{3} \approx$ _____.

An approximate value of π is 3.14.

Plot $\sqrt{3}$, π, and 1.5 on a number line.

Read the numbers from left to right to place them in order from least to greatest.

From least to greatest, the numbers are _____, _____, _____.

TRY THIS!

Order the numbers from least to greatest.

3a. $\sqrt{5}, 2.5, \sqrt{3}$ _____

3b. $\pi^2, 10, \sqrt{75}$ _____

PRACTICE

Approximate each irrational number to the nearest hundredth without using a calculator.

1. $\sqrt{34}$

_____

2. $\sqrt{82}$

_____

3. $\sqrt{45}$

_____

4. $\sqrt{104}$

_____

5. $\sqrt{71}$

_____

6. $\sqrt{19}$

_____

7. $\sqrt{24}$

_____

8. $\sqrt{41}$

_____

Compare. Write <, >, or =.

9. $\sqrt{3} + 2$ ◯ $\sqrt{2} + 3$

10. $\sqrt{11} + 15$ ◯ $\sqrt{15} + 11$

11. $\sqrt{6} + 5$ ◯ $6 + \sqrt{5}$

12. $\sqrt{9} + 3$ ◯ $9 + \sqrt{3}$

13. $\sqrt{15} - 3$ ◯ $-2 + \sqrt{5}$

14. $10 - \sqrt{8}$ ◯ $12 - \sqrt{2}$

15. $\sqrt{7} + 1$ ◯ $\sqrt{10} - 1$

16. $\sqrt{12} + 3$ ◯ $3 + \sqrt{11}$

Order the numbers from least to greatest.

17. $\sqrt{7}, \dfrac{\sqrt{8}}{2}, 2$

_____

18. $\sqrt{10}, \pi, 3.5$

_____

19. $1.5, \dfrac{\sqrt{12}}{3}, \sqrt{3}$

_____

20. $2\sqrt{7}, \sqrt{24}, 2\pi$

_____

Additional Practice

Each square root is between two consecutive integers. Name the integers. Explain your answer.

1. $\sqrt{6}$

_____

2. $\sqrt{20}$

_____

3. $\sqrt{28}$

_____

4. $\sqrt{44}$

_____

5. $\sqrt{31}$

_____

6. $\sqrt{52}$

_____

7. The area of a square piece of cardboard is 70 cm². What is the approximate length of each side of the cardboard?

_____

Approximate each irrational number to the nearest hundredth without using a calculator.

8. $\sqrt{63}$

9. $\sqrt{18}$

10. $\sqrt{87}$

11. $\sqrt{319}$

_____

Compare. Write <, >, or =.

12. $7+\sqrt{3} \boxed{} \sqrt{7}+3$

13. $\sqrt{12}-2 \boxed{} 12-\sqrt{2}$

_____

14. $\sqrt{10}+5 \boxed{} 10-\sqrt{5}$

15. $-3+\sqrt{15} \boxed{} \sqrt{15}-3$

_____

Order the numbers from least to greatest.

16. $\sqrt{20}$, 4, $\dfrac{\sqrt{35}}{2}$

17. 2π, $\sqrt{32}$, $3\sqrt{5}$

_____

18. 2.5, π, $\sqrt{8}$

19. $\sqrt{11}$, $\dfrac{\sqrt{17}}{3}$, π

Problem Solving

The distance to the horizon can be found using the formula

$d = 112.88\sqrt{h}$ **where d is the distance in kilometers and h is the number of kilometers from the ground. Round your answer to the nearest kilometer.**

1. How far is it to the horizon when you are standing on the top of Mt. Everest, a height of 8.85 km?

   _____

2. Find the distance to the horizon from the top of Mt. McKinley, Alaska, a height of 6.194 km.

   _____

3. How far is it to the horizon if you are standing on the ground and your eyes are 2 m above the ground?

   _____

4. Mauna Kea is an extinct volcano on Hawaii that is about 4 km tall. You should be able to see the top of Mauna Kea when you are how far away?

   _____

You can find the approximate speed of a vehicle that leaves skid marks before it stops. The formulas $S = 5.5\sqrt{0.7L}$ and

$S = 5.5\sqrt{0.8L}$ **, where S is the speed in miles per hour and L is the length of the skid marks in feet, will give the minimum and maximum speeds that the vehicle was traveling before the brakes were applied. Round to the nearest mile per hour.**

5. A vehicle leaves a skid mark of 40 feet before stopping. What was the approximate speed of the vehicle before it stopped?

   A 25–35 mi/h   C 29–31 mi/h

   B 28–32 mi/h   D 68–70 mi/h

6. A vehicle leaves a skid mark of 100 feet before stopping. What was the approximate speed of the vehicle before it stopped?

   F 46–49 mi/h   H 62–64 mi/h

   G 50–55 mi/h   J 70–73 mi/h

7. A vehicle leaves a skid mark of 150 feet before stopping. What was the approximate speed of the vehicle before it stopped?

   A 50–55 mi/h   C 55–70 mi/h

   B 53–58 mi/h   D 56–60 mi/h

8. A vehicle leaves a skid mark of 200 feet before stopping. What was the approximate speed of the vehicle before it stopped?

   F 60–63 mi/h   H 72–78 mi/h

   G 65–70 mi/h   J 80–90 mi/h

The Real Numbers
Going Deeper

Essential question: *How can you tell whether a number is rational or irrational?*

Recall that a *rational number* is any number that can be expressed as the quotient of two integers where the divisor is not zero. All rational numbers can be written as fractions or as decimals that either terminate or repeat, such as −1.5 and 9.106106106....

An **irrational number** can only be written as a decimal that neither terminates nor repeats. If a whole number is not a perfect square, then its square root is an irrational number.

All rational and irrational numbers together make up the set of **real numbers**.

CC.8.NS.1

1 EXAMPLE Classifying Real Numbers

Write all names that apply to the number −3.

−3 can be shown on a number line.

So it is _____.

−3 can be written as $-\frac{3}{1}$.
So it is _____.

−3 can be written as −3.0. So it is

a _____ decimal.

−3 is an integer.

−3 is a _____ integer.

Real Numbers
├── Rational Numbers ── Irrational Numbers
│   ├── Terminating Decimals ── Repeating Decimals
│   │   ├── Non-Integers ── Integers
│   │   │   ├── Negative Integers ── Whole Numbers
│   │   │   │   ├── Zero ── Natural Numbers

−3 is _____

TRY THIS!

Write all names that apply to each number.

1. 32 _____

2. $\sqrt{5}$ _____

3. $\frac{-5}{8}$ _____

Write all names that apply to each number.

1. 41 _____

2. 9.020020002... _____

3. −12 _____

4. $\sqrt{25}$ _____

Is the statement *true* or *false*? Give a reason or an example to support your answer.

5. All rational numbers are real numbers.

   _____

6. All integers are real numbers.

   _____

7. All irrational numbers are real numbers.

   _____

8. All real numbers are integers.

   _____

9. The fraction $\frac{22}{7}$ is often used to approximate the irrational number π. So, $\frac{22}{7}$ is also an irrational number.

   _____

10. All negative numbers are rational numbers.

    _____

Write *sometimes true*, *always true*, or *never true*. Give a reason or an example to support your answer.

11. Whole numbers are rational numbers.

    _____

12. Terminating decimals are irrational numbers.

    _____

13. Negative numbers are integers.

    _____

14. **Error Analysis** Derek says that the number 4.05005005... is a rational number because it has a pattern. What do you think?

    _____

    _____

Additional Practice

Write all names that apply to each number.

1. $-\dfrac{7}{8}$

2. $\sqrt{0.15}$

3. $\sqrt{\dfrac{18}{2}}$

_____   _____   _____

_____   _____   _____

4. $\sqrt{45}$

5. -25

6. -6.75

_____   _____   _____

_____   _____   _____

State if the number is rational, irrational, or not a real number.

7. $\sqrt{14}$

8. $\sqrt{-16}$

9. $\dfrac{6.2}{0}$

10. $\sqrt{49}$

_____   _____   _____   _____

11. $\dfrac{7}{20}$

12. $-\sqrt{81}$

13. $\sqrt{\dfrac{7}{9}}$

14. -1.3

_____   _____   _____   _____

Find a real number between each pair of numbers.

15. $7\dfrac{3}{5}$ and $7\dfrac{4}{5}$

16. 6.45 and $\dfrac{13}{2}$

17. $\dfrac{7}{8}$ and $\dfrac{9}{10}$

_____   _____   _____

18. Give an example of a rational number between $-\sqrt{4}$ and $\sqrt{4}$

_____

19. Give an example of an irrational number less than 0.

_____

20. Give an example of a number that is not real.

_____

Problem Solving

Write the correct answer.

1. Twin primes are prime numbers that differ by 2. Find an irrational number between twin primes 5 and 7.

   _____

2. Rounded to the nearest ten-thousandth, $\pi = 3.1416$. Find a rational number between 3 and π.

   _____

3. One famous irrational number is e. Rounded to the nearest ten-thousandth e is 2.7183. Find a rational number that is between 2 and e.

   _____

4. Perfect numbers are those for which the divisors of the number sum to the number itself. The number 6 is a perfect number because $1 + 2 + 3 = 6$. The number 28 is also a perfect number. Find an irrational number between 6 and 28.

   _____

Choose the letter for the best answer.

5. Which is a rational number?

   A the length of a side of a square with area 2 cm^2

   B the length of a side of a square with area 4 cm^2

   C a non-terminating decimal

   D the square root of a prime number

6. Which is an irrational number?

   F a number that can be expressed as a fraction

   G the length of a side of a square with area 4 cm^2

   H the length of a side of a square with area 2 cm^2

   J the square root of a negative number

7. Which is an integer?

   A the number half-way between 6 and 7

   B the average rainfall for the week if it rained 0.5 in., 2.3 in., 0 in., 0 in., 0 in., 0.2 in., 0.75 in. during the week

   C the money in an account if the balance was $213.00 and $21.87 was deposited

   D the net yardage after plays that resulted in a 15 yard loss, 10 yard gain, 6 yard gain and 5 yard loss

8. Which is a whole number?

   F the number half-way between 6 and 7

   G the total amount of sugar in a recipe that calls for $\frac{1}{4}$ cup of brown sugar and $\frac{3}{4}$ cup of granulated sugar

   H the money in an account if the balance was $213.00 and $21.87 was deposited

   J the net yardage after plays that resulted in a 15 yard loss, 10 yard gain, 6 yard gain and 5 yard loss

The Pythagorean Theorem
Extension: In Three Dimensions

Essential question: *How can you use the Pythagorean Theorem to solve problems?*

In a right triangle, the two sides that form the right angle are the **legs**. The side opposite the right angle is the **hypotenuse**.

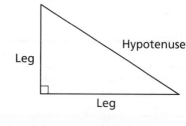

> ### The Pythagorean Theorem
>
> In a right triangle, the sum of the squares of the lengths of the legs is equal to the square of the length of the hypotenuse.
>
> If a and b are legs and c is the hypotenuse, $a^2 + b^2 = c^2$.

CC.8.G.7

1 EXAMPLE **Using the Pythagorean Theorem**

Find the length of the missing side.

A

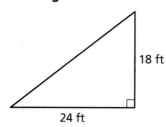

18 ft

24 ft

$$a^2 + b^2 = c^2$$

$24^2 + \boxed{}^2 = c^2$ *Substitute into the formula.*

$\boxed{} + \boxed{} = c^2$ *Simplify.*

$\boxed{} = c^2$ *Add.*

$\boxed{} = c$ *Take the square root of both sides.*

The length of the hypotenuse is _____ ft.

B

26 ft   10 ft

$$a^2 + b^2 = c^2$$

$a^2 + \boxed{}^2 = 26^2$ *Substitute into the formula.*

$a^2 + \boxed{} = 676$ *Simplify.*

$a^2 = \boxed{}$ *Use properties of equality to get a^2 by itself.*

$a = \boxed{}$ *Take the square root of both sides.*

The length of the leg is _____ cm.

REFLECT

1. If you are given the length of the hypotenuse and one leg, does it matter whether you solve for a or b? Explain.

_____

_____

2 **E X A M P L E** **Pythagorean Theorem in the Coordinate Plane**

Approximate the length of the hypotenuse to the nearest tenth without using a calculator.

Find the length of the vertical leg: _____ units

Find the length of the horizontal leg: _____ units

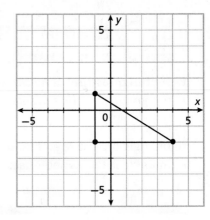

$$a^2 + b^2 = c^2$$

$$\boxed{}^2 + \boxed{}^2 = c^2 \qquad \textit{Substitute into the formula.}$$

$$\boxed{} + \boxed{} = c^2 \qquad \textit{Simplify.}$$

$$\boxed{} = c^2 \qquad \textit{Add.}$$

$$\sqrt{\boxed{}} = c \qquad \textit{Take the square root of both sides.}$$

$\sqrt{\boxed{}}$ is between _____ and _____ , so $\sqrt{\boxed{}} \approx \boxed{}$.

The hypotenuse is about _____ units long.

TRY THIS!

2a. Approximate the length of the hypotenuse to the nearest tenth without using a calculator.

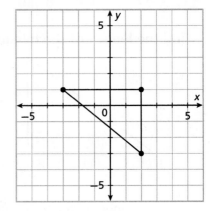

REFLECT

2b. Which side of a right triangle is always the longest side?

_____

2c. How could you find the length of the legs of an isosceles right triangle if you are only given the length of the hypotenuse?

_____

_____

2d. **Conjecture** Explain whether the lengths 2 cm, 3 cm, and 7 cm could be the side lengths of a right triangle.

_____

_____

_____

3 EXAMPLE **Pythagorean Theorem in Three Dimensions**

Mr. Woo wants to ship a fishing rod that is 42 inches long to his son. He has a box that measures 10 inches by 10 inches by 40 inches. Will the fishing rod fit in the box?

$h = 10$ in.
$w = 10$ in.
$\ell = 40$ in.
r
s

Will the rod fit in the bottom of the box?
Let s represent the length of the diagonal across the bottom of the box.

$$w^2 + \ell^2 = s^2$$

$10^2 + \boxed{}^2 = s^2$ *Substitute into the formula.*

$\boxed{} + \boxed{} = s^2$ *Simplify.*

$\boxed{} = s^2$ *Add.*

$\sqrt{\boxed{}} = s$ *Take the square root of both sides.*

$\boxed{} \approx s$ *Use a calculator to round to the nearest tenth.*

Will the rod fit diagonally from one bottom corner to the opposite top corner?
Let r represent the length from a bottom corner to the opposite top corner.

$$h^2 + s^2 = r^2$$

$\boxed{}^2 + \sqrt{\boxed{}^2} = r^2$ *Substitute into the formula. Use the value for s^2.*

$\boxed{} + \boxed{} = r^2$ *Simplify.*

$\boxed{} = r^2$ *Add.*

$\sqrt{\boxed{}} = r$ *Take the square root of both sides.*

$\boxed{} \approx r$ *Use a calculator to round to the nearest tenth.*

Explain whether the rod will fit in the box. If so, tell how.

_____

_____

TRY THIS!

3. Tina ordered a replacement part for her desk. It was shipped in a box that measures 4 in. by 4 in. by 14 in. What is the greatest length in whole inches that the part could have been?

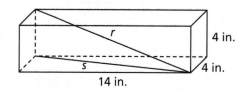

r
s
4 in.
4 in.
14 in.

Find the length of the missing side. Approximate square roots of non-perfect squares to the nearest tenth without using a calculator.

1.

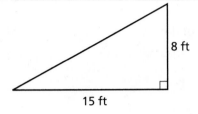

8 ft

15 ft

_____

2.

39 m

15 m

_____

3.

14 in.

8 in.

_____

4.

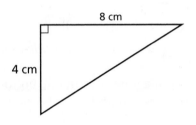

8 cm

4 cm

_____

Approximate the length of the hypotenuse to the nearest tenth without using a calculator.

5.

_____

6.

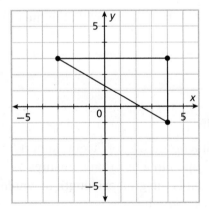

_____

7. What is the longest flagpole (in whole feet) that could be shipped in a box that measures 1 ft by 2 ft by 12 ft?

r

s

12 ft

2 ft

1 ft

_____

Additional Practice

Find the length of the missing side. Round your answers to the nearest tenth if neccessary.

1.

_____

2.

_____

3.

_____

4.

_____

5.

_____

6.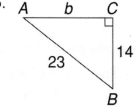

_____

7. A glider flies 8 miles south from the airport and then 15 miles east. Then it flies in a straight line back to the airport. What was the distance of the glider's last leg back to the airport?

_____

8. Approximate the length of the hypotenuse to the nearest tenth without using a calculator.

_____

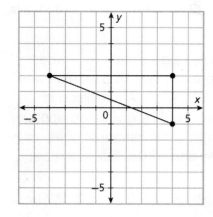

Problem Solving

Write the correct answer. Round to the nearest tenth.

1. A utility pole 10 m high is supported by two guy wires. Each guy wire is anchored 3 m from the base of the pole. How many meters of wire are needed for the guy wires?

   _____

2. A 12 foot-ladder is resting against a wall. The base of the ladder is 2.5 feet from the base of the wall. How high up the wall will the ladder reach?

   _____

3. The base-path of a baseball diamond forms a square. If it is 90 ft from home to first, how far does the catcher have to throw to catch someone stealing second base?

   _____

4. A football field is 100 yards with 10 yards at each end for the end zones. The field is 45 yards wide. Find the length of the diagonal of the entire field, including the end zones.

   _____

Choose the letter for the best answer.

5. The frame of a kite is made from two strips of wood, one 27 inches long, and one 18 inches long. What is the perimeter of the kite? Round to the nearest tenth.

   A 18.8 in.   C 65.7 in.
   B 32.8 in.   D 131.2 in.

6. The glass for a picture window is 8 feet wide. The door it must pass through is 3 feet wide. How tall must the door be for the glass to pass through the door? Round to the nearest tenth.

   F 3.3 ft   H 7.4 ft
   G 6.7 ft   J 8.5 ft

7. A television screen measures approximately 15.5 in. high and 19.5 in. wide. A television is advertised by giving the approximate length of the diagonal of its screen. How should this television be advertised?

   A 25 in.   C 12 in.
   B 21 in.   D 6 in.

8. To meet federal guidelines, a wheelchair ramp that is constructed to rise 1 foot off the ground must extend 12 feet along the ground. How long will the ramp be? Round to the nearest tenth.

   F 11.9 ft   H 13.2 ft
   G 12.0 ft   J 15.0 ft

© Houghton Mifflin Harcourt Publishing Company

Applying the Pythagorean Theorem and Its Converse
Modeling

Essential question: *How can you prove the Pythagorean Theorem and its converse?*

video tutor

CC.8.G.6

1 EXPLORE   Using Area to Prove the Pythagorean Theorem

A   Draw a right triangle on a piece of paper and cut it out. Make one leg shorter than the other.

B   Trace your triangle onto another piece of paper four times, arranging them as shown. For each triangle, label the shorter leg a, the longer leg b, and the hypotenuse c.

C   What is the area of the unshaded square?

_____

Label the unshaded square with its area.

D   Trace your original triangle onto a piece of paper four times again, arranging them as shown. Draw a line outlining a larger square that is the same size as the figure you made in **B** .

E   What is the area of the unshaded square at the top right of the figure in **D** ? at the top left?

_____

Label the unshaded squares with their areas.

F   What is the total area of the unshaded regions of the figure in **D** ?

_____

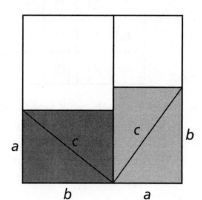

REFLECT

1a.   Explain whether the figures in **B** and **D** have the same area.

_____

1b.   Explain whether the unshaded regions of the figures in **B** and **D** have the same area.

_____

_____

_____

1c. Write an equation relating the area of the unshaded region in step B to the unshaded region in D .

_____

The Pythagorean Theorem says "If a triangle is a right triangle, then $a^2 + b^2 = c^2$."

The _converse_ of the Pythagorean Theorem says "If $a^2 + b^2 = c^2$, then the triangle is a right triangle."

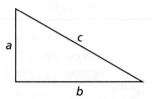

CC.8.G.6

2 EXPLORE Testing the Converse of the Pythagorean Theorem

Decide whether the converse of the Pythagorean Theorem is true.

 A Verify that the following sets of lengths make the equation $a^2 + b^2 = c^2$ true. Record your results in the table.

a	b	c	Is $a^2 + b^2 = c^2$ true?	Makes a right triangle?
3	4	5		
5	12	13		
7	24	25		
8	15	17		
20	21	29		

 B For each set of lengths in the table, cut strips of grid paper with a width of one square and lengths that correspond to the values of a, b, and c.

 C For each set of lengths, use the strips of grid paper to try to form a right triangle. An example using the first set of lengths is shown here.

Record your findings in the table.

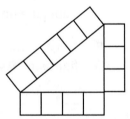

REFLECT

2. Based on your observations, explain whether you think the converse of the Pythagorean Theorem is true.

_____

_____

_____

Additional Practice

Tell whether the given side lengths form a right triangle.

1. 7, 24, 25

   _____

2. 30, 40, 45

   _____

3. 21.6, 28.8, 36

   _____

4. 10, 15, 18

   _____

5. 10.5, 36, 50

   _____

6. 2.5, 6, 6.5

   _____

7. 50, 64, 80

   _____

8. 1.2, 1.6, 2

   _____

9. A map is placed on a coordinate grid. Cincinnati is located at (5, 4) and San Diego is located at (−10, −3). How far apart is Cincinnati from San Diego on the map? Round your answer to the nearest tenth.

   _____

10. Katie, Ralph, and Juan are tossing a football. Katie is 22.5 feet away from Ralph. Ralph is 58.5 feet away from Juan. Juan is 54 feet away from Katie. Do the distances between Katie, Ralph, and Juan form a right triangle? Explain.

    _____

11. A rectangular picture frame has dimensions 6 inches by 8 inches. The diagonal of the frame is 10 inches. Do the sides of the frame meet at a right angle? Explain.

    _____

Problem Solving

Solve each problem.

1. Linda made triangular flags for the spirit club to wave. The sides of each flag were 1.2 feet, 1.6 feet, and 2 feet. Are the flags that Linda made in the shape of a right triangle? Explain.

   _____

2. A wheelchair ramp starts 8 meters from the base of a staircase. The staircase is 1 meter high. What is the length of the wheelchair ramp? Round to the nearest tenth of a meter.

   _____

3. The city of Chicago is located at (4, 8) on a grid. The city of Memphis is located at (6, −12) on the grid. How many units apart are Chicago and Memphis on the grid? Round to the nearest tenth of a unit.

   _____

4. Tony needs to use a ladder to get onto the roof. The height of the house is about 11 feet. The ladder will be placed 6 feet from the house. What is the minimum height, to the nearest foot, that the ladder can be to safely reach the roof of the house?

   _____

Solve each problem.

5. An airplane is 33 miles due south and 56 miles due west of its destination airport. How far is the plane from the destination airport?

   A 9.4 miles   C 65 miles

   B 89 miles   D 4,225 miles

6. The location of a post office is marked at (2, 2) on a coordinate grid. Which point is about 18 units from the location of the post office?

   F L(−12, 9)   H M(12, 9)

   G N(12, −9)   J P(−12, −9)

7. A rectangular tabletop has a length of 3.3 feet and a width of 8.8 feet. Which is the length of its diagonal to the nearest tenth?

   A 88.33 feet   C 29.04 feet

   B 9.4 feet   D 3.5 feet

8. The location of three ships are shown on a coordinate grid by the following points: X(0, 7), Y(−5, −3), and Z(4, −1). Which ships are farthest apart?

   F X and Y   H X and Z

   G Y and Z   J Z and Y

Problem Solving Connections

COMMON
CORE

CC.8.EE.1,
CC.8.EE.3,
CC.8.EE.4

Living on the Moon! Suppose that in the year 2050, it is possible for humans to live on the moon. The resources on the moon will allow for $\sqrt{1 \times 10^{19}}$ people to live there.

The table below gives the projected population for each of the seven continents on Earth in the year 2050.

Projected Population in 2050							
Continent	Africa	Antarctica	Asia	Australia	Europe	North America	South America
Population	2×10^9	1.0×10^3	5.43×10^9	3.09×10^7	6.03×10^8	4.38×10^8	5.36×10^8

1 Can Earth's Total Population Live on the Moon?

Could the total population of Earth live on the moon?

A Write the population of each continent using the same power of 10.

B Add the multipliers for each population. Use the same power of 10 as in **A** to write the world population.

C Write the world population in scientific notation and standard notation.

D Find the number of people who could live on the moon. Use a calculator to find $\sqrt{1 \times 10^{19}}$. Write your answer in standard notation and scientific notation.

E Can the total population of Earth live on the moon? Use your answers from **C** and **D** to perform a calculation and explain how the result justifies your answer.

2 Can the Population of Each Continent Live on the Moon?

The projected population of Antarctica is 1.0×10^3 people. That's just 1000 people on the continent. By comparing this population to the possible population of the moon, you can determine that the entire population of Antarctica could live on the moon. Could the entire population of each of the other continents live on the moon?

A Use subtraction with numbers in scientific notation to compare the populations of Africa, Asia, and Australia to the possible population of the moon. Explain whether the entire population of each these continents could live on the moon.

Africa:

Asia:

Australia:

B Use division with numbers in scientific notation to compare the populations of Europe, North America, and South America to the possible population of the moon. Explain whether the entire population of each these continents could live on the moon.

Europe:

North America:

South America:

C Name the continent(s) for which the entire population could live on the moon.

_____

_____

_____

3 What is the Population Density on the Moon?

Population density is a measure of the number of people per a given area. For example, the population density of Boston, Massachusettes, is about 5,000 people per square kilometer.

The land surface area of Earth is 1.4894×10^8 square kilometers. The surface area of the moon is 3.793×10^7 square kilometers. Assume that humans are able to colonize the entire surface area of the moon. If $\sqrt{1 \times 10^{19}}$ people lived on the moon, would the population density be greater on Earth or on the moon?

A Find the average population density of Earth by dividing the total population of Earth by the land surface area of Earth.

There are about _____ people per square kilometer on Earth.

B Find the average population density of the moon by dividing the possible population of the moon by the surface area of the moon.

There would be about _____ people per square kilometer on the moon.

C Use your answers from **A** and **B** to explain whether Earth or the moon would have a greater population density.

_____

_____

D **Extension** Make a conjecture about why the population density of a city like Boston is greater than the population density of Earth.

_____

_____

_____

_____

Performance Task

CHAPTER 3

COMMON CORE

CC.8.NS.2
CC.8.EE.1
CC.8.EE.2
CC.8.EE.3
CC.8.EE.4
CC.8.G.7
CC.8.G.8

⭐ **1.** Tiny organisms called bacteria can develop a resistance to drugs used to treat them. A scientist has a sample of 3.5×10^5 bacteria, and the scientist estimates that 35% of them are resistant to a certain drug. About how many of the bacteria are *not* resistant to the drug? Write your answer in scientific notation.

⭐ **2.** Cory is making a poster of common geometric shapes. He draws a square with a side of length $4^3 \times 2^{-2}$ cm, an equilateral triangle with a height of $\sqrt{200}$ cm, a circle with a circumference of 8π cm, a rectangle with length $6^2 - 2^3 + 3^{-1}$ cm, and a parallelogram with base $2^3 \times 2^2$ cm.

    a. Which of these numbers are irrational?

    b. Write the numbers in this problem in order from smallest to largest. Use 3.14 as an approximation of π.

⭐ **3.** The formula for the volume of a cube is $V = s^3$, where V is the volume and s is the length of each side. Maureen has a cubic box that has a volume of 512 cubic inches.

    a. Find the length of each side of the box.

b. Maureen wants to line the bottom of the box with paper. How many square inches of paper does she need?

c. Maureen has small ornament boxes with square bases of area 4 square inches. How many of these boxes can she place on the bottom of the large box? Justify your answer.

⭐⭐⭐ **4.** From his home, Myles walked his dog north 5 blocks, east 2 blocks, and stopped at a drinking fountain. He then walked north 3 more blocks and east 4 more blocks. It started to rain so he cut through a field and walked straight home.

a. Draw a diagram of his path.

b. How many blocks did Myles walk in all? How much longer was his walk before it started to rain than his walk home?

Name _____ Class _____ Date _____

SELECTED RESPONSE

1. An industrial machine creates $4^3 \cdot 4^5$ products every year. How many products does the machine create each year?

   A. 4

   B. 16

   C. 64

   D. 65,536

2. Simplify the expression:

   $$(2^2)^4 - \left(\frac{(7-1)^9}{6^2}\right) + (20-17)^3 \times 3^8$$

   F. $2^6 - 6^{11} + 3^{11}$

   G. $4^6 - 6^{11} + 3^5$

   H. $2^8 - 6^7 + 3^{11}$

   J. $8^6 - 36^{11} + 9^{11}$

Use the table for 3 and 4.

Weights of Large Animals			
Animal	African Bush Elephant	Polar Bear	Ostrich
Weight (lb)	27,000	2,000	343.92

3. What is the weight of the ostrich written in scientific notation?

   A. 0.34392×10^4 pounds

   B. 3.4392×10^2 pounds

   C. 3.4392×10^3 pounds

   D. 34.392×10^4 pounds

4. How many times as great as the weight of the polar bear is the weight of the African bush elephant?

   F. 0.135×10^2 pounds

   G. 1.35×10^7 pounds

   H. 1.35×10^1 pounds

   J. 5.4×10^7 pounds

5. In 2009, the population of California was estimated as 3.696×10^7 people. The population of Florida was estimated as 1.854×10^7 people. What was the total estimated population for these two states?

   A. 5.550×10^7 people

   B. 5.550×10^5 people

   C. 1.842×10^7 people

   D. 1.842×10^1 people

6. In 2009, the population of the United States was estimated as 3.07×10^8 people. The population of Maryland was estimated as 5.7×10^6 people. About how many times greater is the population of the U.S. than the population of Maryland?

   F. 2 times

   G. 5 times

   H. 50 times

   J. 200 times

7. A square section of a kitchen floor is made of 49 square tiles. How many tiles are on each side of the square section of the kitchen floor?

   A. 4.9 tiles

   B. 7 tiles

   C. 36 tiles

   D. 42 tiles

8. A sculpture of a giant cube contains 1331 cubes within it. How many smaller cubes are along each edge of the sculpture?

   F. 11 cubes

   G. 13 cubes

   H. 36 cubes

   J. 133 cubes

9. Chen is building a birdhouse. The bottom part is a cube with a volume of $\frac{1}{8}$ cubic foot. What is the length of each edge of the cube in feet?

A. $\frac{1}{2}$ foot   C. $\frac{1}{64}$ foot

B. $\frac{1}{3}$ foot   D. $\frac{1}{512}$ foot

10. Which is approximately equal to $\sqrt{3}$?

F. $\frac{1}{3}$

G. 1.732050808...

H. 3.0

J. 9.732050808...

11. Which fraction is equivalent to $0.\overline{15}$?

A. $\frac{1}{15}$ C. $\frac{10}{15}$

B. $\frac{15}{99}$ D. $\frac{15}{1}$

12. One of the sails of a sailboat is in the shape of a right triangle. What is the height of the sail?

20 ft

12 ft

F. 16 feet   H. 32 feet

G. 23.3 feet   J. 64 feet

13. The table gives the side lengths for four triangles. Which of the triangles is a right triangle?

Triangle	Length of Sides
A	7, 9, 12
B	12, 13, 14
C	10, 23, 25
D	15, 20, 25

A. Triangle A   C. Triangle C

B. Triangle B   D. Triangle D

CONSTRUCTED RESPONSE

14. Explain whether each of the following numbers is rational: 2, $\frac{1}{13}$, $\sqrt{11}$, $0.\overline{3}$.

_____

_____

_____

_____

_____

15. Find a number greater than 1 and less than 1000 that is both a perfect square and a perfect cube. Give the principal square root and the cube root of your number.

_____

16. Explain how you know that $\sqrt{2}$ is less than $2\sqrt{2}$ without performing any calculations.

_____

_____

_____

17. Explain how you know whether $\sqrt{38}$ is closer to 6 or 7 without using a calculator.

_____

_____

18. A 13-foot-long ladder leans against the side of a building. The bottom of the ladder is 5 feet from the base of the building. What height does the ladder reach?

13 ft

5 ft

_____

Ratios, Proportions, and Similarity

Chapter Focus

You will find and compare unit rates. You will use tables to identify and describe proportional relationships. Two triangles are similar if their corresponding angles are congruent and the lengths of their corresponding sides are proportional. You will determine if two triangles are similar. Finally, you will use coordinates to describe the results of a dilation.

Chapter at a Glance

COMMON CORE

Lesson		Standards for Mathematical Content
4-1	Ratios, Rates, and Unit Rates	PREP FOR **CC.8.EE.5**
4-2	Solving Proportions	PREP FOR **CC.8.EE.5**
4-3	Similar Figures	**CC.8.G.5**
4-4	Dilations	**CC.8.G.3**
	Problem Solving Connections	
	Performance Task	
	Assessment Readiness	

Unpacking the Standards

Understanding the standards and the vocabulary terms in the standards will help you know exactly what you are expected to learn in this chapter.

COMMON CORE **CC.8.G.4**

Understand that a two-dimensional figure is similar to another if the second can be obtained from the first by a sequence of rotations, reflections, translations, and dilations; given two similar two-dimensional figures, describe a sequence that exhibits the similarity between them.

Key Vocabulary

similar *(semejantes)* Figures with the same shape but not necessarily the same size are similar.

What It Means to You

You will understand that a dilation changes the size of a figure but not its shape. You will also understand that when two figures have the same shape but different sizes, they are called similar figures.

EXAMPLE

Tell whether each transformation is a dilation. Explain.

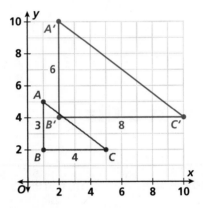

The side lengths of triangle *ABC* multipiled by a scale factor of 2 will produce the side lengths of triangle *A'B'C'*. The side lengths are proportional, so the triangles are similar and triangle *A'B'C'* is a dilation of triangle *ABC*.

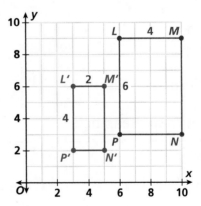

There is not a scale factor that can be multiplied by each side length of rectangle *LMNP* to produce rectangle *L'M'N'P'*. The side lengths are not proportional, so the rectangles are not similar and rectangle *L'M'N'P'* is not a dilation of rectangle *LMNP*.

COMMON CORE **CC.8.G.3**

Describe the effect of dilations, translations, rotations, and reflections on two-dimensional figures using coordinates.

Key Vocabulary

dilation *(dilatación)* A transformation that enlarges or reduces a figure.

translation *(traslación)* A movement (slide) of a figure along a straight line.

rotation *(rotación)* A transformation in which a figure is turned around a point.

reflection *(reflexión)* A transformation of a figure that flips the figure across a line.

What It Means to You

You will describe the effects of transformations to figures in the coordinate plane.

EXAMPLE

Dilate the figure by a scale factor of 2.5. What are the vertices of the image?

$\triangle ABC$ $\qquad\qquad$ $\triangle A'B'C'$

$A(2, 2) \rightarrow A'(2.5 \cdot 2, 2.5 \cdot 2) \rightarrow A'(5, 5)$

$B(3, 4) \rightarrow B'(2.5 \cdot 3, 2.5 \cdot 4) \rightarrow B'(7.5, 10)$

$C(5, 2) \rightarrow C'(2.5 \cdot 5, 2.5 \cdot 2) \rightarrow C'(12.5, 5)$

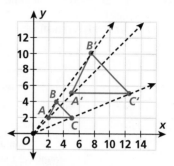

The vertices of the image are
$A'(5, 5)$, $B'(7.5, 10)$, and $C'(12.5, 5)$.

Dilate the figure by a scale factor of $\frac{2}{3}$. What are the vertices of the image?

$\triangle ABC$ $\qquad\qquad$ $\triangle A'B'C'$

$A(3, 9) \rightarrow A'(\frac{2}{3} \cdot 3, \frac{2}{3} \cdot 9) \rightarrow A'(2, 6)$

$B(9, 6) \rightarrow B'(\frac{2}{3} \cdot 9, \frac{2}{3} \cdot 6) \rightarrow B'(6, 4)$

$C(6, 3) \rightarrow C'(\frac{2}{3} \cdot 6, \frac{2}{3} \cdot 3) \rightarrow C'(4, 2)$

The vertices of the image are
$A'(2, 6)$, $B'(6, 4)$, and $C'(4, 2)$.

CHAPTER 4

Key Vocabulary

center of dilation *(centro de una dilatación)* The point of intersection of lines through each pair of corresponding vertices in a dilation.

dilation *(dilatación)* A transformation that enlarges or reduces a figure.

proportion *(proporción)* An equation that states that two ratios are equivalent.

proportional relationship *(relación proporcional)* A relationship between two quantities in which the ratio of one quantity to the other quantity is constant.

scale factor *(factor de escala)* The ratio used to enlarge or reduce similar figures.

unit rate *(tasa unitaria)* A rate in which the second quantity in the comparison is one unit.

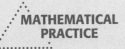
MATHEMATICAL PRACTICE

The Common Core Standards for Mathematical Practice describe varieties of expertise that mathematics educators at all levels should seek to develop in their students. Opportunities to develop these practices are integrated throughout this program.

1. Make sense of problems and persevere in solving them.
2. Reason abstractly and quantitatively.
3. Construct viable arguments and critique the reasoning of others.
4. Model with mathematics.
5. Use appropriate tools strategically.
6. Attend to precision.
7. Look for and make use of structure.
8. Look for and express regularity in repeated reasoning.

CHAPTER 4

Ratios, Rates, and Unit Rates
Going Deeper

Essential question: *How do you find and compare unit rates?*

Recall that a *rate* is a ratio comparing two different units.

$$\frac{2 \text{ dollars}}{5 \text{ pounds}} \leftarrow \text{Read as } \$2 \text{ for } 5 \text{ pounds}$$

A **unit rate** is a rate in which the second quantity is 1. It can be described as the price per 1 unit of an item.

$$\frac{3 \text{ dollars}}{1 \text{ pound}} \leftarrow \text{Read as } \$3 \text{ per pound}$$

video tutor

PREP FOR **CC.8.EE.5**

1 E X A M P L E Finding Unit Rates

Eva can cycle 45 miles in 2.5 hours. What is her rate *r* in miles per hour?

Find Eva's unit rate.

$r = \dfrac{d}{t}$ Find the *ratio* of distance ☐ to time ☐ .

$= \dfrac{45}{2.5}$ Substitute ☐ miles for *d* and ☐ hours for *t*.

$= $ ☐ mi/h   Divide ☐ by ☐ to find her unit rate.

Eva cycles at a rate of _____ .

TRY THIS!

Find each unit rate.

1a. $30 for 4 lb

1b. 3.5 pages in 2 hours

1c. $1\frac{1}{4}$ hours in 5 days

_____   _____   _____

REFLECT

1d. Explain why a rate is a kind of ratio. How does it differ from other ratios?

_____

_____

_____

2 EXAMPLE Comparing Unit Rates

Carl buys 4 gallons of gas for $11. Angela buys 2.5 gallons of the same gas for $6.25. Who is getting the better buy, Carl or Angela?

Compare the unit rates: *Divide* each price by each number of gallons.

Carl's purchase	Angela's purchase

$11 ÷ 4 = $ [   ] ← He pays $ [   ] /gal $6.25 ÷ 2.5 = $ [   ] ← She pays $ [   ] /gal

↑   ↑   ↑   ↑

price   gallons   price   gallons

> The *smaller* unit rate is the better buy.

$ [   ] < $ [   ] . So, _____ is getting the better buy.

TRY THIS!

2a. Which is a better buy: 3 lb for $1.59 or 2.5 lb for $1.41?

_____

2b. Which is faster: 50 mi in 4 h or 35 mi in $2\frac{1}{2}$ h?

_____

REFLECT

2c. What happens when you try to compare the two unit prices shown below?
3-lb bag of peaches for $2.95 *or* one dozen peaches for $3.19

_____

_____

PRACTICE

1. What does one bagel cost if bagels are sold in packages of 0.5 dozen for $2.70? _____

2. Which is the better buy on beef: 1.8 lb for $6.30 *or* 4 lb for $15?

_____

3. In $\frac{1}{4}$ hour, Kyle jogged $2\frac{1}{2}$ mi. Dee jogged $1\frac{3}{4}$ mi in 10 minutes.
Who ran at a faster rate? What is that rate?

_____

4. Error Analysis Milk is on sale at 4 qt for $3.20. Vin says that the unit price is $1.25/qt.
Is he correct? Explain.

_____

Additional Practice

1. Copper weighing 4480 kilograms has a volume of 0.5 cubic meters. What is the density of copper?

   _____

2. Yoshi's yogurt contains 15 calories per ounce. How many calories are in an 8-ounce container of Yoshi's yogurt?

   _____

3. Emily earns $7.50 per hour. How much does she earn in 3 hours?

   _____

4. An antelope can run 152.5 miles in 2.5 hours. What is average speed of the antelope?

   _____

5. Bob and Marquis went on a trip. The first day, they drove 465 miles in 8 hours. What is their average speed for the first day of their trip?

   _____

6. A racecar was attempting to set a record. The racecar went 1000 feet in 4.5 seconds. To the nearest tenth, what is the average speed of the racecar?

   _____

Tell which is the better buy.

7. 8.2 oz of toothpaste for $2.99 or 6.4 oz of toothpaste for $2.49

   _____

8. a 3 lb bag of apples for $2.99 or a 5 lb bag of apples for $4.99

   _____

9. 16 oz bottle of soda for $1.25 or 20 oz bottle of soda for $1.55

   _____

10. Mavis rides the bus every day. She bought a bus pass good for the month of October for $38.75. How much was Mavis charged per day for the bus pass?

    _____

Problem Solving

Scientists have researched the ratio of brain weight to body size in different animals. The results are in the table below.

1. Order the animals by their brain weight to body weight ratio, from smallest to largest.

   _____

   _____

2. It has been hypothesized that the higher the brain weight to body weight ratio, the more intelligent the animal is. By this measure, which animals listed are the most intelligent?

   _____

3. Name two sets of animals that have approximately the same brain weight to body weight ratio.

   _____

Animal	Brain Weight / Body Weight
Cat	$\dfrac{1}{100}$
Dog	$\dfrac{1}{125}$
Elephant	$\dfrac{1}{560}$
Hippo	$\dfrac{1}{2789}$
Horse	$\dfrac{1}{600}$
Human	$\dfrac{1}{40}$
Small birds	$\dfrac{1}{12}$

Find the unit rate. Round to the nearest hundredth.

4. A 64-ounce bottle of apple juice costs $1.35.

   A $0.01/oz   C $0.47/oz

   B $0.02/oz   D $47.4/oz

6. 12 slices of pizza cost $9.00.

   A $0.45/slice   C $0.75/slice

   B $0.50/slice   D $1.33/slice

8. There are 64 beats in 4 measures of music.

   A 16 beats/measure

   B 12 beats/measure

   C 4 beats/measure

   D 0.06 beats/measure

5. Find the unit rate for a 2 lb package of hamburger that costs $3.45.

   F $0.58/lb   H $1.73/lb

   G $1.25/b   J $2.28/b

7. John is selling 5 comic books for $6.00.

   F $0.83/book   H $1.02/book

   G $1.20/book   J $1.45/book

9. The average price of a 30 second commercial for the 2002 Super Bowl was $1,900,000.

   F $120.82/sec

   G $1,242.50/sec

   H $5,839.02/sec

   J $63,333.33/sec

© Houghton Mifflin Harcourt Publishing Company

Solving Proportions
Going Deeper

Essential question: *How can you use tables to identify and describe proportional relationships?*

PREP FOR CC.8.EE.5

1 EXPLORE   Discovering Proportional Relationships

Hedo is playing the drums in a marching band. It takes him 3 minutes to walk 1.5 blocks during a parade.

A   Use the bar diagram to help you determine how many blocks Hedo walks in 1 minute. What operation did you use to find the answer?

_____

B   Complete the table.

Time (min)	1	2	3	4	5
Distance (mi)			1.5		

C   For each column of the table, find the ratio of the distance to the time. Write each ratio in simplest form.

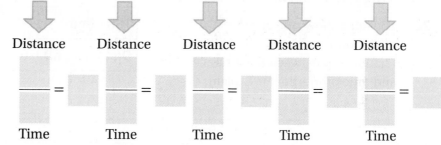

D   What do you notice about the ratios?

_____

E   **Conjecture**   If time was divided by distance, would this ratio be constant?

_____

REFLECT

1.   Suppose the band marches for 20 minutes. Explain how you could find the distance Hedo walks.

_____

_____

A **proportional relationship** is a relationship between two quantities in which the ratio of one quantity to the other quantity is *constant*. A **proportion** is a statement that two ratios are equal.

2 E X A M P L E Identifying Proportional Relationships

Julie's car gets 32 miles per gallon. Is the relationship between the number of miles and the number of gallons a proportional relationship?

A Complete the table.

Fuel Used (gal)	1	2	3	4	5
Distance (mi)	32				

B Complete the ratios.

$$\frac{\text{Distance (mi)}}{\text{Fuel Used (gal)}} = \frac{32}{1} = \underline{\quad} = \underline{\quad} = \underline{\quad} = \underline{\quad} = \boxed{}$$

The ratios are constant. The common ratio is _____.

So, the relationship is/is not proportional.

TRY THIS!

2a. The table shows the distance a cross-country skier travels. Is the relationship between the distance and time proportional? Explain.

Time (min)	1	2	3	4	5
Distance (mi)	0.3	0.6	0.9	1	1.25

_____

2b. The table shows how long it takes Tanya to download data using her cable internet connection. Is the relationship between the data downloaded and time proportional? Explain.

Time (s)	1	2	3	4	5
Data (Kb)	15,000	30,000	45,000	60,000	75,000

_____

REFLECT

2c. At her current download speed, how long will it take Tanya to download 120,000 Kb of data? Explain.

_____

_____

Additional Practice

Tell whether the ratios are proportional.

1. $\dfrac{3}{4} \overset{?}{=} \dfrac{9}{12}$

2. $\dfrac{9}{24} \overset{?}{=} \dfrac{18}{48}$

3. $\dfrac{16}{24} \overset{?}{=} \dfrac{10}{18}$

4. $\dfrac{13}{25} \overset{?}{=} \dfrac{26}{50}$

_____

5. $\dfrac{10}{32} \overset{?}{=} \dfrac{16}{38}$

6. $\dfrac{20}{36} \overset{?}{=} \dfrac{50}{90}$

7. $\dfrac{20}{28} \overset{?}{=} \dfrac{28}{36}$

8. $\dfrac{14}{42} \overset{?}{=} \dfrac{16}{36}$

_____

9. A karate team had 6 girls and 9 boys. Then 2 more girls and 3 more boys joined the team. Did the ratio of girls to boys stay the same? Explain.

_____

10. Janessa bought 4 stamps for $1.48. At this rate, how much would 10 stamps cost?

_____

11. Janelle can mow 5 lawns in 36 minutes. At this rate, how long will it take her to mow 11 lawns?

_____

12. An animal shelter wants their ratio of dogs to cats to be 3:2. If the animal shelter has 78 dogs, how many cats should they have?

_____

13. On a field trip, the ratio of teachers to students must be 2:9. If there are 81 students on the field trip, how many teachers must there be?

_____

14. A gallery owner is hanging up 444 pictures for an art exhibit. She has put up 37 pictures in 9 minutes. If she continues at the same rate how many more minutes will it take her to hang the rest of the pictures?

_____

Problem Solving

Use the ratios in the table to answer each question. Round to the nearest tenth.

Body Part	$\dfrac{\text{Body Part}}{\text{Height}}$
Femur	$\dfrac{1}{4}$
Tibia	$\dfrac{1}{5}$
Hand span	$\dfrac{2}{17}$
Arm span	$\dfrac{1}{1}$
Head circumference	$\dfrac{1}{3}$

1. Which body part is the same length as the person's height?

   _____

2. If a person's tibia is 13 inches, how tall would you expect the person to be?

   _____

3. If a person's hand span is 8.5 inches, about how tall would you expect the person to be?

   _____

4. If a femur is 18 inches long, how many feet tall would you expect the person to be?

   _____

5. What would you expect the head circumference to be of a person who is 5.5 feet tall?

   _____

6. What would you expect the hand span to be of a person who is 5 feet tall?

   _____

Choose the letter for the best answer.

7. Five milliliters of a children's medicine contains 400 mg of the drug amoxicillin. How many mg of amoxicillin does 25 mL contain?

   A 0.3 mg   C 2000 mg

   B 80 mg   D 2500 mg

8. A basketball player for the Seattle Supersonics averages about 2 three-pointers for every 5 he shoots. If he attempts 10 three-pointers in a game, how many would you expect him to make?

   F 4   H 8

   G 5   J 25

9. In 2002, a 30-second commercial during the Super Bowl cost an average of $1,900,000. At this rate, how much would a 45-second commercial cost?

   A $1,266,666   C $3,500,000

   B $2,850,000   D $4,000,000

10. A medicine for dogs indicates that the medicine should be administered in the ratio 2 teaspoons per 5 lb, based on the weight of the dog. How much should be given to a 70 lb dog?

   F 5 teaspoons   H 14 teaspoons

   G 12 teaspoons   J 28 teaspoons

video tutor

Similar Figures
Going Deeper: Similar Triangles

Essential question: *How can you determine when two triangles are similar?*

Recall that similar figures have the same shape, but may have different sizes. Two triangles are similar if their corresponding angles are congruent and the lengths of their corresponding sides are proportional.

CC.8.G.5

1 EXPLORE **Discovering Angle-Angle Similarity**

A Use your protractor and a straightedge to draw a triangle. Make one angle measure 45° and another angle measure 60°.

B Compare your triangle to those drawn by your classmates. How are the triangles the same?

_____

How are they different?

_____

C Use the Triangle Sum Theorem to find the measure of the third angle of your triangle.

_____

REFLECT

1a. If two angles in one triangle are congruent to two angles in another triangle, what do you know about the third pair of angles?

_____

_____

1b. Are two pairs of congruent angles enough information to conclude that two triangles are similar? Explain.

_____

_____

Angle-Angle (AA) Similarity Postulate

If two angles of one triangle are congruent to two angles of another triangle, then the triangles are similar.

2 EXAMPLE   Using the AA Similarity Postulate

Explain whether the triangles are similar.

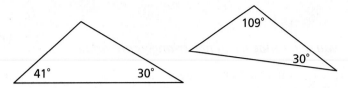

The figure shows only one pair of congruent angles. Find the measure of the third angle in each triangle. Label the angle measures in the figure.

$41° + 30° + m\angle 3 = 180°$

$71° + m\angle 3 = 180°$

$71° + m\angle 3 - \boxed{} = 180° - \boxed{}$

$m\angle 3 = \boxed{}$

$\boxed{} + \boxed{} + m\angle 3 = 180°$

$\boxed{} + m\angle 3 = 180°$

$\boxed{} + m\angle 3 - \boxed{} = 180° - \boxed{}$

$m\angle 3 = \boxed{}$

Because _____ in one triangle are congruent to _____ in the other triangle, the triangles are _____.

You can also determine whether two triangles are similar by deciding whether the lengths of the corresponding sides are proportional.

3 EXAMPLE   Using Proportional Side Lengths

Explain whether △ABC and △DEF are similar.

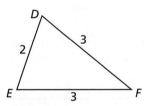

Corresponding parts of triangles are listed in the same order, so $\overline{AB}$ corresponds to $\overline{DE}$, $\overline{BC}$ corresponds to _____, and $\overline{AC}$ corresponds to _____.

Determine whether the lengths of corresponding sides are proportional.

$\dfrac{AB}{DE} = \dfrac{BC}{EF} \rightarrow \dfrac{6}{\boxed{}} \overset{?}{=} \dfrac{\boxed{}}{\boxed{}}$ *Substitute the lengths from the figure.*

$\dfrac{\boxed{}}{\boxed{}} \overset{?}{=} \dfrac{\boxed{}}{\boxed{}}$ *Simplify the ratios.*

AC is congruent to BC and DF is congruent to EF, so you do not need to set up a second proportion. Because the lengths of corresponding sides are _____, the triangles are _____.

4 EXAMPLE Finding Missing Measures in Similar Triangles

While playing tennis, Matt is 12 meters from the net that is 0.9 meter high. He needs to hit the ball so that it just clears the net and lands 6 meters beyond the base of the net. At what height in meters should Matt hit the tennis ball?

A Both triangles contain $\angle A$; $\angle A$ in $\triangle ABC$ is congruent to _____ in $\triangle ADE$.

The net ($\overline{BC}$) is perpendicular to the ground ($\overline{AB}$), so $\triangle ABC$ is a right angle. The line representing the height of the ball ($\overline{DE}$) is perpendicular to the ground ($\overline{AD}$), so $\angle ADE$ is a _____.

There are two pairs of _____ angles, so $\triangle ABC$ and $\triangle ADE$ are _____.

B In similar triangles, corresponding side lengths are proportional.

$$\frac{AD}{AB} = \frac{DE}{BC} \quad \rightarrow \quad \frac{6+12}{\boxed{}} = \frac{h}{\boxed{}}$$ *Substitute the lengths from the figure.*

$$\boxed{} \times \frac{18}{\boxed{}} = \frac{h}{\boxed{}} \times \boxed{}$$ *Use properties of equality to get h by itself.*

$$0.9 \times \boxed{} = h$$ *Simplify.*

$$\boxed{} = h$$ *Multiply.*

Matt should hit the ball at a height of _____ meter(s).

TRY THIS!

4. What if you set up a proportion so that each ratio compares parts of one triangle?

height of $\triangle ABC$ → $\dfrac{BC}{AB} = \dfrac{DE}{AD}$ ← height of $\triangle ADE$
base of $\triangle ABC$ → $\phantom{\dfrac{BC}{AB}}$ ← base of $\triangle ADE$

Show that this proportion leads to the same value for h as in **B**.

1. Two transversals intersect two parallel lines as shown. Explain whether △*ABC* and △*DEC* are similar.

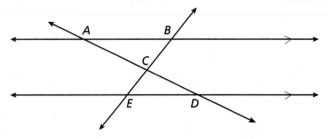

_____

_____

_____

_____

2. A flagpole casts a shadow 23.5 feet long. At the same time of day, Mrs. Gilbert, who is 5.5 feet tall, casts a shadow that is 7.5 feet long. How tall in feet is the flagpole? Round your answer to the tenths place.

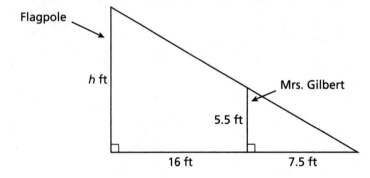

3. △*LMN* and △*QRS* are similar. Find the value of *x*.

Additional Practice

1. Which triangles are similar?

_____

2. Explain whether the triangles are similar.

_____

_____

3. An isosceles triangle has a base of 20 cm
   and legs measuring 36 cm. How long are the legs
   of a similar triangle with base measuring 50 cm? _____

4. Explain why ΔABC and ΔADE are similar. Then find CE.

_____

_____

Problem Solving

Write the correct answer.

1. Mr. Hernstrom stands next to the Illinois Centennial Monument at Logan Square in Chicago and casts a shadow that is 18 feet long. The shadow of the monument is 204 feet long. If Mr. Hernstrom is 6 feet tall, how tall is the monument?

_____

2. If two angles in one triangle are congruent to two angles in another triangle, what do you know about the third pair of angles?

_____

3. The two shortest sides of a right triangle are 10 in. and 24 in. long. What is the length of the shortest side of a similar right triangle whose two longest sides are 36 in. and 39 in.?

_____

Choose the letter for the best answer.

4. A 9-foot street sign casts a shadow that is 12 feet long. The lamppost next to it casts a shadow that is 24 feet long. How tall is the lamppost?

   A 15 feet

   B 18 feet

   C 24 feet

   D 36 feet

5. Two tables shaped like triangles are similar. The measure of one of the larger table's angles is 38°, and another angle is half that size. What are the measures of all the angles in the smaller table?

   F 19°, 9.5°, and 61.5°

   G 38°, 19°, and 123°

   H 38°, 38°, and 104°

   J 76°, 38°, and 246°

4-4

Dilations
Going Deeper

Essential question: *How can you use coordinates to describe the result of a dilation?*

A **dilation** is a transformation that changes the size, but not the shape, of a geometric figure. The center of the figure is known as the **center of dilation**. When dilating in the coordinate plane, the center of dilation is usually the origin.

CC.8.G.3

1 EXPLORE Applying Dilations

The square is the preimage (input). The center of dilation is the origin.

A List the coordinates of the vertices of the square.

  A: (_____, _____)   C: (_____, _____)

  B: (_____, _____)   D: (_____, _____)

B Multiply each coordinate by 2. List the resulting ordered pairs.

  A': (_____, _____)   C': (_____, _____)

  B': (_____, _____)   D': (_____, _____)

C Sketch the image of the dilation. Label each vertex of the image.

D How does multiplying the coordinates of the preimage by 2 affect the image?

_____

_____

E Multiply each coordinate from the preimage by $\frac{1}{2}$. List the resulting ordered pairs.

  A'': (_____, _____)   C'': (_____, _____)

  B'': (_____, _____)   D'': (_____, _____)

F Sketch the image of the dilation. Label each vertex of the image.

G How does multiplying the coordinates of the preimage by $\frac{1}{2}$ affect the image?

_____

_____

A **scale factor** describes how much larger or smaller the image of a dilation is than the preimage.

> ### Rule for Dilation
>
> For a dilation centered at the origin with scale factor k, the image of point $P(x, y)$ is found by multiplying each coordinate by k.
> $$(x, y) \rightarrow (kx, ky)$$
> - If $k > 1$, then the image is larger than the preimage.
> - If $0 < k < 1$, then the image is smaller than the preimage.

CC.8.G.3

2 EXAMPLE Enlargements

The figure is the preimage. The center of dilation is the origin.

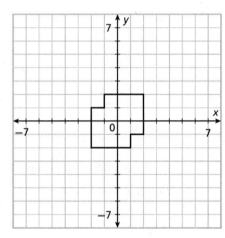

A List the coordinates of the vertices of the preimage in the first column of the table.

Preimage	Image
(2, 2)	(6, 6)

B What is the scale factor for the dilation $(x, y) \rightarrow (3x, 3y)$? _____

C Apply the dilation to the preimage and write the coordinates of the vertices of the image in the second column of the table.

D Sketch the image under the dilation on the coordinate grid.

REFLECT

2a. How does the dilation affect the length of line segments?

_____

_____

2b. How does the dilation affect angle measures?

_____

3 EXAMPLE Reductions

The arrow is the preimage. The center of dilation is the origin.

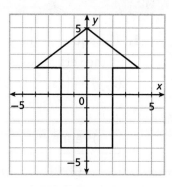

A List the coordinates of the vertices of the preimage in the first column of the table.

Preimage	Image

B What is the scale factor for the dilation $(x, y) \rightarrow \left(\frac{1}{2}x, \frac{1}{2}y\right)$? _____

C Apply the dilation to the preimage and write the coordinates of the vertices of the image in the second column of the table.

D Sketch the image under the dilation on the coordinate grid.

REFLECT

3a. How does the dilation affect the length of line segments?

_____

_____

3b. How would a dilation with scale factor 1 affect the preimage?

_____

_____

TRY THIS!

3c. Identify the scale factor of the dilation shown.

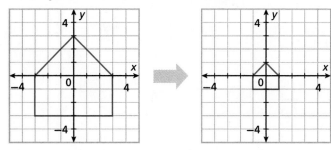

_____

1. The square is the preimage. The center of dilation is the origin. Write the coordinates of the vertices of the preimage in the first column of the table. Then apply the dilation $(x, y) \rightarrow \left(\frac{3}{2}x, \frac{3}{2}y\right)$ and write the coordinates of the vertices of the image in the second column. Sketch the image of the figure under the dilation.

Preimage	Image
(2, 0)	**(3, 0)**

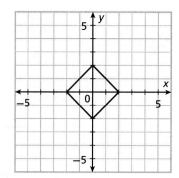

Sketch the image of the figure under the given dilation.

2. $(x, y) \rightarrow (2x, 2y)$

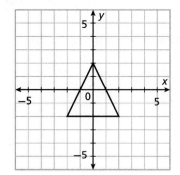

3. $(x, y) \rightarrow \left(\frac{2}{3}x, \frac{2}{3}y\right)$

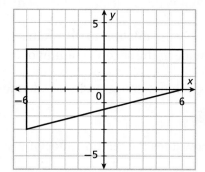

Identify the scale factor of the dilation shown.

4. scale factor =

5. scale factor =

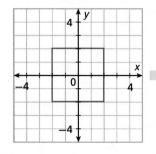

Additional Practice

Tell whether each transformation is a dilation.

1.

_____

2.

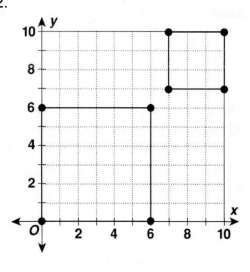

_____

Dilate each figure by the given scale factor with the origin as the center of dilation. What are the vertices of the image?

3. scale factor of 2

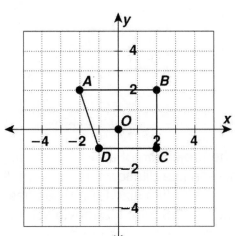

_____

_____

4. scale factor of $\frac{1}{2}$

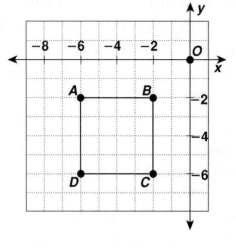

_____

_____

Problem Solving

Write the correct answer.

1. When you enlarge something on a photocopy machine, is the image a dilation?

_____

2. When you make a photocopy that is the same size, is the image a dilation? If so, what is the scale factor?

_____

3. In the movie *Honey, I Blew Up the Kid*, a two-year-old-boy is enlarged to a height of 112 feet. If the average height of a two-year old boy is 3 feet, what is the scale factor of this enlargement?

_____

4. In the movie *Honey, I Shrunk the Kids,* an inventor shrinks his kids by a scale factor of about $\frac{1}{240}$. If his kids were about 5 feet tall, how many inches tall were they after they were shrunk?

_____

Use the coordinate plane for Exercises 5–6. Round to the nearest tenth. Choose the letter for the best answer.

5. What will be the coordinates of *A'*, *B'* and *C'* after △*ABC* is dilated by a factor of 5?

   A *A'* (5, 10), *B'* (7, 8), *C'* (3, 8)

   B *A'* (0, 25), *B'* (10, 15), *C'* (−10, 15)

   C *A'* (0, 5), *B'* (10, 3), *C'* (−10, 3)

   D *A'* (0, 15), *B'* (2, 15), *C'* (−2, 15)

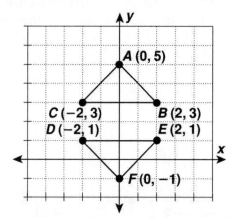

6. What will be the coordinates of *D'*, *E'* and *F'* after △*DEF* is dilated by a factor of 5?

   F *D'* (−10, 5), *E'* (10, 5), *F'* (0, −5)

   G *D'* (10, 5), *E'* (5, 5), *F'* (0, 5)

   H *D'* (10, 0), *E'* (5, 0), *F'* (−5, 0)

   J *D'* (10, 5), *E'* (5, 5), *F'* (−10, 0)

7. The projection of a movie onto a screen is a dilation. The universally accepted film size for movies has a width of 35 mm. If a movie screen is 12 m wide, what is the dilation factor?

   A 420   C 342.9

   B 0.3   D 2916.7

CHAPTER 4

Problem Solving Connections

COMMON CORE

CC.8.G.3
CC.8.G.4

Sign Design   Tyler has been hired by the owner of a 3-D movie theater to create a neon sign for the theater. The owner asks Tyler to design a logo and then turn it into a large neon sign that covers most of an outside wall. How much will it cost to produce the neon sign?

1   Draw the Logo

Because the theater shows 3-D movies, Tyler decides that the logo should look like three rectangular movie screens.

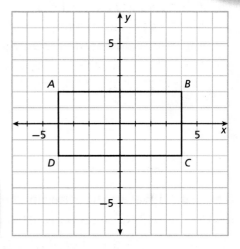

A   Tyler begins by drawing a rectangle, as shown. Write the coordinates of the vertices of the rectangle.

B   To draw the second rectangle, Tyler dilates rectangle *ABCD* using a dilation with scale factor $\frac{3}{2}$. Sketch the image and label the vertices *A'*, *B'*, *C'*, and *D'*. Then write the coordinates of the vertices of the image.

C   Write the dilation using the notation (x, y) (kx, ky). Then use the value of *k* to explain whether the dilation is an enlargement or a reduction.

D   To draw the third rectangle, Tyler dilates rectangle *A'B'C'D'* using the dilation $(x, y) \rightarrow (\frac{1}{3} x, \frac{1}{3} y)$. Sketch the image and label the vertices *A''*, *B''*, *C''*, and *D''*. Then write the coordinates of the vertices of the image.

2 Find the Height of the Wall

The neon sign will be placed on an outside wall of the movie theater. In order to determine the dimensions of the sign, Tyler first needs to know the height of the wall.

Outside Wall of Theater

A Tyler is 6 feet tall. He stands near the theater and finds that his shadow is 7.5 feet long. The shadow of the wall is 62.5 feet long. He makes the sketch shown here. Name two triangles that are similar and explain why they are similar.

B What are the corresponding sides in the triangles?

C Write and solve a proportion to find the height of the wall. Show your work.

D Tyler decides that the top of the neon sign should be 10 feet below the top of the wall and the bottom of the neon sign should 10 feet above the ground. What is the overall height of the neon sign? Explain.

3 Find the Dimensions of the Sign

The neon sign will be an enlargement of the logo that Tyler designed. Tyler needs to know the dimensions of the logo when it is enlarged.

A Tyler has already determined the overall height of the neon sign. In his drawing of the logo, this height is represented by the height of the outer rectangle, rectangle A′B′C′D′. Look back at your work to complete the following.

Overall height of the neon sign: _____ feet

Height of rectangle A′B′C′D′ on coordinate plane: _____ units

B What length on the neon sign is represented by one unit on the coordinate plane? Explain.

C Complete the table.

Length on the Coordinate Plane (units)	1	2	3	4	5	6
Length on the Neon Sign (ft)						

D Is the relationship in the table a proportional relationship? Why or why not?

E Use your drawing of the logo on a coordinate plane and the above table to help you find the height and width of each rectangle in the neon sign.

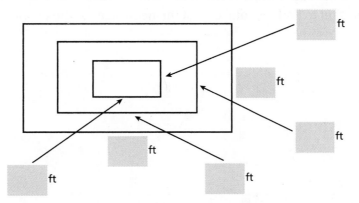

4 Answer the Question

Neon signs are made from glass tubing that is bent into the desired shapes. The cost of a sign depends upon the length of the tubing.

A What is the total length of the tubing that will be needed to make the neon sign for the movie theater? Explain.

B Tyler gathers pricing information from two different companies that make neon signs. The prices are shown in the tables. For which company is the relationship between price and length a proportional relationship? Why?

Nancy's Neon					
Length of Tubing (ft)	4	8	12	16	20
Price of Sign ($)	14.00	24.00	42.00	52.00	60.00

A-Plus Neon					
Length of Tubing (ft)	3	6	9	12	15
Price of Sign ($)	7.50	15.00	22.50	30.00	37.50

C Which company seems to offer a better deal on neon signs? Why?

D Tyler chooses the company that offers a better deal. Show how he can use a proportion to find the total cost of the neon sign for the movie theater.

CHAPTER 4

Performance Task

COMMON CORE

CC.8.EE.5
CC.8.G.3
CC.8.G.4

⭐ **1.** Janelle runs a steady pace from the parking lot down a 5-mile trail. She makes the graph shown to describe her run. Tim jogs the same 5-mile trail, but writes the equation $d = \frac{1}{8}t$ to describe his distance d miles after jogging t minutes.

a. Write an equation to represent Janelle's graph.

b. How would Tim's graph compare to Janelle's graph? Who runs at a faster average rate? Explain.

⭐ **2.** Peggy holds a rubber band between her thumb and index finger, then pulls from one point to form a triangle. When she pulls harder, the triangle gets bigger. She drew the triangles on the coordinate plane as shown.

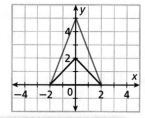

a. Are the triangles similar? How do you know?

b. Is this an example of a dilation? Explain.

3. A triangle on the coordinate plane has vertices (0, 0), (5, 0), and (5, 4).

   a. The figure is dilated by a scale factor of 1.5 with the origin as the center of dilation. Find the coordinates of the dilated figure.

   b. What is the effect of the dilation on the side lengths of the figure?

   c. Are the triangles similar? Explain.

4. Fernando has a fence represented by rectangle *LMNP* on the coordinate plane. He asks for a new fence to enclose 6 times as much area as the current fence. He would also like the shape enclosed by the fence to be similar to shape enclosed by the current fence. The contractors construct the fence shown by the rectangle *L'M'N'P'*.

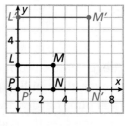

   a. Did the contractors increase the area by the amount Fernando wanted? Explain.

   b. Does the new fence enclose a shape similar to the old shape? How do you know?

Name _____ Class _____ Date _____

SELECTED RESPONSE

1. Temperatures were taken after every 10 minutes for 4 experiments.

Experiment 1	52°	26°	13°

Experiment 2	28°	56°	84°

Experiment 3	14°	28°	56°

Experiment 4	67°	54°	41°

Which of the experiments' temperatures have a proportional relationship with time?

A. Experiment 1

B. Experiment 2

C. Experiment 3

D. Experiment 4

2. Which value would complete the table to make the relationship between the two quantities proportional?

x	y
1	22.4
2	44.8
3	?
4	89.6
5	112

F. 44.8   **H.** 89.6

G. 67.2   **J.** 56

3. Determine whether the ratios $\frac{8}{12}$ and $\frac{10}{18}$ are proportional.

A. not proportional   **B.** proportional

4. A factory worker can package 150 games in 15 minutes. How many games can he package per minute?

F. 20   **H.** 8.33

G. 135   **J.** 10

5. Sarah's pay for two weeks was $158.16. If she worked 8 hours the first week and 4 hours the second, what was her rate of pay?

A. $3.23 per hr   **C.** $22.60 per hr

B. $13.18 per hr   **D.** $31.64 per hr

6. Which of these is a lower unit price than 8 for $15?

F. 3 for $7   **H.** 10 for $20

G. 5 for $9   **J.** 12 for $25

7. Which of these prices is a lower unit price than 5 for $9.00?

A. 3 for $6.00   **C.** 6 for $10.00

B. 8 for $16.00   **D.** 10 for $19.00

8. Ignacio is going on vacation. He needs to drive 520 miles in 8 hours. What is his average speed in miles per hour?

F. 63 miles per hour

G. 65 miles per hour

H. 67 miles per hour

J. 69 miles per hour

9. Three pounds of ground beef costs $2.00. What is the unit rate?

A. $0.50/pound   **C.** $1.50/pound

B. $0.67/pound   **D.** $2.00/pound

© Houghton Mifflin Harcourt Publishing Company

10. Triangle *ABC* is similar to triangle *DEF*. What is the value of *x*?

 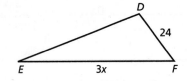

    F. 15   **H.** 30

    G. 20   **J.** 60

11. A figure is dilated by a scale factor of 3. If the origin is the center of dilation, what is the image of a vertex located at $(3, 4)$?

    A. $(1, 1\frac{1}{2})$ **C.** $(9, 4)$

    B. $(3, 12)$ **D.** $(9, 12)$

CONSTRUCTED RESPONSE

12. Dilate the figure by a scale factor of 2.5 with the origin as the center of dilation. Graph the new figure on the coordinate plane, and list the vertices of the image. Show your work.

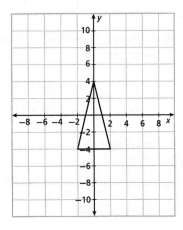

_____

_____

_____

13. A figure is dilated by a scale factor of 2. If the origin is the center of dilation, what are the coordinates in the original figure of a vertex located at $(12, 8)$ in the enlarged figure?

_____

14. Su, who is 5 feet tall, is standing at point *D* in the drawing. The top of her head is at point *E*. A tree in the yard is at point *B* with the top of the tree at point *C*. Su stands so her shadow meets the end of the tree's shadow at point *A*.

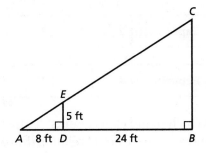

    a. Which triangles are similar? How do you know?

_____

_____

_____

_____

    b. What is the ratio of the triangles?

_____

    c. Find the height of the tree.

_____

Geometric Relationships

Chapter Focus

You will use angle pairs to solve problems. You will explore angles formed by parallel lines that are cut by a transversal and the measures of the angles in a triangle. A dilation is a transformation in which a figure and its image are similar. You will use coordinates to find the scale factor used in a dilation and to describe the result of a translation, reflection, or rotation. You will also consider what properties of a figure are preserved under a translation, reflection, or rotation. The Side-Side-Side Postulate and the Side-Angle-Side Postulate will be used to prove that two triangles are congruent. Finally, you will explore the connection between transformations and congruent figures and transformations and similar figures.

Chapter at a Glance

COMMON CORE

Lesson		Standards for Mathematical Content
5-1	Angle Relationships	PREP FOR **CC.8.G.1**
5-2	Parallel and Perpendicular Lines	**CC.8.G.5**
5-3	Triangles	**CC.8.G.5**
5-4	Coordinate Geometry	PREP FOR **CC.8.G.3**
5-5	Congruence	PREP FOR **CC.8.G.2**
5-6	Transformations	**CC.8.G.3**
5-7	Similarity and Congruence Transformations	**CC.8.G.1**
5-8	Identifying Combined Transformations	**CC.8.G.2, CC.8.G.4**
	Problem Solving Connections	
	Performance Task	
	Assessment Readiness	

CHAPTER 5

Unpacking the Standards

Understanding the standards and the vocabulary terms in the standards will help you know exactly what you are expected to learn in this chapter.

COMMON CORE CC.8.G.5

Use informal arguments to establish facts about the angle sum and exterior angle of triangles, about the angles created when parallel lines are cut by a transversal, and the angle-angle criterion for similarity of triangles.

Key Vocabulary

transversal *(transversal)* A line that intersects two or more lines.

What It Means to You

You will learn about the special angle relationships formed when parallel lines are intersected by a third line called a transversal.

EXAMPLE

Copy and measure the angles formed by the transversal and the parallel lines. Which angles seem to be congruent?

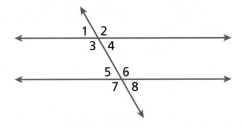

$\angle 1$, $\angle 4$, $\angle 5$, and $\angle 8$ all measure 60°.

$\angle 2$, $\angle 3$, $\angle 6$, and $\angle 7$ all measure 120°.

$\angle 1 \cong \angle 4 \cong \angle 5 \cong \angle 8$

$\angle 2 \cong \angle 3 \cong \angle 6 \cong \angle 7$

COMMON CORE CC.8.G.4

Understand that a two-dimensional figure is similar to another if the second can be obtained from the first by a sequence of rotations, reflections, translations, and dilations; given two similar two-dimensional figures, describe a sequence that exhibits the similarity between them.

Key Vocabulary

similar *(semejantes)* Figures with the same shape but not necessarily the same size are similar.

What It Means to You

You will understand that a dilation changes the size of a figure but not its shape. You will also understand that when two figures have the same shape but different sizes, they are called similar figures.

EXAMPLE

Identify the combined transformations from the original to the final image, and tell whether the two figures are similar or congruent.

ABCD → *A'B'C'D'*: This is a 90° clockwise rotation around the origin.

A'B'C'D' → *A"B"C"D"*: This is a dilation by a factor of 2 with the origin as the center of dilation. The original and final images are similar.

COMMON CORE **CC.8.G.3**

Describe the effect of dilations, translations, rotations, and reflections on two-dimensional figures using coordinates.

Key Vocabulary

dilation *(dilatación)* A transformation that enlarges or reduces a figure.

translation *(traslación)* A movement (slide) of a figure along a straight line.

rotation *(rotación)* A transformation in which a figure is turned around a point.

reflection *(reflexión)* A transformation of a figure that flips the figure across a line.

What It Means to You

You will describe the effects of transformations to figures in the coordinate plane.

EXAMPLE

Identify the transformation from the original to the image, and tell whether the two figures are similar or congruent.

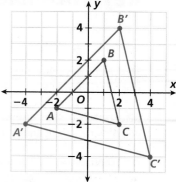

Original △ABC

Image △A'B'C'

Original vertex	Image vertex
A (−2, −1)	A' 2(−2, −1) = (−4, −2)
B (1, 2)	B' 2(1, 2) = (2, 4)
C (2, −2)	C' 2(2, −2) = (4, −4)

The coordinates of A', B', and C' are double the original coordinates of A, B, and C. So the transformation is a dilation and the triangles are similar.

COMMON CORE **CC.8.G.2**

Understand that a two-dimensional figure is congruent to another if the second can be obtained from the first by a sequence of rotations, reflections, and translations; given two congruent figures, describe a sequence that exhibits the congruence between them.

Key Vocabulary

congruent *(congruentes)* Having the same size and shape; the symbol for congruent is ≅.

What It Means to You

You will describe the sequence of rotations, reflections, and translations used to transform one figure into a second congruent figure.

EXAMPLE

Identify the combined transformations from the original to the final image, and tell whether the two figures are similar or congruent.

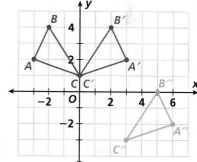

Original △ABC

First image △A'B'C'

Final image △A''B''C''

△**ABC** → △**A'B'C'**: This is a reflection across the *y*-axis.

△**A'B'C'** → △**A''B''C''**: This is a translation.

Each transformation is a congruence transformation. original and final images are congruent.

CHAPTER 5

Key Vocabulary

adjacent angles *(ángulos adyacentes)* Angles in the same plane that have a common vertex and a common side.

alternate exterior angles *(ángulos alternos externos)* For two lines intersected by a transversal, a pair of angles that lie on opposite sides of the transversal and outside the other two lines.

alternate interior angles *(ángulos alternos internos)* For two lines intersected by a transversal, a pair of nonadjacent angles that lie on opposite sides of the transversal and between the other two lines.

complementary angles *(ángulos complementarios)* Two angles whose measures add to 90°.

congruent *(congruentes)* Having the same size and shape; the symbol for congruent is ≅.

corresponding angles *(ángulos correspondientes)* For two lines intersected by a transversal, a pair of angles that lie on the same side of the transversal and on the same sides of the other two lines.

dilation *(dilatación)* A transformation that enlarges or reduces a figure.

exterior angle *(ángulo exterior)* An angle formed by one side of a polygon and the extension of an adjacent side.

image *(imagen)* A figure resulting from a transformation.

interior angles *(ángulos internos)* Angles on the inner sides of two lines cut by a transversal.

line of reflection *(línea de reflexión)* A line that a figure is flipped across to create a mirror image of the original figure.

reflection *(reflexión)* A transformation of a figure that flips the figure across a line.

remote interior angle *(ángulo interior remoto)* An interior angle that is not adjacent to the exterior angle.

rotation *(rotación)* A transformation in which a figure is turned around a point.

same-side interior angles *(ángulo de interior del mismo lado)* For two lines intersected by a transversal, a pair of angles that lie on the same side of the transversal, between the parallel lines.

scale factor *(factor de escala)* The ratio used to enlarge or reduce similar figures.

similar *(semejantes)* Figures with the same shape but not necessarily the same size are similar.

supplementary angles *(ángulos suplementarios)* Two angles whose measures have a sum of 180°.

transformation *(transformación)* A change in the size or position of a figure.

translation *(traslación)* A movement (slide) of a figure along a straight line.

transversal *(transversal)* A line that intersects two or more lines.

vertical angles *(ángulos verticales)* A pair of opposite congruent angles formed by intersecting lines.

Angle Relationships
Going Deeper

Essential question: *How can you use angle pairs to solve problems?*

PREP FOR CC.8.G.1

1 E X P L O R E   **Measuring and Describing Angles**

A When lines intersect, several angles are formed. Use a ruler or straightedge to draw a pair of intersecting lines. Label each angle in order clockwise from 1 to 4.

B Use a protractor to find each angle measure.

Angle	Angle Measure
1	
2	
3	
4	

C What can you say about m∠1 and m∠3? _____

Angles 1 and 3 are **vertical angles**. They are *opposite* one another. Vertical angles have equal measures, *no* sides in common, and *no* common interior points.

What is the other pair of vertical angles in **A** ? _____

D What can you say about m∠1 and m∠2? About m∠2 and m∠3?

_____

Angles 1 and 2 and angles 2 and 3 are **adjacent angles**. They share a common vertex and a common side.

What are the two other pairs of adjacent angles in the figure?

_____

E What can you say about the sum of the degree measures of each pair of

adjacent angles? _____

Two angles whose measures add up to **180°** are called **supplementary angles**.

Each pair of adjacent angles in the figure you made are _____ angles.

Two angles whose measures add up to **90°** are called **complementary angles**.

REFLECT

1. Angles *A* and *B* are supplementary. m∠*A* = 80°. m∠*B* = _____

2 EXAMPLE Finding Angle Measures

Find the measure of ∠EHF.

∠EHF and _____ are _____ angles.

The sum of their measures is _____.

Write and solve an equation to find m∠EHF.

$$\boxed{} + \boxed{} = 180$$

$$2x \quad = \boxed{}$$

m∠EHF = _____

TRY THIS!

2. Write and solve an equation to find the value of $3x$ and m∠JML.

_____

_____

m∠JML = $3x$ = _____

PRACTICE

For 1–6, use the figure. $\overleftrightarrow{SQ} \perp \overleftrightarrow{TN}$.

1. Name a pair of vertical angles. _____

2. Name a pair of adjacent angles. _____

3. Name a pair of supplementary angles.

_____

4. Name a pair of complementary angles.

_____

5. Angle SUT measures 90°. What is m∠QUN? _____

6. Angle RUN measures 51°. What is m∠SUR? _____

7. Two streets intersect. One of the angles formed measures 136°. The angles adjacent to the 136° angle each measure $2x°$. What does x equal? What is the degree measure of each of these adjacent angles?

_____

8. **Error Analysis** James claims that when two adjacent angles measure 90° together, the two angles are supplementary. Explain why James is wrong.

_____

_____

5-1

Additional Practice

Use the diagram to name each figure.

1. a right angle

_____

2. two acute angles

_____

3. two obtuse angles

_____

4. a pair of complementary angles

_____

_____

_____

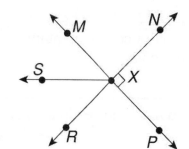

5. three pairs of supplementary angles

_____

_____

_____

Use the diagram to find each angle measure.

6. If m∠2 = 110°, find m∠4.

_____

7. If m∠1 = n°, find m∠3.

_____

8. The diagram shows the intersection of three
roadways on a map. Based on the diagram, what
should be the measure of ∠ECD?

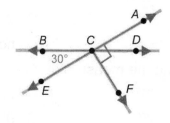

Problem Solving

Use the flag of the Bahamas to solve the problems.

1. Name a right angle in the flag.

   _____

2. Name a pair of complementary
   angles in the flag.

   _____

3. Name two acute angles in the flag.

   _____

4. Name a pair of supplementary
   angles in the flag.

   _____

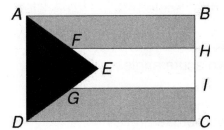

**The diagram illustrates a ray of light being reflected off a
mirror. The angle of incidence is congruent to the angle of
reflection. Choose the letter for the best answer.**

5. Name a pair of supplementary angles.

   A ∠CMA, ∠AMN,

   B ∠NMB, ∠AMB

   C ∠NMC, ∠DMN

   D ∠AMN, ∠NMD

6. Name a pair of complementary
   angles.

   F ∠NMB, ∠BMD

   G ∠AMN, ∠NMB

   H ∠CMA, ∠AMD

   J ∠CMA, ∠DMB

7. Which angle is congruent to ∠2?

   A ∠1   C ∠3

   B ∠4   D none

9. Find the measure of ∠1.

   A 65°   C 25°

   B 35°   D 90°

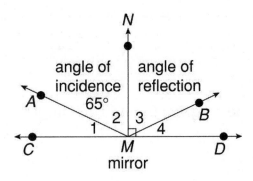

8. Find the measure of ∠4.

   F 65°   H 25°

   G 35°   J 90°

10. Find the measure of ∠3.

    F 90°   H 35°

    G 45°   J 65°

Parallel and Perpendicular Lines
Going Deeper

Essential question: *What can you conclude about the angles formed by parallel lines that are cut by a transversal?*

A **transversal** is a line that intersects two lines in the same plane at two different points. Transversal *t* and lines *a* and *b* form eight angles.

video tutor

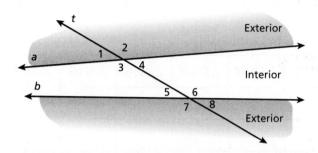

Angle Pairs Formed by a Transversal

Term	Example
Corresponding angles lie on the same side of the transversal *t*, on the same side of lines *a* and *b*.	∠1 and ∠5
Alternate interior angles are nonadjacent angles that lie on opposite sides of the transversal *t*, between lines *a* and *b*.	∠3 and ∠6
Alternate exterior angles lie on opposite sides of the transversal *t*, outside lines *a* and *b*.	∠1 and ∠8
Same-side interior angles lie on the same side of the transversal *t*, between lines *a* and *b*.	∠3 and ∠5

CC.8.G.5

1 EXPLORE Parallel Lines and Transversals

Use geometry software to explore the angles formed when a transversal intersects parallel lines.

A Construct a line and label two points on the line *A* and *B*.

B Create point *C* not on $\overleftrightarrow{AB}$. Then construct a line parallel to $\overleftrightarrow{AB}$ through point *C*. Create another point on this line and label it *D*.

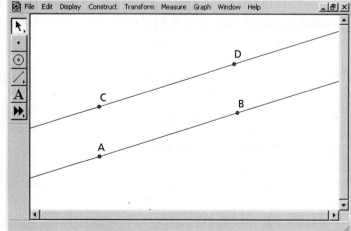

C Create two points outside the two parallel lines and label them *E* and *F*. Construct transversal $\overleftrightarrow{EF}$. Label the points of intersection *G* and *H*.

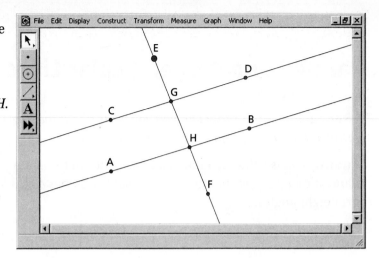

D Measure the angles formed by the parallel lines and the transversal. Write the angle measures in the table below.

E Drag point *E* or point *F* to a different position record the new angle measures in the table.

Angle	∠CGE	∠DGE	∠CGH	∠DGH	∠AHG	∠BHG	∠AHF	∠BHF
Measure								
Measure								

REFLECT

1a. Identify the pairs of corresponding angles in the diagram. Then make a conjecture about their angle measures. Drag a point in the diagram to confirm your conjecture.

_____

_____

1b. Identify the pairs of alternate interior angles in the diagram. Then make a conjecture about their angle measures. Drag a point in the diagram to confirm your conjecture.

_____

1c. Identify the pairs of alternate exterior angles in the diagram. Then make a conjecture about their angle measures. Drag a point in the diagram to confirm your conjecture.

_____

1d. Identify the pairs of same-side interior angles in the diagram. Then make a conjecture about their angle measures. Drag a point in the diagram to confirm your conjecture.

_____

_____

© Houghton Mifflin Harcourt Publishing Company

You can use your knowledge of transformations to informally justify the angle relationships formed by parallel lines and a transversal.

CC.8.G.5

2 EXPLORE   Justifying Angle Relationships

Lines *a* and *b* are parallel. (The blue arrows on the diagram indicate parallel lines.)

A Trace line *a* and line *t* on a piece of paper. Label ∠1. Translate your traced angle down so that line *a* aligns with line *b* and line *t* aligns with itself. Which angle does ∠1 align with? _____

B Because there is a translation that transforms ∠1 to _____, ∠1 and _____ are congruent.

TRY THIS!

2. Name a pair of alternate interior angles. What transformation(s) could you use to show that that those angles are congruent?

_____

_____

CC.8.G.5

3 EXAMPLE   Finding Unknown Angle Measures

Find each angle measure.

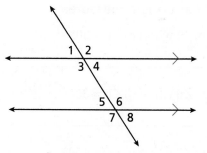

A m∠5 when m∠4 = 55°

∠4 is congruent to ∠5 because they are

_____.

m∠5 = _____°

B m∠*SVW*

∠*SVW* is _____ to ∠*YVW* because they are a linear pair.

$\angle SVW + \angle YVW = 180°$

$4x° + \boxed{}° = 180°$

$\boxed{}x = 180°$

$\dfrac{\boxed{}x}{} = \dfrac{180}{12}$

$x = \boxed{}$

$\angle SVW = \angle 8x° = \left(8 \cdot \boxed{}\right)° = \boxed{}°$

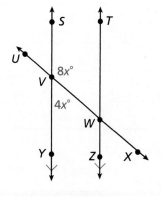

Use the figure for 1–4.

1. Name a pair of corresponding angles.

_____

2. Name a pair of alternate exterior angles.

_____

3. Name the relationship between ∠3 and ∠6.

_____

4. Name the relationship between ∠4 and ∠6.

_____

For parallel lines intersected by a transversal, tell whether each type of angle pair is congruent or supplementary.

5. alternate interior angles

_____

6. linear pair

_____

7. corresponding angles

_____

8. same-side interior angles

_____

9. vertical angles

_____

10. alternate exterior angles

_____

Find each angle measure.

11. m∠2 when m∠1 = 30°

_____

12. m∠6 when m∠1 = 30°

_____

13. m∠7 when m∠3 = 150°

_____

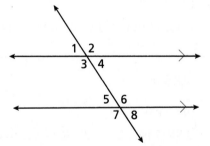

14. m∠EGB

_____

15. m∠AGH

_____

16. m∠DHF

_____

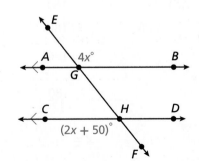

5-2

Additional Practice

1. Measure the angles formed by the transversal and the parallel lines. Which angles seem to be congruent?

_____

_____

In the figure, line *m* || line *n*. Find the measure of each angle. Justify your answer.

2. ∠1   3. ∠2

_____   _____

4. ∠5   5. ∠6

_____   _____

6. ∠8   7. ∠7

_____   _____

In the figure, line *a* || line *b*. Find the measure of each angle. Justify your answer.

8. ∠2   9. ∠5

_____   _____

10. ∠6   11. ∠7

_____   _____

12. ∠4   13. ∠3

_____   _____

In the figure, line *r* || line *s*.

14. Name all angles congruent to ∠2.

15. Which line is the transversal?

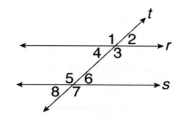

_____

Problem Solving

The figure shows the layout of parking spaces in a parking lot.
$\overline{AB} \parallel \overline{CD} \parallel \overline{EF}$

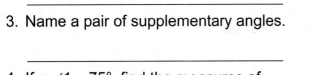

1. Name all angles congruent to ∠1.

   _____

2. Name all angles congruent to ∠2.

   _____

3. Name a pair of supplementary angles.

   _____

4. If m∠1 = 75°, find the measures of
   the other angles.

   _____

   _____

   _____

5. Name a pair of vertical angles.

   _____

6. If m∠1 = 90°, then $\overline{GH}$ is
   perpendicular to

   _____

The figure shows a board that will be cut along parallel
segments GB and CF. $\overline{AD} \parallel \overline{HE}$. Choose the letter for the best
answer.

7. Find the measure of ∠1.

   A 45°   C 60°

   B 120°   D 90°

8. Find the measure of ∠2.

   F 30°   H 60°

   G 120°   J 90°

10. Find the measure of ∠4.

    F 45°   H 60°

    G 120°   J 90°

12. Find the measure of ∠6.

    F 30°   H 60°

    G 120°   J 90°

9. Find the measure of ∠3.

   A 30°   C 60°

   B 120°   D 90°

11. Find the measure of ∠5.

    A 30°   C 60°

    B 120°   D 90°

13. Find the measure of ∠7.

    A 45°   C 60°

    B 120°   D 90°

Triangles
Going Deeper: Triangle Angle Theorems

Essential question: *What can you conclude about the measures of the angles of a triangle?*

5-3

CC.8.G.5

1 EXPLORE Sum of the Angle Measures in a Triangle

There is a special relationship between the measures of the interior angles of a triangle.

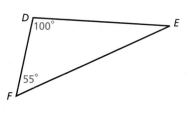

A Draw a triangle and cut it out. Label the angles *A*, *B*, and *C*.

B Tear off each "corner" of the triangle. Each corner includes the vertex of one angle of the triangle.

C Arrange the vertices of the angle around a point so that none of your corners overlap and there are no gaps between them.

D What do you notice about how the angles fit together around a point?

_____

E What is the measure of a straight angle? _____

F Describe the relationship among the measures of the angles of △*ABC* in words.

_____

 The Triangle Sum Theorem states that for △*ABC*,
m∠*A* + m∠*B* + m∠*C* = _____.

TRY THIS!

Find the missing angle measure.

1a.

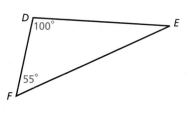

$$55° + \boxed{} + m\angle E = 180°$$
$$155° + m\angle E = 180°$$
$$155° - \boxed{} + m\angle E = 180° - \boxed{}$$
$$m\angle E = \boxed{}$$

1b.

You can use your knowledge of parallel lines intersected by a transversal to informally justify the Triangle Sum Theorem.

2 EXPLORE Justifying the Triangle Sum Theorem

Follow the steps to informally prove the Triangle Sum Theorem. You should draw each step on your own paper. The figures below are provided for you to check your work.

A Draw a triangle and label the angles as ∠1, ∠2, and ∠3 as shown.

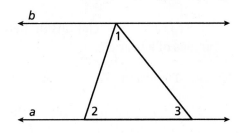

B Draw line *a* through the base of the triangle.

C The Parallel Postulate states that through a point not on a line ℓ, there is exactly one line parallel to line ℓ. Draw line *b* parallel to line *a*, through the vertex opposite the base of the triangle.

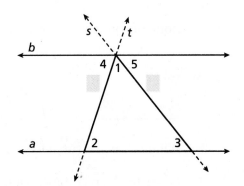

D Extend the other sides of the triangles to form transversal *s* and transversal *t*. Transversals *s* and *t* intersect parallel lines *a* and *b*.

E Label the angles formed by line *b* and the transversals as ∠4 and ∠5.

F ∠4 and _____ are alternate interior

angles, so they are _____.

Label ∠4 with the number of the angle it

is congruent to.

G ∠5 and _____ are alternate interior angles, so they

are _____. Label ∠5 with the number of the

angle it is congruent to.

H The three angles that lie along line *b* at the vertex of the

triangle are ∠1 and two angles that have the same measures

as ∠2 and ∠3. Because these three angles lie along a line,

the sum of their measures is _____.

$$m\angle 1 + m\angle 2 + m\angle 3 = \text{_____}$$

The sum of the angle measures in a triangle is always _____.

An **interior angle** of a triangle is formed by two sides of the triangle. An **exterior angle** of a triangle is formed by one side of the triangle and the extension of an adjacent side. Each exterior angle has two *remote interior angles*. A **remote interior angle** is an interior angle that is not adjacent to the exterior angle.

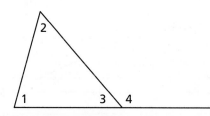

- ∠1, ∠2, and ∠3 are interior angles.
- ∠4 is an exterior angle.
- ∠1 and ∠2 are remote interior angles to ∠4.

CC.8.G.5

3 EXPLORE   **Exterior Angles and Remote Interior Angles**

There is a special relationship between the measure of an exterior angle and the measures of its remote interior angles.

A Extend the base of the triangle and label the exterior angle as ∠4.

B The Triangle Sum Theorem states:

$$m\angle 1 + m\angle 2 + m\angle 3 = \underline{\hspace{2cm}}$$

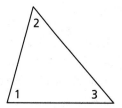

C ∠3 and ∠4 form a _____,

so $m\angle 3 + m\angle 4 = \underline{\hspace{2cm}}$.

D Use the equations in **B** and **C** to complete the following equation:

$$m\angle 1 + m\angle 2 + \underline{\hspace{1.5cm}} = \underline{\hspace{1.5cm}} + m\angle 4$$

E Use properties of equality to simplify the equation in **D** :

_____

 The Exterior Angle Theorem states that the measure of an _____ angle is equal to the sum of its _____ angles.

REFLECT

3a. Sketch a triangle and draw all of its exterior angles. How many exterior angles does a triangle have at each vertex?

_____

3b. How many total exterior angles does a triangle have?

_____

Find the missing angle measure.

1.

m∠M = _____

2.

m∠Q = _____

Use the Triangle Sum Theorem to find the measure of each angle in degrees.

3.

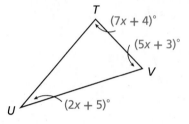

m∠T = _____

m∠U = _____

m∠V = _____

4.

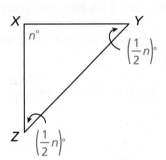

m∠X = _____

m∠Y = _____

m∠Z = _____

Use the Exterior Angles Theorem to find the measure of each angle in degrees.

5.

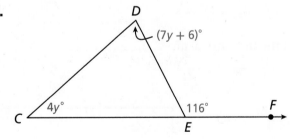

m∠C = _____

m∠D = _____

m∠DEC = _____

6.

m∠L = _____

m∠MKL = _____

m∠MKJ = _____

Additional Practice

1. Find $x°$ in the right triangle.

_____

2. Find $y°$ in the obtuse triangle.

_____

3. Find $m°$ in the acute triangle.

_____

4. Find $w°$ in the acute triangle.

_____

5. Find $t°$ in the scalene triangle.

_____

6. Find $n°$ in the scalene triangle.

_____

7. Find $x°$ in the isosceles triangle.

_____

8. Find y in the equilateral triangle.

_____

9. Find r in the isosceles triangle.

_____

10. The second angle in a triangle is one third as large as the first. The third angle is two thirds as large as the first angle. Find the angle measures. Draw a possible picture of the triangle.

_____

Problem Solving

The American flag must be folded according to certain rules
that result in the flag being folded into the shape of a triangle.
The figure shows a frame designed to hold an American flag.

1. Is the triangle acute, right, or obtuse?

   _____

2. Is the triangle equilateral, isosceles,
   or scalene?

   _____

3. Find $x°$.

   _____

4. Find $y°$.

   _____

The figure shows a map of three streets. Choose the letter for
the best answer.

5. Find $x°$.

   A 22°   C 30°

   B 128°   D 68°

6. Find $w°$.

   F 22°   H 30°

   G 128°   J 52°

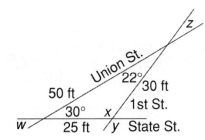

7. Find $y°$.

   A 22°

   B 30°

   C 128°

   D 143°

8. Find $z°$.

   F 22°

   G 30°

   H 128°

   J 143°

9. Which word best describes the
   triangle formed by the streets?

   A acute

   B right

   C obtuse

   D equilateral

Coordinate Geometry
Going Deeper

Essential question: *How can you use coordinates to find scale factors?*

A **dilation** is a transformation in which a figure and its *image* are similar. The ratio between the image and the original figure is called the **scale factor**.

PREP FOR **CC.8.G.3**

1 EXAMPLE Finding and Graphing a Dilation

The vertices of quadrilateral *ABCD* are *A*(–4, –2), *B*(–2, 2), *C*(1, 2), and *D*(2, –2).

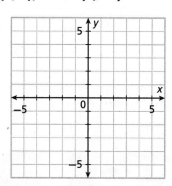

A Plot points *A, B, C,* and *D*. Connect them in order to graph this polygon on the coordinate plane.

B Quadrilateral *A′B′C′D′* is an image of quadrilateral *ABCD*. Vertex *A′* in *A′B′C′D′* has coordinates (–6, –3).

Find the scale factor: Divide the *x*- and *y*-coordinates of Vertex *A′* by the *x*- and *y*-coordinates of Vertex *A*.

x-coordinates y-coordinates

$$\frac{\text{image} \rightarrow A'}{\text{original} \rightarrow A} \qquad \frac{-6}{-4} = \underline{\quad} \qquad \underline{\quad} = \underline{\quad} \qquad \text{The scale factor is } \underline{\quad}.$$

C Use the scale factor to find the *x*- and *y*-coordinates of vertices *B′, C′,* and *D′*.

$$B(-2, 2) \rightarrow B'\left(\frac{3}{2} \times -2, \frac{3}{2} \times 2\right) = \left(\underline{\quad}, \underline{\quad}\right)$$

$$C(1, 2) \rightarrow C'\left(\underline{\quad} \times \underline{\quad}, \underline{\quad} \times \underline{\quad}\right) = \left(\underline{\quad}, \underline{\quad}\right)$$

$$D(2, -2) \rightarrow D'\left(\underline{\quad} \times \underline{\quad}, \underline{\quad} \times \underline{\quad}\right) = \left(\underline{\quad}, \underline{\quad}\right)$$

D On the coordinate plane in **A**, graph quadrilateral *A′B′C′D′*.

REFLECT

1a. Describe the figures you have graphed. What kind of quadrilateral is each one? How are they related?

_____

_____

1b. What are the coordinates of the image of quadrilateral *EFGH* after a dilation with a scale factor of $\frac{1}{2}$?

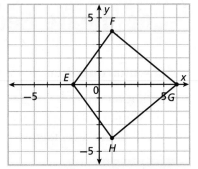

$E(-2, 0) \rightarrow E'\left(\frac{1}{2} \times \boxed{}, \frac{1}{2} \times \boxed{}\right) = \left(\boxed{}, \boxed{}\right)$

$F\left(1, \boxed{}\right) \rightarrow F'\left(\frac{\boxed{}}{\boxed{}} \times 1, \frac{\boxed{}}{\boxed{}} \times \boxed{}\right) = \left(\frac{\boxed{}}{\boxed{}}, \boxed{}\right)$

$G\left(\boxed{}, \boxed{}\right) \rightarrow G'\left(\frac{\boxed{}}{\boxed{}} \times \boxed{}, \frac{\boxed{}}{\boxed{}} \times \boxed{}\right) = \left(\boxed{}, \boxed{}\right)$

$H\left(\boxed{}, \boxed{}\right) \rightarrow H'\left(\frac{\boxed{}}{\boxed{}} \times \boxed{}, \frac{\boxed{}}{\boxed{}} \times \boxed{}\right) = \left(\frac{\boxed{}}{\boxed{}}, \boxed{}\right)$

1c. Graph *E′F′G′H′* on the coordinate plane. What kind of quadrilateral have you drawn? _____

PRACTICE

Use the diagram for Exercises 1–3.

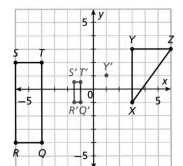

1. *Q′R′S′T′* is the image of *QRST*. Find the scale factor.
$\dfrac{\text{image} \rightarrow Q'}{\text{original} \rightarrow Q}$ _____

2. *Y′* is the image of *Y* in a dilation of $\triangle XYZ$. Find the scale factor.
$\dfrac{\text{image} \rightarrow Y'}{\text{original} \rightarrow Y}$ _____

3. Use the scale factor to graph $\triangle X'Y'Z'$.

$X(3, -1) \rightarrow X'\left(\boxed{}, -\frac{\boxed{}}{\boxed{}}\right) \quad Z(6, 3) \rightarrow Z'\left(\boxed{}, \boxed{}\right)$

4. Given quadrilateral *MNOP* with vertices $M(-2, -1)$, $N(2, 0)$, $O(2, 2)$, and $P(-1, 2)$, find the coordinates of its image after a dilation with a scale factor of 2.

_____

5. In triangle *ABC*, $AB = 7$ cm, $BC = 6$ cm, and $CD = 10$ cm. After a dilation, the length of $A'B' = 21$ cm. What is the scale factor of the dilation? What is the perimeter of $A'B'C'$?

_____

Additional Practice

Graph the polygons with the given vertices. What are the coordinates of the image after a dilation with a scale factor of 2?

1. $S(-3, -3)$, $T(-3, 4)$, $U(4, -3)$

2. $M(-1, 2)$, $N(2, 0)$, $Q(2, -4)$, $P(-1, -2)$

 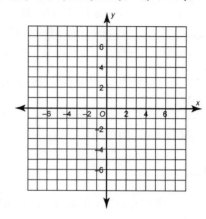

_____

3. Quadrilateral *JKLM* is a square. Find the coordinates of the missing vertex.

   Then find the coordinates of the image after a dilation with a scale factor of $\frac{1}{2}$.

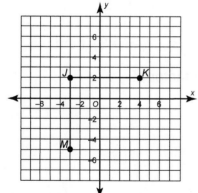

_____

4. The vertices of triangle *FGH* are $F(4, 6)$, $G(8, 8)$, and $H(12, 4)$. Triangle *F'G'H'* is an image of triangle *FGH*. Vertex *F'* has coordinates $(2, 3)$. What is the scale factor of the dilation? What are the coordinates of vertices *G'* and *H'*?

_____

_____

Problem Solving

Nguyen and his family went to Washington D.C. Nguyen graphed the sites he and his family visited on a coordinate grid.

1. On Saturday, Nguyen and his family visited the Lincoln Memorial (*L*), the Washington Monument (*W*), the White House (*H*), and the National Academy of Sciences (*N*) The coordinates for each site are *L*(–4, 2), *W*(2, 2), *H*(2, 6) and *N*(–3, $3\frac{1}{2}$). Graph and label the coordinates. Connect the vertices. Give the most specific name for the polygon formed.

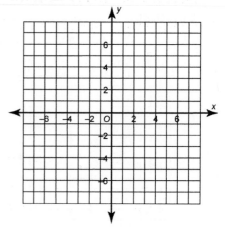

_____

2. Polygon *L'W'H'N'* is the image of the polygon graphed above after a dilation. Vertex *N'* has coordinates (–9, $10\frac{1}{2}$). What is the scale factor of the dilation? What are the coordinates of the remaining vertices of *L'W'H'N'*?

_____

_____

3. Rectangle *ABCD* has vertices *A*(–6, 0), *B*(6, 0), *C*(6, –3), *D*(–6, –3). Find the coordinates of the image after a dilation with a scale factor of $\frac{1}{3}$.

_____

_____

Choose the letter for the best answer.

4. An architect is trying to draw an isosceles right triangle on a grid to use in his next blueprint. He has a point at (6, 3) and a point at (–2, 3). What could be the third point?

  A (–2, 0)   C (2, –2)

  B (6, –5)   D (6, 8)

5. Triangle QRS has vertices *Q*(–7, 3), *R*(9, 8), and *S*(2, 16). What is the scale factor if the vertices after a dilation are *Q'*(–10.5, 4.5), *R'*(13.5, 12), and *S*(3, 24)?

  F $\frac{1}{3}$ H $\frac{2}{3}$

  G $\frac{1}{2}$ J $\frac{3}{2}$

Congruence
Going Deeper

Essential question: *How can you prove that two triangles are congruent?*

Congruent triangles are triangles with the same *size* and *shape*. But to prove that two triangles are congruent, you do not need to show that all corresponding sides and angles are congruent.

PREP FOR **CC.8.G.2**

1 EXPLORE Side-Side-Side Congruence

One way of making congruent triangles is to use only the lengths of the sides.

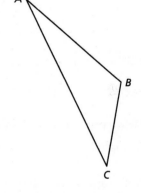

A Using a compass and a straightedge, copy the lengths of the three sides of triangle *ABC*.

B Cut out the sides you made. Use these line segments to form triangle *DEF*.

What can you say about the size and shape of triangles *ABC* and *DEF*?

_____

Are triangles *ABC* and *DEF* congruent?_____

How can you demonstrate that triangles *ABC* and *DEF* are congruent?

_____

Using the same three side lengths, is it possible to make a triangle that is *not* congruent to triangle *ABC*? Try it to find out. _____

Side-Side-Side Postulate (SSS Postulate)

If three sides of one triangle are congruent to three sides of another triangle, the two triangles are congruent.

We write △*ABC* ≅ △*DEF*.

REFLECT

1. Are two triangles congruent if only *two* corresponding sides of the triangles are congruent? Explain your reasoning.

_____

_____

Another way of proving that two triangles are congruent
is to use two sides and the angle between them.

A Using a protractor and a ruler, draw triangle
RST in the space provided. Make side
RS = 4 cm and side *RT* = 6 cm. Make the
measure of the included angle, ∠*R*, 50°. Draw
side *ST* to complete the triangle.

B Draw triangle *RST* again using a new piece
of paper, and label the triangle *XYZ*.

Are triangles *RST* and *XYZ* congruent? How do
you know?

_____

_____

REFLECT

2a. Using the side lengths of *RS* and *RT*, and the angle in between, try to make a
triangle that is *not* congruent to *RST*. Can you do it? _____

2b. Make a new triangle *RST* using the given side lengths of *RS* and *RT* and
m∠*S* = 50° (which is not included between *RS* and *RT*). Can you make a
triangle using the same measurements that is not congruent to *RST*? Try
it to find out. _____ Then compare your findings with a classmate's.

2c. Suppose you were given the measures of *all three* angles of a triangle but
had no information about side lengths. How many triangles can you
draw using this information? _____
So, is angle-angle-angle (AAA) a method you could use for proving two
triangles congruent? _____

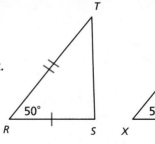

Side-Angle-Side Postulate (SAS Postulate)

If two sides and the included angle
of one triangle are congruent to two
sides and the included angle of another
triangle, the two triangles are congruent.

We write △*RST* ≅ △*XYZ*.

Additional Practice

Write a congruence statement for the pair of congruent triangles.

1.

_____

_____

In the figure, triangle *PRT* ≅ triangle *FJH*.

2. Find *a*.

_____

3. Find *b*.

_____

4. Find *c*.

_____

5. Find *x*.

_____

6. Find *y*.

_____

7. Find *z*.

_____

Problem Solving

Use the American patchwork quilt block design called Carnival to answer the questions. Triangle *AIH* ≅ Triangle *AIB*, Triangle *ACJ* ≅ Triangle *AGJ*, Triangle *GFJ* ≅ Triangle *CDJ*.

1. What is the measure of ∠*IAB*?

   _____

2. What is the measure of $\overline{AH}$?

   _____

3. What is the measure of $\overline{AG}$?

   _____

4. What is the measure of ∠*JDC*?

5. What is the measure of $\overline{FG}$?

   _____

The sketch is part of a bridge. Trapezoid *ABEF* ≅ Trapezoid *DEBC*. Choose the letter for the best answer.

6. What is the measure of $\overline{DE}$?

   A 4 feet

   B 8 feet

   C 16 feet

   D Cannot be determined

7. What is the measure of $\overline{FE}$?

   F 4 feet   H 8 feet

   G 16 feet   J 24 feet

8. What is the measure of ∠*FAB*?

   A 45°   C 60°

   B 90°   D 120°

9. What is the measure of ∠*ABE*?

   F 45°   H 60°

   G 90°   J 120°

10. What is the measure of ∠*EBC*?

    A 45°   C 60°

    B 90°   D 120°

11. What is the measure of ∠*BED*?

    F 45°   H 60°

    G 90°   J 120°

12. What is the measure of ∠*BCD*?

    A 45°   C 60°

    B 90°   D 120°

5-6

Transformations
Modeling

Essential question: *How can you use coordinates to describe the result of a translation, reflection, or rotation?*

You learned that a function is a rule that assigns exactly one output to each input. A **transformation** is a type of function that describes a change in the position or size of a figure. The input of a transformation is called the **preimage**, and the output of a transformation is called the **image**.

A **translation** is a transformation that slides a figure along a straight line. The image has the same size and shape as the preimage.

video tutor

CC.8.G.3
1 EXPLORE Applying Translations

The triangle is the preimage (input). The arrow shows the motion of a translation and how point *A* is translated to point *A'*.

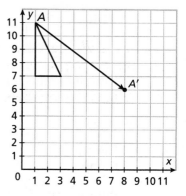

A Trace the triangle on a piece of paper. Slide point *A* of your traced triangle down the arrow to model the translation.

B Sketch the image (output) of the translation.

C Describe the motion modeled by the translation.

Move _____ units right and _____ units down.

D Complete the ordered pairs to describe the effect of the translation on point *A*.

$(1, 11)$ becomes $\left(1 + \boxed{}, \ 11 + \boxed{}\right) = \left(\boxed{}, \boxed{}\right)$

E You can give a general rule for a translation by telling the number of units to move up or down and the number of units to move left or right. Complete the ordered pairs to write a general rule for this transformation.

$(x, y) \rightarrow \left(x + \boxed{}, \ y + \boxed{}\right)$

TRY THIS!

1. Apply the translation $(x, y) \rightarrow (x - 2, y + 3)$ to the figure shown. Give the coordinates of the vertices of the image. (The image of point *A* is point *A'*.)

A': (_____, _____)

B': (_____, _____)

C': (_____, _____)

D': (_____, _____)

A **reflection** is a transformation that flips a figure across a line called the **line of reflection**. Each point and its image are the same distance from the line of reflection. The image has the same size and shape as the preimage.

2 EXPLORE   Applying Reflections

The triangle is the preimage. You will use the *x*- or *y*-axis as the line of reflection.

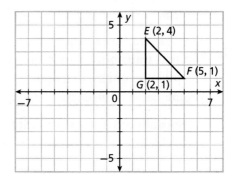

Reflection across the *x*-axis:

A Trace the triangle and the *x*- and *y*-axes on a piece of paper. Fold your paper along the *x*-axis and trace the image of the triangle on the opposite side of the *x*-axis.

B Sketch the image of the reflection. Label each vertex of the image. (The image of point *E* is point *E'*.)

C Complete the table.

Preimage	(2, 4)	(2, 1)	(5, 1)
Image			

D How does reflecting the figure across the *x*-axis change the *x*-coordinates? How does it change the *y*-coordinates?

_____

E Complete the ordered pair to write a general rule for reflection across the *x*-axis. $(x, y) \rightarrow \left(x, y \times \boxed{} \right)$

Reflection across the *y*-axis:

F Fold your traced image along the *y*-axis and trace the image of the triangle on the opposite side of the *y*-axis.

G Sketch the image of the reflection. Label each vertex of the image. (For clarity, label the image of point *E* as point *E''*.)

H Complete the table.

Preimage	(2, 4)	(2, 1)	(5, 1)
Image			

I How does reflecting the figure across the *y*-axis change the *x*-coordinates? How does it change the *y*-coordinates?

_____

J Complete the ordered pair to write a general rule for reflection across the *y*-axis. $(x, y) \rightarrow \left(\boxed{}, \boxed{} \right)$

Rules for Reflections

Across the *x*-axis	$(x, y) \rightarrow (x, -y)$
Across the *y*-axis	$(x, y) \rightarrow (-x, y)$

A **rotation** is a transformation that turns a figure around a given point called the center of rotation. The image has the same size and shape as the preimage.

CC.8.G.3

3 EXPLORE   Applying Rotations

The triangle is the preimage. You will use the origin as the center of rotation.

A Trace the triangle on a piece of paper. Rotate the triangle 90° counterclockwise about the origin. The side of the triangle that lies along the *x*-axis should now lie along the *y*-axis.

B Sketch the image of the rotation. Label each vertex of the image. (The image of point *H* is point *H′*.)

C Give the coordinates of the vertices of the image.

H′: (_____, _____)

J′: (_____, _____)

K′: (_____, _____)

TRY THIS!

3a. Rotate the original triangle 180° counterclockwise about the origin. Sketch the result on the coordinate grid above. Label each vertex of the image. (For clarity, label the image of point *H* as point *H″*.)

3b. Give the coordinates of the vertices of the image.

H″: (_____, _____)

J″: (_____, _____)

K″: (_____, _____)

REFLECT

3c. Compare the image of a counterclockwise rotation of 180° about the origin to the image of a clockwise rotation of 180° about the origin.

_____

3d. Through how many degrees would you need to rotate a figure for the image to coincide with the preimage? Explain.

_____

_____

**Sketch the image of the figure after the given transformation.
Label each vertex.**

1. Translation: $(x, y) \rightarrow (x - 3, y + 1)$

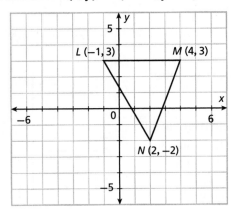

2. Reflection: $(x, y) \rightarrow (x, -y)$

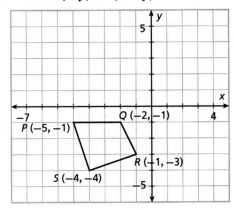

3. Rotation: 90° clockwise about the origin

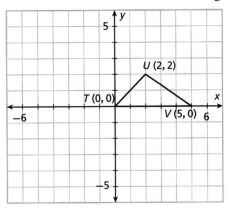

4. Reflection: $(x, y) \rightarrow (-x, y)$

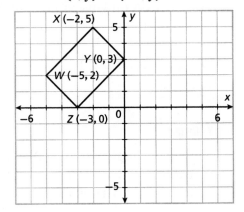

**Apply each transformation to the vertices of the original rectangle,
and give the coordinates of each vertex of the image.**

Vertices of Rectangle	(2, 2)	(2, 4)	(−3, 4)	(−3, 2)
5. $(x, y) \rightarrow (x, -y)$				
6. $(x, y) \rightarrow (x + 2, y - 5)$				
7. $(x, y) \rightarrow (-x, y)$				
8. $(x, y) \rightarrow (-x, -y)$				
9. $(x, y) \rightarrow (x - 3, y + 1)$				

Additional Practice

Graph each translation.

1. 3 units left and 9 units down

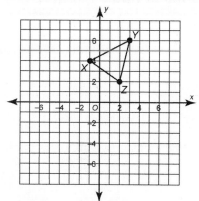

2. 3 units right and 6 units up

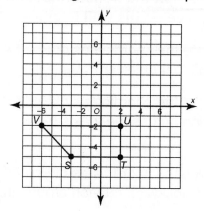

Graph each reflection.

3. across the *x*-axis

4. across the *y*-axis

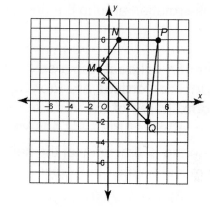

Graph each rotation around the origin.

5. 90° clockwise

6. 180°

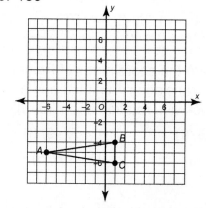

7. A parallelogram has vertices $A(-1, 3)$, $B(4, 3)$, $C(6, -1)$, and $D(1, -1)$. After a transformation, the coordinates of the image are $A'(1, 3)$, $B'(-4, 3)$, $C'(-6, -1)$, and $D'(-1, -1)$. Describe the transformation. _____

Problem Solving

Drew is going to hang a flag in his bedroom that is in the shape of a trapezoid. The grid below represents Drew's wall. The flag, a trapezoid *ABCD,* has vertices *A*(−1, −1), *B*(2, −1), *C*(4, −4), and *D*(−1, −4). Graph the transformations that Drew performs to find the right place on his wall to answer the questions.

1. What are the coordinates of Point *A* after a translation 4 units left? _____

2. What are the coordinates of Point *B* after a reflection across the *y*-axis?

   _____

3. What are the coordinates of Point *C* after a 90° counterclockwise rotation around the origin?

   _____

4. What are the coordinates of Point *D* after a 180° clockwise rotation around the origin?

   _____

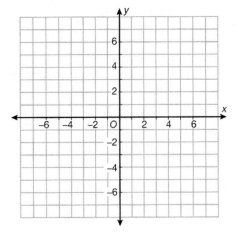

A blueprint of a sailboat has a sail in the shape of a right triangle, *RST*. On the blueprint the vertices are *R*(−4, 6), *S*(−4, 2) and *T*(1, 2). Use the rules to find the coordinates of the vertices of the sailboat as it changes position. Choose the letter for the best answer.

5. What are the coordinates of the sail after a reflection over the *x*-axis?

   A *R*(−4, 6), *S*(−4, 2), *T*(1, 2)
   B *R*(−4, −6), *S*(−4, −2), *T*(1, −2)
   C *R*(6, −4), *S*(2, −4), *T*(2, 1)
   D *R*(−6, −4), *S*(−2, −4), *T*(2, 1)

6. What are the coordinates of the sail after a translation left 3 units and a reflection over the *y*-axis?

   F *R*(7, 6), *S*(7, 2), *T*(2, 2)
   G *R*(7, −6), *S*(7, −2), *T*(2, −2)
   H *R*(−7, −6), *S*(−7, −2), *T*(−2, −2)
   J *R*(−6, −7), *S*(−2, −7), *T*(−2, −2)

7. What are the coordinates of Point *R* after a translation 1 unit left and a 90° clockwise rotation about (0, 0)?

   A *R*(5, 6)   C *R*(−5, 6)
   B *R*(−6, −5)   D *R*(6, 5)

8. What are the coordinates of Point *S* after a translation 4 units to the right and 5 units down?

   F *S*(−3, 0)   H *S*(0, 3)
   G *S*(0, −3)   J *S*(3, 0)

5-7

Similarity and Congruence Transformations
Reasoning

Essential question: *What properties of a figure are preserved under a translation, reflection, or rotation?*

video tutor

CC.8.G.1

1 EXPLORE Properties of Translations

A Trace the rectangle and triangle on a piece of paper. Then cut out your traced figures.

B Place your copy of the rectangle on top of the rectangle in the figure. Then translate the rectangle by sliding your copy 6 units to the right and 1 unit down. Draw the new location of the rectangle on the coordinate plane and label the vertices A', B', C', and D'.

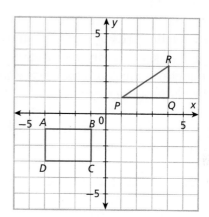

C Place your copy of the triangle on top of the triangle in the figure. Then translate the triangle by sliding your copy 5 units to the left and 2 units up. Draw the new location of the triangle on the coordinate plane and label the vertices P', Q', and R'.

D Use a ruler to measure line segments $\overline{AD}$ and $\overline{PR}$. Then, measure $\overline{A'D'}$ and $\overline{P'R'}$. What do you notice?

_____

E Use a protractor to measure $\angle C$ and $\angle R$. Then, measure $\angle C'$ and $\angle R'$. What do you notice?

_____

F Count the pairs of parallel lines in rectangle $ABCD$. Count the pairs of parallel lines in rectangle $A'B'C'D'$. What do you notice?

_____

_____

REFLECT

1. Use your results from **D** , **E** , and **F** to write a conjecture about translations.

_____

2 EXPLORE   Properties of Reflections

A   Trace the rectangle and triangle on a piece of paper. Then, cut out your traced figures.

B   Place your copy of the rectangle on top of the rectangle in the figure. Then reflect the rectangle across the *x*-axis by flipping your copy across the *x*-axis. Draw the new location of the rectangle on the coordinate plane and label the vertices *A′*, *B′*, *C′*, and *D′*.

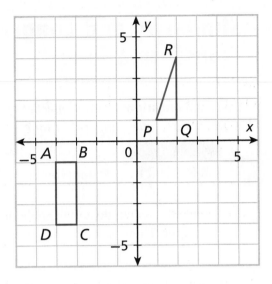

C   Place your copy of the triangle on top of the triangle in the figure. Then reflect the triangle across the *y*-axis by flipping your copy across the *y*-axis. Draw the new location of the triangle on the coordinate plane and label the vertices *P′*, *Q′*, and *R′*.

D   Use a ruler to measure line segments $\overline{BC}$ and $\overline{PR}$. Then, measure $\overline{B'C'}$ and $\overline{P'R'}$. What do you notice?

_____

E   Use a protractor to measure ∠*D* and ∠*P*. Then, measure ∠*D′* and ∠*P′*. What do you notice?

_____

F   Count the pairs of parallel lines in rectangle *ABCD*. Count the pairs of parallel lines in rectangle *A′B′C′D′*. What do you notice?

_____

REFLECT

2a.   Use your results from **D**, **E**, and **F** to write a conjecture about reflections.

_____

TRY THIS!

2b.   Rotate your copy of the triangle from **A** 180° around the origin and draw the new location of the triangle. Make measurements and observations to help you state a conjecture about rotations.

_____

_____

_____

Additional Practice

Identify each transformation from the original to the image, and tell whether the two figures are congruent. Justify your answer.

1. Original: $A(0, 2)$, $B(3, 4)$, $C(7, -2)$, $D(4, -4)$

   Image: $A'(0, -2)$, $B'(-3, -4)$, $C'(-7, 2)$, $D'(-4, 4)$

   _____

   _____

   _____

2. Original: $A(-3, -4)$, $B(-1, -2)$, $C(1, -4)$, $D(0, -7)$, $E(-2, -7)$

   Image: $A'(2, -5)$, $B'(4, -3)$, $C'(6, -5)$, $D'(5, -8)$, $E'(3, -8)$

   _____

   _____

   _____

3. Original: $A(-3, -3)$, $B(-2, 3)$, $C(2, -2)$

   Image: $A'(-9, -9)$, $B'(-6, 6)$, $C'(6, -6)$

   _____

   _____

   _____

4. Original: $A(-4, 8)$, $B(4, 7)$, $C(-4, 6)$

   Image: $A'(-4, -8)$, $B'(4, -7)$, $C'(-4, -6)$

   _____

   _____

   _____

Problem Solving

Identify each transformation and tell whether the two figures are congruent. Justify your answer.

1. Original: $A(-5, 6)$, $B(3, 6)$, $C(-3, 2)$

   Image: $A'(5, 6)$, $B'(-3, 6)$, $C'(3, 2)$

   _____

   _____

2. Original: $A(4, -2)$, $B(7, -1)$, $C(4, -7)$

   Image: $A'(1, 1)$, $B'(4, 2)$, $C'(1, -4)$

   _____

   _____

Choose the letter for the best answer.

3. A figure is transformed. Which best describes the transformation of the figure?

   Original: $A(7, 3)$, $B(5, -3)$, $C(3, 0)$

   Image: $A'(-7, 3)$, $B'(-5, -3)$, $C'(-3, 0)$

   A rotation

   B reflection

   C translation

   D dilation

4. A figure is transformed. Which best describes the transformation of the figure?

   Original: $A(4, 8)$, $B(6, 4)$, $C(0, 2)$

   Image: $A'(3, 6)$, $B'(4.5, 3)$, $C'(0, 1.5)$

   F rotation

   G reflection

   H translation

   J dilation

5. Which coordinate map describes a 90° counterclockwise rotation?

   A $(x, y) \rightarrow (x, -y)$

   B $(x, y) \rightarrow (y, -x)$

   C $(x, y) \rightarrow (-y, x)$

   D $(x, y) \rightarrow (-x, y)$

6. Which transformation would not necessarily result in a congruent figure?

   F rotation

   G reflection

   H translation

   J dilation

Identifying Combined Transformations
Going Deeper

Essential question: *What is the connection between transformations and congruent figures and transformations and similar figures?*

CC.8.G.2

1 EXPLORE Combining Transformations

Apply the indicated series of transformations to the triangle. Each transformation is applied to the image of the previous translation, not the original figure. Label each image with the letter of the transformation applied.

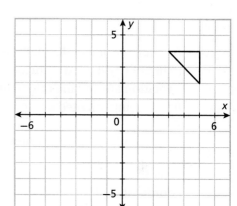

A Reflection across the *x*-axis

B $(x, y) \rightarrow (x - 3, y)$

C Reflection across the *y*-axis

D $(x, y) \rightarrow (x, y + 4)$

E Rotation 90° clockwise around the origin

F Compare the size and shape of the final image to that of the original figure.

_____

Two figures are said to be **congruent** if one can be obtained from the other by a sequence of translations, reflections, and rotations. Congruent figures have the same size and shape.

When you are told that two figures are congruent, there must be a sequence of translations, reflections, and/or rotations that transforms one into the other.

CC.8.G.2

2 EXAMPLE Congruent Figures

A Identify a sequence of transformations that will transform figure *A* into figure *B*.

_____

B Identify another sequence of transformations that transforms figure *A* into figure *B*.

_____

C Any sequence of transformations that changes figure *B* into figure *C* will need to include a rotation. Identify a rotation around the origin that would result in the figure being oriented as figure *C*.

_____° clockwise / counterclockwise

D After the rotation you identified in **C**, what transformation is necessary to result in figure *C*?

_____

_____

E A sequence of transformations that changes figure *D* to figure *E* will need to include a rotation. Describe a rotation around the origin that would result in the figure being oriented as figure *E*.

_____° clockwise / counterclockwise

F After the rotation you identified in **E**, what are the coordinates of the vertices of the rotated figure?

_____

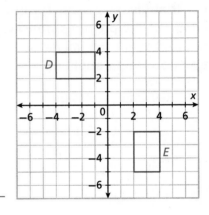

G After the rotation you identified in **E**, what transformation is necessary to result in figure *E*?

_____

_____

TRY THIS!

2a. Explain whether the figures are congruent.

_____

_____

_____

_____

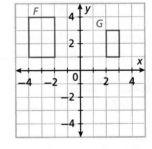

2b. Describe a sequence of translations, reflections, or rotations that would transform figure *F* into figure *G*.

_____

_____

_____

© Houghton Mifflin Harcourt Publishing Company

Apply the indicated series of transformations to the rectangle. Each transformation is applied to the image of the previous transformation, not to the original figure. Label each image with the letter of the transformation applied.

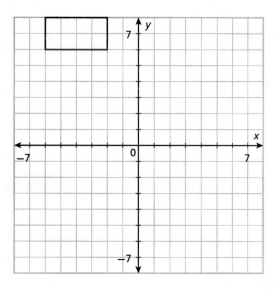

A $(x, y) \rightarrow (x + 7, y - 2)$

B $(x, y) \rightarrow (x, -y)$

C rotation 90° clockwise around the origin

D $(x, y) \rightarrow (x + 5, y + 3)$

E $(x, y) \rightarrow (3x, 3y)$

F List the coordinates of the vertices of rectangle E.

_____

G Compare the following attributes of rectangle E to those of the original figure.

Shape	
Size	
Angle Measures	

Two figures are **similar** if one can be obtained from the other by a sequence of translations, reflections, rotations, and dilations. Similar figures have the same shape but may be different sizes.

When you are told that two figures are similar, there must be a sequence of translations, reflections, rotations, and/or dilations that can transform one to the other.

4 EXPLORE Similar Figures

A Identify a sequence of transformations that will transform figure *A* into figure *B*.

_____

_____

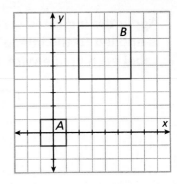

B What happens if you reverse the order of the sequence you defined in **A**?

_____

_____

C Tell whether figures *A* and *B* are congruent. Tell whether they are similar.

_____

_____

D Identify a sequence of transformations that will transform figure *C* into figure *D*. Include a reflection.

_____

_____

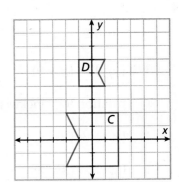

E Identify a sequence of transformations that will transform figure *C* into figure *D*. Include a rotation.

_____

_____

TRY THIS!

4. Circle the figures that are similar to each other.

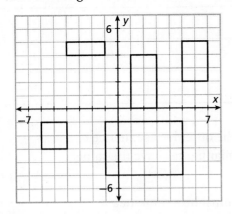

Use the diagram for Exercises 1 and 2.

1. Describe a sequence of translations, reflections, or rotations that would transform figure E into figure F.

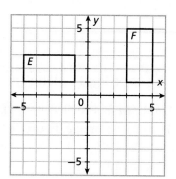

_____

_____

_____

_____

2. Are figures F and E congruent or similar? Explain.

_____

Use the diagram for Exercises 3 and 4.

3. Describe a sequence of translations, reflections, or rotations that would transform figure G into figure H.

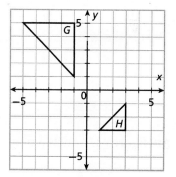

_____

_____

_____

_____

4. Are figures H and G congruent or similar? Explain.

_____

Use the diagram for Exercises 5 and 6.

5. Describe a sequence of translations, reflections, or rotations that would transform figure J into figure K.

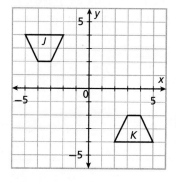

_____

_____

_____

6. Are figures K and J congruent or similar? Explain.

_____

7. **Error Analysis** Sidney drew figure A, with vertices (–4, –1), (–1, 3), and (–1, –2). Then she drew its image, figure A′, with vertices (1, –1), (4, 3), and (4, –2). She described the transformation as a translation across the x-axis, and she described the change using the rule $(x, y) \rightarrow (x, y + 5)$. Is she correct? Explain.

_____

_____

Use the coordinate plane for Exercises 8–10.

8. Figure M has vertices (–4, 1), (–3, 1), (–3, –2), and (–4, –2). Its image, figure M′, has vertices (–3, 3), (–3, 5), (3, 5), and (3, 3). Graph both figures on the coordinate plane.

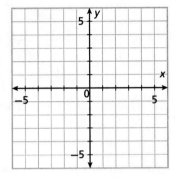

9. Describe a sequence of translations, reflections, or rotations that would transform figure M into figure M′.

_____

_____

_____

_____

_____

10. Are figures M and M′ congruent? Explain.

_____

_____

Solve.

11. Choose one of the sequences of transformation you have described in the preceding exercises. Present a different sequence that would also describe the change from the first figure to the second.

_____

_____

_____

_____

5-8

Additional Practice

Identify the combined transformations from the original to the final image, and tell whether the two figures are similar or congruent.

1.

_____

2.

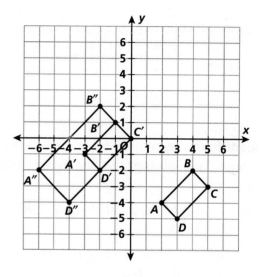

_____

Find a sequence of at least two combined transformations for transforming the original to the final image. Justify your answer.

3.

_____

4.

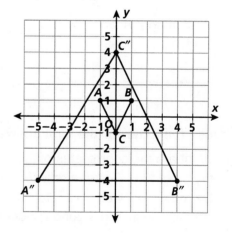

_____

Problem Solving

For each sequence of transformations, find the coordinates of the final image and state whether the two figures are similar or congruent.

1. Original *ABC*: *A*(–3, 1), *B*(–1, 5), *C*(1, 1)

   A reflection across the *y*-axis, followed by a 90° clockwise rotation around the origin.

   _____

2. Original *ABCD*: *A*(6, –3), *B*(2, –2), *C*(–1, –2), *D*(–5, –1)

   A 180° rotation around the origin, followed by a dilation by a scale factor of 0.5, with the origin as the center of dilation.

   _____

Identify the combined transformations from the original to the final image. Tell whether the two figures are similar or congruent. Justify your answer.

3. Original *ABCDE* with *A*(–2, 2), *B*(0, 3), *C*(1, 2), *D*(1, 0), *E*(–1, 1)

   Final Image: *A″B″C″D″E″* with *A″*(–4, –6), *B″*(–5, –4), *C″*(–4, –3), *D″*(–2, –3), *E″*(–3, –5)

   _____

4. Original *ABC* with *A*(–6, –4), *B*(3, 6), *C*(3, –4)

   Final Image: *A″B″C″* with *A″*(10, –9), *B″*(1, 1), *C″*(1, –9)

   _____

5. Original *ABCD* with *A*(0, 1), *B*(1, 2), *C*(3, 0), *D*(2, –1)

   Final Image: *A″B″C″D″* with *A″*(2, 2), *B″*(1, 3), *C″*(–1, 3), *D″*(0, 0)

   _____

6. Original *ABCD* with *A*(0, 1), *B*(2, 1), *C*(2, –4), *D*(0, –4)

   Final Image: *A″B″C″D″* with *A″*(1.5, 0), *B″*(1.5, –3), *C″*(–6, –3), *D″*(–6, 0)

   _____

Choose the letter for the best answer.

7. What are the coordinates of the image of the point (2, –4) after a reflection across the *x*-axis followed by a rotation of 90° counter-clockwise around the origin?

   A (–4, –2)

   B (–4, 2)

   C (4, –2)

   D (4, 2)

8. What are the coordinates of the image of the point (–2, 1) after being dilated by a scale factor of 3 with the origin set as the center of dilation and then translated 2 units left and 3 units up?

   F (–3, 1)

   G (–6, 3)

   H (–4, 0)

   J (–1, 7)

CHAPTER 5

Problem Solving Connections

COMMON CORE

CC.8.G.1
CC.8.G.2
CC.8.G.3
CC.8.G.4

Stitch Perfect Ellie is making a cross-stitch pattern for a butterfly. She uses translations, reflection, rotations, and dilations to design the parts of the butterfly. Perform the transformations as described. Then, draw the images on the final answer grid on the last page of the Problem Solving Connections.

1 Making the Body and Wings

A The coordinates of the vertices of the rectangle that represents the body of the butterfly are $(-1, 7)$, $(1, 7)$, $(1, -7)$, $(-1, -7)$. Draw the body on the final answer grid.

B What would the body of the butterfly look like if it were rotated clockwise by 180°?

_____

_____

C Ellie draws one upper wing of the butterfly. The coordinates of the vertices of the wing are given in the table. Draw the wing on the final answer grid.

First Upper Wing	$(-10, 9)$	$(-4, 9)$	$(-1, 5)$	$(-1, 0)$	$(-10, 2)$
Image					

To find the coordinates of the other upper wing, perform a reflection across the y-axis. Draw the image of the first wing on the final answer grid.

D Ellie draws one lower wing of the butterfly. The coordinates of the vertices of the wing are given in the table. Draw the wing on the final answer grid.

First Lower Wing	$(1, 0)$	$(5, 0)$	$(9, -2)$	$(10, -9)$	$(5, -9)$	$(1, -2)$
Image						

To find the coordinates of the other lower wing, perform a reflection across the y-axis. Draw the image of the first wing on the final answer grid.

E Is the first upper wing congruent to its image? Is the first lower wing congruent to its image? Explain how you know.

_____

_____

2 Designing the Upper-Wing Pattern

A On the grid below, draw a square centered at the origin, with side lengths of 6 units.

B Ellie transforms the figure from **A** under the dilation $(x, y) \rightarrow \left(\frac{1}{3}x, \frac{1}{3}y\right)$. Write the coordinates of the image. Then, draw the image on the grid below.

_____

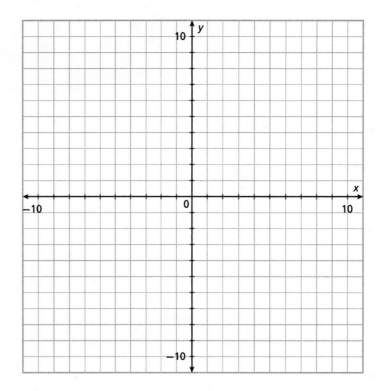

C Ellie transforms the figure from **B** under the translation $(x, y) \rightarrow (x + 5, y + 4)$. Write the coordinates of the image. Then, draw the image on the final answer grid.

_____

D Ellie transforms the figure from **C** by reflecting it across the y-axis. Write the coordinates of the image. Then, draw the image on the final answer grid.

_____

E On the final answer grid, there is a black square. Ellie reflects the square across the y-axis. Write the coordinates of the image. Then, draw the image on the final answer grid.

_____

3 Designing the Lower-Wing Pattern

A On the final answer grid, there is a black triangle. Ellie reflects the triangle across the y-axis. Write the coordinates of the image. Then, draw the image on the final answer grid.

_____

B Ellie rotates the original triangle by 180° about the origin. Write the coordinates of the image. Then, draw the image on the grid below.

_____

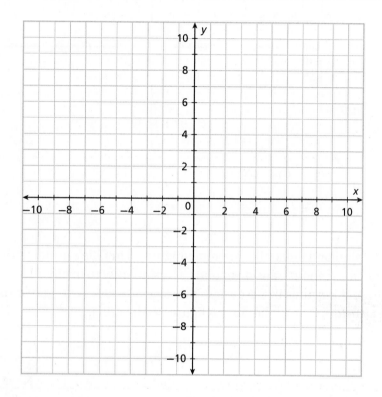

C Ellie transforms the figure from **B** under the translation $(x, y) \rightarrow (x - 13, y - 11)$. Write the coordinates of the image. Then, draw the image on the final answer grid.

_____

D Ellie transforms the figure from **C** by reflecting it across the y-axis. Write the coordinates of the image. Then, draw the image on the final answer grid.

_____

Use this final answer grid to draw Ellie's completed butterfly design.

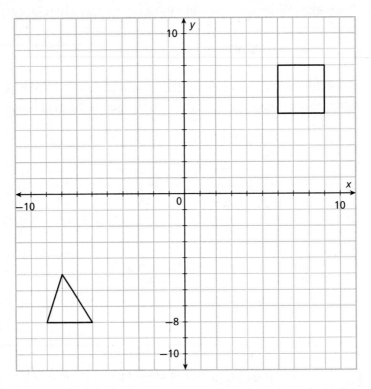

Are there any similar figures (that are not congruent) in Ellie's butterfly design?
Use what you know about transformations and similarity to justify your answer.
(If there are similar figures in the design, describe a sequence of transformations
that would transform one of the similar figures to the other.)

_____

_____

_____

_____

_____

_____

_____

© Houghton Mifflin Harcourt Publishing Company

Performance Task

COMMON
CORE

CC.8.G.2
CC.8.G.3
CC.8.G.4
CC.8.G.5

★ **1.** A computer graphic used to represent a mountain in a game is shown. The triangle is isosceles.

108°

a. Find the angle measures of the triangle. Explain your reasoning.

b. In the game, a series of increasingly large similar triangles are used to create the appearance of the player moving toward the mountain. What happens to the angle measures of the triangles as the size of the triangles increase?

★ **2.** A transformation of the black triangle to the blue triangle is shown in the coordinate plane.

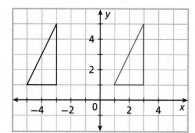

a. Bart says the transformation is a reflection over the y-axis. Is he correct? If not, describe the actual transformation.

b. Are the two figures congruent? Explain.

A rectangle is shown in the coordinate plane.

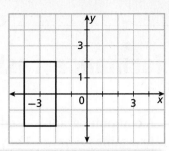

   a. The figure is rotated 90° clockwise about the origin. Give the coordinates of the image of the rectangle. Then draw its image in the coordinate plane.

   b. Describe two ways you could use transformations that would move the image from part a back to the original figure. One or both ways can involve more than one transformation if you want.

A pentagon is drawn on the coordinate plane. It is then rotated 180° about the origin, translated 5 units left, and dilated by a factor of 2.

   a. A vertex of the original figure was at (–2, 2). Where is this vertex after the three transformations? Describe each step.

   b. Describe a different series of transformations that would lead to the same final image. Use two reflections, a dilation, and finally a translation.

© Houghton Mifflin Harcourt Publishing Company

Name _____ **Class** _____ **Date** _____

SELECTED RESPONSE

1. Which is the image of $(2, 3)$ under the translation $(x, y) \rightarrow (x - 5, y - 2)$?

   A. $(-5, -2)$ **C.** $(3, 5)$

   B. $(-3, 1)$ **D.** $(3, -1)$

2. Which is the image of $(2, 3)$ under a reflection across the y-axis?

   F. $(2, 3)$ **H.** $(2, -3)$

   G. $(-2, 3)$ **J.** $(-2, -3)$

3. Which is the image of $(2, 3)$ under a 180° rotation about the origin?

   A. $(3, 2)$ **C.** $(-2, -3)$

   B. $(2, -3)$ **D.** $(-3, -2)$

4. Which sequence of translations, reflections, rotations, and/or dilations transforms figure A into figure B?

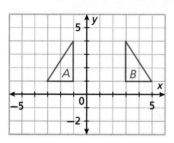

   F. 180° rotation; reflection across y-axis

   G. dilation with center at origin with scale factor of 2; translation 6 units left

   H. reflection across the y-axis; translation 2 units right

   J. reflection across the x-axis; dilation with center as origin with scale factor of $\frac{1}{2}$

Use the figure to answer 5 and 6.

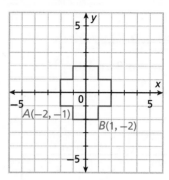

5. Which is the image of point A under a dilation centered at the origin described by the rule $(x, y) \rightarrow (4x, 4y)$?

   A. $(8, 4)$ **C.** $\left(-\frac{1}{2}, -\frac{1}{4}\right)$

   B. $\left(\frac{1}{2}, \frac{1}{4}\right)$ **D.** $(-8, -4)$

6. Which is the image of point B under a dilation centered at the origin with scale factor $\frac{1}{3}$?

   F. $\left(\frac{1}{3}, -\frac{2}{3}\right)$ **H.** $\left(\frac{4}{3}, -\frac{5}{3}\right)$

   G. $(3, -6)$ **J.** $(-3, 6)$

7. What is the measure of angle x?

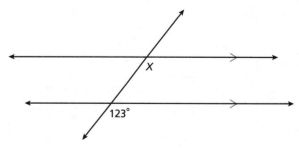

   A. 57°   **C.** 123°

   B. 66°   **D.** 180°

8. What is the value of *x*?

   F. 30°   **H.** 87°

   G. 63°   **J.** 93°

CONSTRUCTED RESPONSE

Use the figure for 9 and 10.

9. Explain how to find the value of *x*.

_____

_____

_____

_____

10. Explain how to find the value of *y*.

_____

_____

_____

Use the figure for 11 through 14.

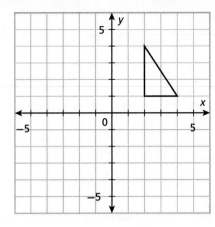

11. Sketch the image of the triangle under a reflection across the *x*-axis.

12. Sketch the image of the triangle after a rotation 90° counterclockwise about the origin followed by a translation left 1 unit.

13. Sketch the image of the triangle after a reflection across the *y*-axis followed by a reflection across the *x*-axis.

14. Identify another transformation or sequence of transformations that results in the same image as the result of Problem 13.

_____

_____

© Houghton Mifflin Harcourt Publishing Company

Measurement and Geometry

Chapter Focus

You will find the area of a circle. You will also solve problems using the formulas for the volume of a cylinder, cone, and sphere.

Chapter at a Glance

COMMON
CORE

Lesson	Standards for Mathematical Content
6-1 Circles	PREP FOR **CC.8.G.9**
6-2 Volume of Prisms and Cylinders	**CC.8.G.9**
6-3 Volume of Pyramids and Cones	**CC.8.G.9**
6-4 Spheres	**CC.8.G.9**
Problem Solving Connections	
Performance Task	
Assessment Readiness	

CHAPTER 6

Unpacking the Standards

Understanding the standards and the vocabulary terms in the standards will help you know exactly what you are expected to learn in this chapter.

COMMON CORE **CC.8.G.9**

Know the formulas for the volumes of cones, cylinders, and spheres and use them to solve real-world and mathematical problems.

Key Vocabulary

sphere *(esfera)* A three-dimensional figure with all points the same distance from the center.

What It Means to You

You will learn the formula for volume of a sphere.

EXAMPLE

To lay their eggs, green turtles travel hundreds of miles to the beach where they were born. The eggs are buried on the beach in a hole about 40 cm deep. The eggs are approximately spherical, with an average diameter of 4.5 cm, and each turtle lays an average of 113 eggs at a time. Estimate the total volume of eggs laid by a green turtle at one time.

Find the volume of one egg.

$$V = \frac{4}{3}\pi r^3$$

$$V = \frac{4}{3}\pi (2.25)^3$$

$$V = 15.1875 \, \pi \, \text{cm}^3$$

$$V \approx 47.7 \, \text{cm}^3$$

Multiply to find the volume of 113 eggs.

$$47.7 \cdot 113 \approx 5{,}390 \, \text{cm}^3$$

The total volume of eggs is approximately 5,390 cm³.

COMMON CORE **CC.8.G.9**

Know the formulas for the volumes of cones, cylinders, and spheres and use them to solve real-world and mathematical problems.

Key Vocabulary

formula *(fórmula)* A rule showing relationships among quantities.
volume *(volumen)* The number of cubic units needed to fill a given space.
cylinder *(cilindro)* A three-dimensional figure with two parallel, congruent circular bases connected by a curved lateral surface.

What It Means to You

You will learn the formula for volume of a cylinder.

EXAMPLE

The Asano Taiko Company of Japan built the world's largest drum in 2000. The drum's diameter is 4.8 meters, and its height is 4.95 meters. Estimate the volume of the drum.

$d = 4.8 \approx 5$

$h = 4.95 \approx 5$

$r = \dfrac{d}{2} = \dfrac{5}{2} = 2.5$

$V = (\pi r^2)h$ *Volume of a cylinder.*

$= (3)(2.5)^2 \cdot 5$ *Use 3 for π.*

$= (3)(6.25)(5)$

$= 18.75 \cdot 5$

$= 93.75$

≈ 94

The volume of the drum is approximately 94 m³.

COMMON CORE **CC.8.G.9**

Know the formulas for the volumes of cones, cylinders, and spheres and use them to solve real-world and mathematical problems.

Key Vocabulary

cone *(cono)* A three-dimensional figure with one vertex and one circular base.

What It Means to You

You will learn the formula for volume of a cone.

EXAMPLE

Find the volume of the cone. Use 3.14 for π.

6 in.

2 in.

$B = \pi\left(2^2\right) = 4\pi$ in²

$V = \dfrac{1}{3} \cdot 4\pi \cdot 6$ $V = \dfrac{1}{3}Bh$

$V = 8\pi$ *Use 3.14 for π.*

≈ 25.1 in³

The volume of the cone is approximately 25.1 in³.

Key Vocabulary

circle *(círculo)* The set of all points in a plane that are the same distance from a given point called the center.

circumference *(circunferencia)* The distance around a circle.

diameter *(diámetro)* A line segment that passes through the center of a circle and has endpoints on the circle, or the length of that segment.

radius *(radio)* A line segment with one endpoint at the center of the circle and the other endpoint on the circle, or the length of that segment.

MATHEMATICAL PRACTICE The Common Core Standards for Mathematical Practice describe varieties of expertise that mathematics educators at all levels should seek to develop in their students. Opportunities to develop these practices are integrated throughout this program.

1. Make sense of problems and persevere in solving them.
2. Reason abstractly and quantitatively.
3. Construct viable arguments and critique the reasoning of others.
4. Model with mathematics.
5. Use appropriate tools strategically.
6. Attend to precision.
7. Look for and make use of structure.
8. Look for and express regularity in repeated reasoning.

CHAPTER 6

Circles
Going Deeper

Essential question: *How do you find the area of a circle?*

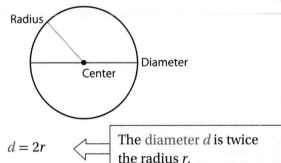

video tutor

A **circle** is a set of points in a plane that are a fixed distance from a given point, called the center.

The **circumference** of a circle is the distance around it.

A **radius** is a line segment that connects the center of a circle to any point on the circle.

A **diameter** is a line segment that connects two points on the circle and passes through the center.

Radius

Center

Diameter

$d = 2r$ ⟸ The diameter *d* is twice the radius *r*.

PREP FOR **CC.8.G.9**

1 EXPLORE **Modeling the Area of a Circle**

The ratio of the circumference to the length of the diameter is about 3.14. The Greek letter π (pi) is the symbol for this constant ratio. You can use π and what you know about circles to find the formula for the area of a circle.

Step 1: Use a compass to draw a circle and cut it out.

Step 2: Fold the circle three times as shown to get equal wedges.

Step 3: Unfold and shade one-half of the circle.

Step 4: Cut out the wedges and fit the pieces together to form a figure that looks like a parallelogram.

The figure has the _____ area as the circle does.

Its *base b* is approximately equal to _____ the circumference of the circle. ($\frac{1}{2}\pi d = \pi r$)

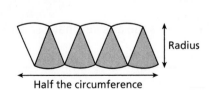

Radius

Half the circumference

Its *height h* is approximately equal to the _____ *r* of the circle.

To find the area of a parallelogram, use the formula *A* = _____.

To find the area of a circle, substitute for b and h in the area formula.

$A = bh$

$A = \boxed{}\, h$ *Substitute πr for b.*

$A = \pi r\, \boxed{}$ *Substitute r for h.*

$A = \pi\, \boxed{}$ $r \cdot r = r^2$

So, the area of a circle is equal to π times the radius squared: _____

REFLECT

1. Explain why your answer will be an approximation when you use 3.14 for pi to find the area of a circle.

_____

_____

2 EXAMPLE   Finding the Area of a Circle

The Anasazi of the American Southwest built underground circular rooms called kivas. The Great Kiva at Chetro Ketl in Chaco Canyon in New Mexico has a diameter of about 50 feet. What is its approximate area?

Step 1: First find the radius. $d = 2r$

$\boxed{} = 2r$ *Substitute 50 for the diameter d.*

$\dfrac{\boxed{}}{2} = \dfrac{2r}{2}$ *Divide both sides by 2 to isolate r.*

$\boxed{} = r$

Step 2: Next find the diameter. $A = \pi r^2$

$\approx \boxed{} \cdot \boxed{} \cdot \boxed{}$ *Substitute 25 for the radius r. Use 3.14 for π.*

$\approx 3.14 \cdot \boxed{}$ *Simplify.*

$\approx \boxed{}$

The area of the Great Kiva is about _____ ft^2.

REFLECT

2a. Does the answer make sense? Explain.

_____

_____

TRY THIS!

2b. The radius of a crop circle is 52 feet. What is the area of the crop circle?

_____

3 **E X A M P L E** **Finding a Radius or Diameter Given the Area**

The area of Jerome's cake plate is about 50.24 in². He places his 7-inch fork across the plate after eating. Can the fork fit without going over the edge?

To solve the problem, find the diameter of the plate.

Step 1: First find the radius. $A = \pi r^2$

$$\boxed{} \approx \boxed{} \cdot r^2$$
Substitute. Use 3.14 for π.

$$\frac{50.24}{\boxed{}} \approx \frac{3.14 \cdot r^2}{\boxed{}}$$
Divide both sides by 3.14 to isolate r^2.

$$\boxed{} \approx r^2$$
Take the square root of each side.

$$\boxed{} \approx r$$
Keep only the positive value for r.

Step 2: Next find the diameter. $d = 2r$

$$d = 2 \cdot \boxed{}$$
Substitute into the formula.

$$d = \boxed{}$$

The diameter of the plate is _____ inches. So, the fork will/will not fit.

REFLECT

3a. Given the area of a circle, how do you find its radius? its diameter?

_____

_____

_____

TRY THIS!

3b. What is the radius of a circus ring with an area of 78.5 m²? What is the diameter of the ring?

_____

PRACTICE

Solve. Use 3.14 for π.

1. What is the area of a circle whose radius is 3 cm?

_____

2. What is the area of circular region with a diameter of about 18 kilometers?

_____

3. What is the radius of a circle whose area is about 40.69 cm²?

_____

4. What is the diameter of a circle with an area of about 15.2 square yards?

_____

5. The diameter of a large pizza is 14 inches. What is its area?

_____

6. To the nearest tenth, what is the area of a circular ring with a radius of 3.5 meters?

_____

7. The 3-point line on a middle-school basketball court forms a semi-circle. Its diameter is the out-of-bounds line under the basket. That line measures 34 feet. To the nearest square foot, what is the area of the semi-circle?

_____

8. One of the circular kivas at Pueblo Bonita in Chaco Canyon has a diameter of 8 feet. Another has a diameter of 47 feet. What is the difference between the areas of those two kivas?

_____

9. **Think Critically** The answer to Problem 8 is an approximation. How can you express the answer as an exact number?

_____

10. What is the area of the shaded ring? How did you figure it out?

_____

_____

11. A running track and field is composed of a rectangle and two semi-circles. The length of the rectangular part is 70 meters. The radius of each circular part is 40 meters. Using 3 for π, estimate the area of the track and field.

_____

12. A square coaster has side lengths of 3 inches. A circular coaster has a diameter of 3 inches. Which coaster is larger? About how much larger?

_____

13. **Error Analysis** Arthur claims that a circle with a diameter of 12 inches has twice the area of a circle with a diameter of 6 inches. Is he correct? Explain.

_____

_____

Additional Practice

Find the area of each circle, both in terms of π and to the nearest tenth. Use 3.14 for π.

1. circle with radius 9 in.

   _____

2. circle with diameter 14 cm

   _____

3. circle with radius 20 ft

   _____

4. circle with diameter 17 m

   _____

5. circle with diameter 15.4 m

   _____

6. circle with radius 22 yd

   _____

Solve. Use 3.14 for π.

7. A circle has an area of about 28.26 in^2. What is the radius of the circle?

   _____

8. What is the diameter of a circle whose area is about 113.04 cm^2?

   _____

9. A round tablecloth has a radius of 36 inches. What is the area of the tablecloth?

   _____

10. Graph a circle with center (0, 0) that passes through (0, −3). Find the area and circumference, both in terms of π and to the nearest tenth. Use 3.14 for π.

    _____

    _____

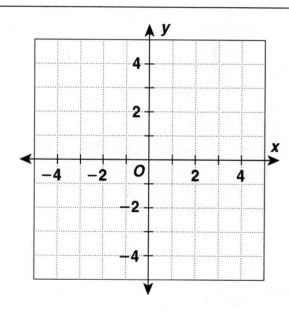

Problem Solving

Round to the nearest tenth. Use 3.14 for π. Write the correct answer.

1. A frying pan has a diameter of 11 inches. What is the area to the nearest square inch of the smallest cover that will fit on top of the pan?

   _____

2. A dog is on a 15-foot chain that is anchored to the ground. How much area can the dog cover while he is on the chain?

   _____

3. A small pizza has a diameter of 10 inches, and a medium has a diameter of 12 inches. How much more pizza do you get with the medium pizza?

   _____

4. How much more crust do you get with a medium pizza with a diameter of 12 inches than a small pizza with a 10 inch diameter?

   _____

Round to the nearest tenth. Use 3.14 for π. Choose the letter for the best answer.

5. The wrestling mat for college NCAA competition has a wrestling circle with a diameter of 32 feet, while a high school mat has a diameter of 28 feet. How much more area is there in a college wrestling mat than a high school mat?

   A 12.6 ft^2

   B 188.4 ft^2

   C 234.8 ft^2

   D 753.6 ft^2

6. A round dining table has a radius of 24 inches. A round tablecloth has a diameter of 60 inches. What is the area to the nearest tenth of an inch of the part of the tablecloth that will hang down the side of the table?

   F 19 in^2

   G 113 in^2

   H 1017 in^2

   J 9495 in^2

7. In men's Olympic discus throwing competition, an athlete throws a discus with a diameter of 8.625 inches. What is the circumference of the discus?

   A 13.5 in.

   B 27.1 in.

   C 58.4 in.

   D 233.6 in.

8. An athlete in a discus competition throws from a circle that is approximately 8.2 feet in diameter. What is the area of the discus throwing circle?

   F 52.8 ft^2

   G 25.7 ft^2

   H 12.9 ft^2

   J 211.1 ft^2

Volume of Prisms and Cylinders
Going Deeper

video tutor

Essential question: *How can you solve problems using the formula for the volume of a cylinder?*

A cylinder has two parallel congruent circular bases. The area of a base is πr^2.

Volume of a Cylinder

The volume of a cylinder with base area
B, radius r, and height h is $V = Bh$,
or $V = \pi r^2 h$.

CC.8.G.9

1 EXAMPLE Volume of a Cylinder

Find the volume of each cylinder. Round your answers to the nearest tenth if necessary. Use 3.14 for π.

> **A** A cylindrical oatmeal canister has a radius of 3 inches and a height of 10 inches.
>
> $V = \pi r^2 h$
>
> $\approx 3.14 \cdot \boxed{}^2 \cdot \boxed{}$ *Substitute into the formula.*
>
> $\approx 3.14 \cdot \boxed{} \cdot \boxed{}$ *Simplify the exponent.*
>
> $\approx \boxed{}$ in^3 *Multiply.*
>
> The volume of the canister is about _____ in^3.

10 in.

3 in.

> **B** A drink can has a diameter of 6.4 centimeters and a height of 13 centimeters.
>
> First, find the radius: _____ cm.
>
> $V = \pi r^2 h$
>
> $\approx 3.14 \cdot \boxed{}^2 \cdot \boxed{}$ *Substitute into the formula.*
>
> $\approx 3.14 \cdot \boxed{} \cdot \boxed{}$ *Simplify the exponent.*
>
> $\approx \boxed{}$ cm^3 *Multiply.*
>
> The volume of the can is about _____ cm^3.

13 cm

6.4 cm

TRY THIS!

1a. The top layer of a wedding cake has a diameter of 10 inches and a height of 6 inches. Find the volume of the top layer of the cake. Round your answer to the nearest tenth if necessary. Use 3.14 for π.

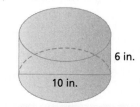

6 in.

10 in.

PRACTICE

Find the volume of each figure. Round your answers to the nearest tenth if necessary. Use 3.14 for π.

1.

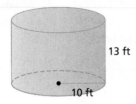

13 ft

10 ft

_____

2.

12 ft

4 ft

_____

3. The area of the circular base of a can of dog food is 12.5 in². The can is 6 inches high. What is its volume?

_____

4. A can of soup has a volume of 2,797.74 cm³. It is 11 cm high. What is the length of the radius of its base?

_____

5. A cookie container is in the shape of a cylinder. Its diameter is 9 inches and its height is 3 inches. To the nearest cubic inch, what is its volume?

_____

6. The volume of a rooftop cylindrical water tank is 1,493 ft³. The tank is 30 feet high. To the nearest square foot, what is the area of its base?

_____

7. A cake has three cylindrical layers, and each layer is 5 inches tall. The top layer has a 12-inch diameter. Each of the other layers has a diameter 2 inches greater than the layer above it. To the nearest cubic inch, what is the cake's volume?

_____

8. How is finding the volume of a cylinder like finding the volume of a prism? How is it different?

_____

_____

_____

9. A cylinder and a prism both have the same base area and height. Which has the greater volume?

_____

10. Which gives a cylinder greater volume: a radius of 16 cm and a height of 20 cm, or a radius of 20 cm and a height of 16 cm? Explain.

_____

11. **Error Analysis** Diane says that tripling the diameter of the base of a can of soup will increase its volume by a factor of 6. Is she correct? Explain.

_____

Additional Practice

Find the volume of each figure to the nearest tenth.
Use 3.14 for π.

1.
6.5 cm

16 cm

_____

2.
15 cm

32 cm

_____

3.
4 mm

7.5 mm

_____

4.
6 in.

11 in.

_____

5. A cylinder has a diameter of 8 feet and height of 40 feet.

_____

6. A cylinder has a diameter of 16 meters and height of 4 meters.

_____

7. A cylindrical paint can is 19 centimeters tall and has a radius of
8 centimeters. What is the volume of the paint can? Round your
answer to the nearest tenth.

_____

8. A cylinder has a radius of 6 ft and a height of 25 ft. Explain
whether tripling the height will triple the volume of the cylinder.

_____

_____

Problem Solving

A rectangular box is 2 inches high, 3.5 inches wide and 4 inches long. A cylindrical box is 3.5 inches high and has a diameter of 3.2 inches. Use 3.14 for π. Round to the nearest tenth.

1. Which box has a larger volume?

   _____

2. How much bigger is the larger box?

   _____

Use 3.14 for π. Choose the letter for the best answer.

3. A can has diameter of 9.8 cm and is 13.2 cm tall. What is the capacity of the can? Round to the nearest tenth.

   A 203.1 cm³

   B 995.2 cm³

   C 3980.7 cm³

   D 959.2 cm³

4. How many cubic feet of air are in a room that is 15 feet long, 10 feet wide and 8 feet high?

   F 33 ft³

   G 1200 ft³

   H 1500 ft³

   J 3768 ft³

5. How many gallons of water will the water trough hold? Round to the nearest gallon. (Hint: 1 cubic foot of water is approximately 7.5 gallons.)

2 ft
6 ft

   A 19 gallons

   B 71 gallons

   C 141 gallons

   D 565 gallons

6. A child's wading pool has a diameter of 5 feet and a height of 1 foot. How much water would it take to fill the pool? Round to the nearest gallon. (Hint: 1 cubic foot of water is approximately 7.5 gallons.)

   F 79 gallons

   G 589 gallons

   H 59 gallons

   J 147 gallons

6-3

Volume of Pyramids and Cones
Going Deeper

Essential question: *How can you solve problems using the formula for the volume of a cone?*

A cone has one circular base. The area of the base is πr^2.

> ### Volume of a Cone
>
> The volume of a cone with base area B, radius r, and height h is $V = \frac{1}{3}Bh$, or $V = \frac{1}{3}\pi r^2 h$.

CC.8.G.9

1 EXAMPLE Volume of a Cone

Find the volume of each cone. Round your answers to the nearest tenth if necessary. Use 3.14 for π.

A A candle in the shape of a cone has a height of 8 inches and a radius of 2 inches.

$V = \frac{1}{3}\pi r^2 h$

$\approx \frac{1}{3} \cdot 3.14 \cdot \boxed{}^{2} \cdot \boxed{}$ *Substitute into the formula.*

$\approx \frac{1}{3} \cdot 3.14 \cdot \boxed{} \cdot \boxed{}$ *Simplify the exponent.*

$\approx \boxed{}$ in^3 *Multiply.*

The volume of the candle is about _____ in^3.

8 in.
2 in.

B Jacob has a tent that is cone-shaped. It has a height of 9 feet and a diameter of 8 feet.

First, find the radius: _____ ft.

$V = \frac{1}{3}\pi r^2 h$

$\approx \frac{1}{3} \cdot 3.14 \cdot \boxed{}^{2} \cdot \boxed{}$ *Substitute into the formula.*

$\approx \frac{1}{3} \cdot 3.14 \cdot \boxed{} \cdot \boxed{}$ *Simplify the exponent.*

$\approx \boxed{}$ ft^3 *Multiply.*

The volume of the tent is about _____ ft^3.

9 ft
8 ft

TRY THIS!

1. What is the relationship between the volume of a cylinder and a cone with the same height and same radius?

_____

Find the volume of each figure. Round your answers to the nearest tenth if necessary. Use 3.14 for π.

1.

7 ft

6 ft

2.

100 in.

33 in.

_____

3. A cone-shaped living space is 9.8 feet high. Its base has a diameter of 8.8 feet. What is the volume of the living space?

_____

4. Waffle cones have a volume of about 234 cm^3. If a cone is 14 cm tall, what is the approximate diameter of its base?

_____

5. Nuala is making a volcano for a science experiment. First, she constructs the cone. The circumference of its base is 125.6 inches. The height of the cone is 33 inches. What is the volume of Nuala's cone? *Remember: C = πd.*

_____

6. A pyramid has a rectangular base with sides of 6.28 m and 8 m. If you wished to make a cone with the same height and volume, what radius should your cone have?

_____

7. How is finding the volume of a cone like finding the volume of a pyramid? How is it different?

_____

_____

_____

8. A cone and a pyramid both have the same base area and height. Which has the greater volume?

_____

9. A cone and a cylinder have the same size base. The cone's height is 6 times the height of the cylinder. How much greater is the volume of the cone?

_____

10. **Error Analysis** Pierre says that doubling the dimensions of a cone will double its volume. Is he correct? Explain.

Additional Practice

Find the volume of each figure to the nearest tenth. Use 3.14 for π.

1.

15 in.

27 in.

2.

20.5 m

12.4 m

_____

_____

3.

7 ft

4 ft

4.

17 cm

16 cm

_____

_____

5. The radius of a cone is 19.4 cm and its height is 24 cm. Find the volume of the cone to the nearest tenth.

_____

6. A funnel has a diameter of 9 in. and is 16 in. deep. Use a calculator to find the volume of the funnel to the nearest hundredth.

_____

7. A cone has a diameter of 6 ft and a height of 11.5 ft. Find the volume of the cone. Round your answer to the nearest tenth.

_____

Problem Solving

Round to the nearest tenth. Use 3.14 for π. Write the correct answer.

1. An oil funnel is in the shape of a cone. It has a diameter of 4 inches and a height of 6 inches. If the end of the funnel is plugged, how much oil can the funnel hold before it overflows?

_____

2. One quart of oil has a volume of approximately 57.6 in^3. Does the oil funnel in exercise 3 hold more or less than 1 quart of oil?

_____

3. The Feathered Serpent Pyramid is located in Teotihuacan, Mexico. Its base is a square that measures 65 m on each side. The pyramid is 19.4 m high. What is the volume of the Feathered Serpent Pyramid?

_____

4. The Sun Pyramid in Teotihuacan, Mexico, is larger than the Feathered Serpent Pyramid. The sides of the square base and the height are each about 3.3 times larger than the Feathered Serpent Pyramid. How many times larger is the volume of the Sun Pyramid than the Feathered Serpent Pyramid?

_____

Round to the nearest tenth. Use 3.14 for π. Choose the letter for the best answer.

5. An ice cream cone has a diameter of 4.2 cm and a height of 11.5 cm. What is the volume of the cone?

   A 18.7 cm^3

   B 25.3 cm^3

   C 53.1 cm^3

   D 212.3 cm^3

7. What is the volume of the hourglass at the right?

   A 13.1 in^3

   B 26.2 in^3

   C 52.3 in^3

   D 102.8 in^3

6. When decorating a cake, the frosting is put into a cone-shaped bag and then squeezed out a hole at the tip of the cone. How much frosting is in a bag that has a radius of 1.5 inches and a height of 8.5 inches?

   F 5.0 in^3 H 15.2 in^3

   G 13.3 in^3 J 20.0 in^3

8 in.

2.5 in.

Spheres
Going Deeper

Essential question: *How can you solve problems using the formula for the volume of a sphere?*

video tutor

All the points in a sphere are the same distance from the center of the sphere.

Volume of a Sphere

The volume of a sphere with radius r is $V = \frac{4}{3}\pi r^3$.

r

CC.8.G.9

1 EXAMPLE Volume of a Sphere

Find the volume of each sphere. Round your answers to the nearest tenth if necessary. Use 3.14 for π.

A The radius of a golf ball is 2.1 centimeters.

$$V = \frac{4}{3}\pi r^3$$

$$\approx \frac{4}{3} \cdot 3.14 \cdot \boxed{}^3 \qquad \textit{Substitute into the formula.}$$

$$\approx \frac{4}{3} \cdot 3.14 \cdot \boxed{} \qquad \textit{Simplify the exponent.}$$

$$\approx \boxed{} \text{ cm}^3 \qquad \textit{Multiply.}$$

2.1 cm

The volume of a golf ball is about _____ cm^3.

B The diameter of a tennis ball is 7 centimeters.

First, find the radius: _____ cm.

$$V = \frac{4}{3}\pi r^3$$

$$\approx \frac{4}{3} \cdot 3.14 \cdot \boxed{}^3 \qquad \textit{Substitute into the formula.}$$

$$\approx \frac{4}{3} \cdot 3.14 \cdot \boxed{} \qquad \textit{Simplify the exponent.}$$

$$\approx \boxed{} \text{ cm}^3 \qquad \textit{Multiply.}$$

7 cm

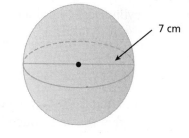

The volume of the tennis ball is about _____ cm^3.

REFLECT

1. A hemisphere is half of a sphere. Explain how you would find the volume of a hemisphere.

_____

_____

Solve. Use 3.14 for π.

1. A ball has a diameter of 20 inches. What is the volume of the ball? Give your answer to the nearest cubic inch.

2. The radius of a soccer ball is 11 cm. What is the volume of the ball? Give your answer to the nearest cubic centimeter.

3. An enormous spherical structure houses a planetarium. The diameter of the building is 60 yards. To the nearest cubic yard, what is the volume of the structure?

4. A steel ball with a diameter of 4 cm is placed in a water-filled cylinder that is 10 cm high and 5 cm in diameter. What is the volume of the water the ball will displace?

5. The diameter of an official squash ball ranges from 39.5 mm to 40.5 mm. What is the approximate difference in volume between the largest and smallest official squash ball?

6. A sphere and a cylinder have the same diameter, and the cylinder's height is the same as its diameter. How will their volumes compare? First guess, then try a few examples to find out.

7. You double the radius of a sphere. How does this affect the volume?

8. Three tennis balls, each with a diameter of 2.6 inches, are packaged in a cylindrical container.

   a. What is the total volume of the balls, to the nearest cubic inch?

   b. What is the volume of the container to the nearest cubic inch, assuming that the balls touch its sides, top, and bottom?

9. **Error Analysis** Curtis claims that the volume of this ball is about 1,436.03 in³. Is he correct? If not, what was his error?

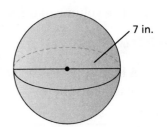

7 in.

Additional Practice

Find the volume of each sphere, both in terms of π and to the nearest tenth. Use 3.14 for π.

1. $r = 9$ ft

2. $r = 21$ m

3. $d = 30$ cm

_____

_____

_____

_____

_____

_____

4. $d = 24$ cm

5. $r = 15.4$ in.

6. $r = 16.01$ ft

_____

_____

_____

_____

_____

_____

Find the volume of each sphere. Round your answers to the nearest tenth. Use 3.14 for π.

7.
6.2 ft

8.
10 cm

9.
12 in.

_____

_____

_____

_____

_____

_____

10. A baseball has a diameter of 2.9 inches. Find the volume of the baseball. Round your answer to the nearest tenth. Use 3.14 for π.

_____

11. A ball with a diameter of 10 inches is placed in a box that is 11 inches by 11 inches by 11 inches. What is the volume of the box that is not filled by the ball? Round your answer to the nearest tenth. Use 3.14 for π.

_____

Problem Solving

Early golf balls were smooth spheres. Later it was discovered that golf balls flew better when they were dimpled. On January 1, 1932, the United States Golf Association set standards for the weight and size of a golf ball. The minimum diameter of a regulation golf ball is 1.680 inches. Use 3.14 for π. Round to the nearest hundredth.

1. Find the volume of a smooth golf ball with the minimum diameter allowed by the United States Golf Association.

_____

2. Would the dimples on a golf ball increase or decrease the volume of the ball?

_____

Use 3.14 for π. Use the following information for Exercises 3–4. A track and field expert recommends changes to the size of a shot put. One recommendation is that a shot put should have a diameter between 90 and 110 mm. Choose the letter for the best answer.

3. Find the volume of a shot put with a diameter of 90 mm.

   A 25,434 mm^3

   B 101,736 mm^3

   C 381,510 mm^3

   D 3,052,080 mm^3

4. Find the volume of a shot put with diameter 110 mm.

   F 37,994 mm^3

   G 696,557 mm^3

   H 2,089,670 mm^3

   J 5,572,453 mm^3

5. Find the volume of the earth if the average diameter of the earth is 7926 miles.

   A 2.0×10^8 mi^3

   B 2.6×10^{11} mi^3

   C 7.9×10^8 mi^3

   D 2.1×10^{12} mi^3

6. An ice cream cone has a diameter of 4.2 cm and a height of 11.5 cm. One spherical scoop of ice cream is put on the cone that has a diameter of 5.6 cm. If the ice cream were to melt in the cone, how much of it would overflow the cone? Round to the nearest tenth.

   F 0 cm^3 H 38.8 cm^3

   G 12.3 cm^3 J 54.3 cm^3

© Houghton Mifflin Harcourt Publishing Company

Problem Solving Connections

Where in the Park is Xander? Xander plans a hiking trip in a national park. Instead of obtaining an accurate trail map from the National Park Service, he downloaded *Bob's Hiking Guide* from a website. Xander's hiking guide eventually gets him lost. Can you help find Xander?

COMMON CORE

CC.8.G.5
CC.8.G.6
CC.8.G.7
CC.8.G.8
CC.8.G.9
CC.8.EE.6

1 Packing for the Trip

Xander fills his backpack with his hiking guide, a book of matches, a flashlight, and two bottles of water. General guidelines suggest that a person drink at least eight 8-oz servings of water per day. Depending on a person's activity level, their body may require more water.

A Xander plans to be hiking for most of the day, so hiking resources suggest that he have at least 3 liters of water with him. The bottles he brought with him are cylinders with a radius of 3 cm and a height of 30 cm. What is the volume of one bottle in cubic centimeters?

B One cubic centimeter has the same volume as one milliliter. There are 1000 milliliters in 1 liter. Does Xander have enough water with him?

C One milliliter has the same volume as about 0.034 fluid ounces. Does Xander have at least eight 8-oz servings of water packed?

2 Following the Map

Xander follows the maps in *Bob's Hiking Guide* and starts out on South Springs Trail.

A Xander wants to take Crossover Trail northeast to intersect with North Rim Trail. A note on Xander's map reads:

> "There are a bunch of trails that split off from the intersection of South Springs Trail and Crossover Trail. I didn't draw them all on my map. But I know North Rim Trail and South Springs Trail run parallel and that the angle in the southeast corner of North Rim Trail and Crossover Trail measures 120°. Good Luck! —Bob"

When Xander gets to the intersection of South Springs Trail and Crossover Trail, the only signs on the four trails he sees are given in degrees. How can Xander determine which trail to take when he gets to the intersection of South Springs and Crossover Trail?

_____

_____

_____

_____

_____

Trail A 15°	Trail B 60°	Trail C 120°	Trail D 135°

B The trail markers at the intersection of South Springs Trail and Crossover Trail are the ones above. Which trail should Xander take?

_____

_____

3 Finding a Landmark

Xander makes a mistake and takes the trail marked 60°. After hiking for a while, he realizes that he is lost and his cell phone battery is almost dead.

A Xander stands 50 feet in front of a young tree and looks up across the top of the tree to the top of a mountain in the distance. Xander estimates the height of the tree as 15 feet. Draw a diagram involving similar triangles that shows the relationship between the tree and the mountain from Xander's perspective.

B Explain how you know that the triangles in your diagram are similar triangles.

_____

_____

_____

C How can the diagram help Xander?

_____

_____

4 Finding Xander

Xander's cell phone battery has just enough life to make a brief call to 911. He quickly tells the dispatcher about the mountain and the tree. The dispatcher tells Xander to stay in the same spot and then Xander's phone dies.

A The dispatcher contacts a ranger at the National Park Service. The ranger knows that the height of the mountain is 3000 feet. Use the height of the mountain and your diagram to find Xander's distance from the mountain.

Xander is about _____ feet from the mountain.

Xander did not mention a lake or waterfall, but did mention being near trees. The ranger uses his knowledge of the park to assume that Xander is south of the mountain. He contacts ranger stations in that area of the park and tells them to look for signs of a lost hiker.

B Xander makes a fire while he waits for rescue. The fire is spotted by two park rangers in towers that are 2000 feet apart. The rangers use the line between the towers as the base of a triangle and determine that the angle to the fire from each tower measures 45°.

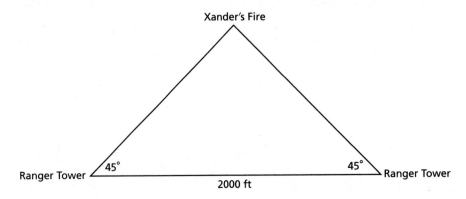

C Classify the triangle as acute, right, or obtuse. Explain how you know.

_____

_____

_____

D When two angles in a triangle have the same measure, the sides opposite those angles have the same length. How can you find the lengths of the missing sides?

_____

_____

E Find Xander's distance from the ranger towers.

Xander is about _____ feet from either ranger tower.

Performance Task

COMMON
CORE

CC.8.G.9

⭐ **1.** A candle maker has a block of paraffin that is 4 centimeters high by 8 centimeters long by 6 centimeters wide. He melts it into a cone-shaped candle that is 5 centimeters wide at the base and 25 centimeters tall. Does the candle maker use all of the paraffin from the original block? How do you know?

⭐ **2.** An inflatable spherical exercise ball and an inflatable cylindrical ottoman both have a diameter of 24 inches. Both hold the same amount of air. What is the height of the ottoman? Use 3.14 for π. Justify your answer.

⭐⭐ **3.** A potter makes a cylindrical vase that is 14 inches high and 8 inches wide. The base and sides of the vase are 0.25 inch thick.

a. How tall and wide is the hollow cylindrical interior of this vase? Explain your reasoning.

b. What is the volume of the interior? Use 3.14 for π. Round your answer to the nearest cubic inch.

c. Another vase having the same outside dimensions has thicker sides. Choose a side thickness and calculate the volume. Is the inside volume of this vase greater or less than the volume of the original vase?

4. A company makes snow globes. Each snow globe is in the shape of a sphere, and the diameter of the sphere is 8 centimeters.

a. One cubic centimeter of water has a mass of about 1 gram. If the snow globe is filled with water, what is the total mass of the water in the snow globe? Explain how you found your answer. Use 3.14 for π and round to the nearest whole gram.

b. The company has another snow globe with a diameter of 9 centimeters and a mass of 934 grams. The plastic shell, decorations, and base make up 454 grams of that mass. Is the snow globe filled with water? Explain your reasoning.

Name _____ Class _____ Date _____

SELECTED RESPONSE

1. Find the area of the circle to the nearest tenth. Use 3.14 for π.

3.4 mm

   A. 114 m^2 **C.** 145.2 m^2

   B. 36.3 m^2 **D.** 21.4 m^2

2. Find the volume of the cylinder. Round your answer to the nearest tenth.

7 mm

4 mm

   F. 87.9 mm^3 **H.** 153.9 mm^3

   G. 175.8 mm^3 **J.** 615.4 mm^3

3. Find the volume of the figure. Use 3.14 for π. If necessary, round your answer to the nearest tenth.

18 ft

8.5 ft

   A. 160.1 ft^3 **C.** 75.6 ft^3

   B 1361.2 ft^3 **D.** 4083.6 ft^3

4. A county has constructed a conical building to store sand. The cone has a height of 195 ft and a diameter of 307 ft. Find the volume of this building to the nearest hundredth.

   F. 1,531,546.25 ft^3 **H.** 31,329.35 ft^3

   G. 14,427,165.67 ft^3 **J.** 4,809,055.23 ft^3

5. To the nearest tenth, find the volume of a sphere with a diameter of 10 cm. Use 3.14 for π.

   A. 314.2 cm^3 **C.** 1256.6 cm^3

   B. 523.3 cm^3 **D.** 4188.8 cm^3

6. Find the volume of a sphere with a radius of 6 cm to the nearest tenth. Use 3.14 for π.

   F. 37.7 cm^3 **H.** 904.3 cm^3

   G. 452.2 cm^3 **J.** 226.1 cm^3

7. A cylinder is 5 centimeters tall and has a radius of 2.1 centimeters. Find the volume to the nearest tenth. Use 3.14 for π.

   A. 33.0 cm^3 **C.** 65.9 cm^3

   B. 61.2 cm^3 **D.** 69.2 cm^3

8. The diameter of the base of a cylinder is 10 cm and the height is 20 cm. What is the volume of the cylinder? Use 3.14 for π.

   F. 628 cm^3 **H.** 1,570 cm^3

   G. 1,256 cm^3 **J.** 6,280 cm^3

9. Find the area of a circle with diameter 31.6 cm, both in terms of π and to the nearest tenth. Use 3.14 for π.

   A. $A = 249.64\pi$ cm$^2 \approx 783.9$ cm^2

   B. $A = 63.2\pi$ cm$^2 \approx 198.4$ cm^2

   C. $A = 31.6\pi$ cm$^2 \approx 99.2$ cm^2

   D. $A = 998.56\pi$ cm$^2 \approx 3135.5$ cm^2

10. The diameter of an ice-hockey puck is 3.0 inches. To the nearest tenth, what is the area of the flat upper surface? Use 3.14 for π.

   F. 3.5 in^2 **H.** 7.1 in^2

   G. 9.4 in^2 **J.** 28.3 in^2

11. Riggoletto's Portraits specializes in making circular portraits of people. A large portrait is 78 in. in diameter. A medium portrait is 26 in. in diameter. Estimate the difference between the areas of the two sizes of portraits. Use 3.14 for π. Round your answer to the nearest whole number.

A. about 82 in^2 **C.** about 16981 in^2

B. about 4245 in^2 **D.** about 163 in^2

12. A farmer is building a new silo. The circular silo is 27 meters tall and has a radius of 14 meters. What is the area of the base of the silo? Round your answer to the nearest tenth. Use 3.14 for π.

F. 615.4 m^2 **H.** 2,461.8 m^2

G. 1,230.9 m^2 **J.** 16,616.9 m^2

Constructed Response

13. Your soccer club wants to sell frozen yogurt to raise money for new uniforms. The club has the choice of the two different size containers shown. Each container costs the club the same amount. The club plans to charge customers $2.50. Which container should the club buy? Explain.

_____

_____

_____

_____

_____

14. Find the volume of the cylinder to the nearest hundredth. Use 3.14 for π.

3 cm

6 cm

_____

15. A new movie theater is going to sell popcorn. The manager has the choice of the three different size containers shown. The manager plans to charge $4.75 for a container of popcorn.

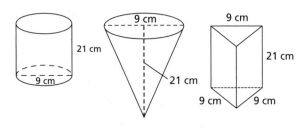

9 cm   9 cm

21 cm

21 cm

9 cm

9 cm   9 cm

Which container would you choose as the manager of the movie theater? Explain.

_____

_____

_____

_____

_____

_____

Multi-Step Equations

Chapter Focus

You will simplify algebraic expressions. You will solve equations by combining like terms and multiplying expressions. When you simplify some equations, you may find that they do not have one solution. You will be asked to give examples of equations with a given number of solutions. Finally, you will solve a system of equations algebraically.

Chapter at a Glance

COMMON CORE

Lesson	Standards for Mathematical Content
7-1 Simplifying Algebraic Expressions	PREP FOR **CC.8.EE.7**
7-2 Solving Multi-Step Equations	**CC.8.EE.7b**
7-3 Solving Equations with Variables on Both Sides	**CC.8.EE.7a, CC.8.EE.7b**
7-4 Systems of Equations	**CC.8.EE.8b, CC.8.EE.8c**
Problem Solving Connections	
Performance Task	
Assessment Readiness	

CHAPTER 7

Unpacking the Standards

Understanding the standards and the vocabulary terms in the standards will help you know exactly what you are expected to learn in this chapter.

COMMON CORE CC.8.EE.7a

Give examples of linear equations in one variable with one solution, infinitely many solutions, or no solutions. Show which of these possibilities is the case by successively transforming the given equation into simpler forms, until an equivalent equation of the form $x = a$, $a = a$, or $a = b$ results (where a and b are different numbers).

Key Vocabulary

linear equation *(ecuación lineal)* An equation whose solutions form a straight line on a coordinate plane.
variable *(variable)* A symbol used to represent a quantity that can change.

What It Means to You

You will learn to recognize how many solutions a given equation has.

EXAMPLE
Solve.

$$-4x + 3(x - 1) = -(x + 3)$$

$$
\begin{aligned}
-4x + 3(x - 1) &= -(x + 3) \\
-4x + 3x - 3 &= -x - 3 \\
-x - 3 &= -x - 3 \\
+x &= +x \\
\hline
-3 &= -3
\end{aligned}
$$

Because $-3 = -3$ is always a true statement, the equation is always true for *any value* of x. There are *infinitely* many solutions.

COMMON CORE CC.8.EE.8b

Solve systems of two linear equations in two variables algebraically, and estimate solutions by graphing the equations. Solve simple cases by inspection.

Key Vocabulary

system of equations *(sistema de ecuaciones)* A set of two or more equations that contain two or more variables.

What It Means to You

You will solve systems of equations algebraically.

EXAMPLE
Solve the system of equations.
$$y = x + 3$$
$$y = 2x + 5$$

The expressions $x + 3$ and $2x + 5$ both equal y. So by the Transitive Property they are equal to each other.

$$y = x + 3 \qquad\qquad y = 2x + 5$$
$$x + 3 = 2x + 5$$

Solve the equation to find x.

$$
\begin{aligned}
x + 3 &= 2x + 5 \\
3 &= x + 5 \qquad \textit{Subtract x from both sides.} \\
-2 &= x \qquad \textit{Add } -5 \textit{ to both sides.}
\end{aligned}
$$

To find y, substitute -2 for x in one of the original equations.
$$y = x + 3 = -2 + 3 = 1$$
The solution is $(-2, 1)$.

CC.8.EE.7b

Solve linear equations with rational number coefficients, including equations whose solutions require expanding expressions using the distributive property and collecting like terms.

Key Vocabulary

Distributive Property *(Propiedad distributiva)* For all real numbers *a, b,* and *c, a(b + c) 5 ab + ac,* and *a(b − c) = ab − ac.*

What It Means to You

You will solve equations using properties of equality and operations.

EXAMPLE

Solve.

$$3(x + 10) + 6 = 12$$

$$3(\,x + 10\,) + 6 = 12$$
$$3x + 30 + 6 = 12$$
$$3x + 36 = 12$$
$$3x \qquad = 224$$
$$x = 28$$

COMMON CORE **CC.8.EE.8c**

Solve real-world and mathematical problems leading to two linear equations in two variables.

What It Means to You

You will write and solve systems of linear equations to solve real-world problems.

EXAMPLE

Tickets for a high school football game were $8 for adults and $5 for students. A total of 1970 tickets were sold. The total ticket sales were $12,220. How many adult tickets were sold and how many student tickets were sold? Let a represent the number of adult tickets sold and s represent the number of student tickets sold.

$$a + s = 1970$$
$$\underline{-a \qquad = \qquad -a}$$
$$s = 1970 - a$$

$$8a + 5s = 12,220$$
$$\underline{-8a \qquad = \qquad -8a}$$
$$5s = 12,220 - 8a$$
$$s = 2,444 - \frac{8}{5}a$$

$$1970 - a = 2,444 - \frac{8}{5}a$$
$$\underline{+\frac{8}{5}a = \qquad +\frac{8}{5}a}$$
$$1970 + \frac{3}{5}a = 2,444$$
$$\underline{-1970 \qquad = -1970}$$
$$\frac{3}{5}a = 474$$
$$\frac{5}{3} \cdot \frac{3}{5}a = 474 \cdot \frac{5}{3}$$
$$a = 790$$

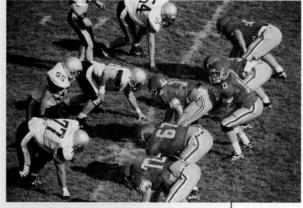

$$790 - s = 1970$$
$$s = 1,180$$

790 adult tickets and 1,180 student tickets were sold.

CHAPTER 7

Key Vocabulary

like terms *(términos semejantes)* Terms that have the same variable raised to the same exponent.

system of equations *(sistema de ecuaciones)* A set of two or more equations that contain two or more variables.

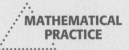

MATHEMATICAL PRACTICE The Common Core Standards for Mathematical Practice describe varieties of expertise that mathematics educators at all levels should seek to develop in their students. Opportunities to develop these practices are integrated throughout this program.

1. Make sense of problems and persevere in solving them.
2. Reason abstractly and quantitatively.
3. Construct viable arguments and critique the reasoning of others.
4. Model with mathematics.
5. Use appropriate tools strategically.
6. Attend to precision.
7. Look for and make use of structure.
8. Look for and express regularity in repeated reasoning.

CHAPTER 7

Simplifying Algebraic Expressions
Going Deeper

Essential question: *How do you simplify algebraic expressions?*

Like terms, such as **3t** and **4t**, or **3m^3** and **2.5m^3**, have the *same* variables raised to the *same* exponents.

To simplify an expression means to combine, or collect, its like terms to form an equivalent expression with as few terms as possible. You can use number properties to combine like terms.

PREP FOR **CC.8.EE.7**

1 EXAMPLE   Writing and Simplifying Single-Variable Expressions

Alex bought 2.5 pounds of apples and Derrick bought 3.5 pounds of apples. Write and simplify an expression that represents how much they spent on apples.

A   Write expressions for how much Alex and Derrick spent on apples. Let p represent the price of apples per pound.

Alex: ▢ p Derrick: ▢ p

B   Add both expressions to represent the total amount they spent.

▢p + ▢p = (▢ + ▢)p *Use the* _____ *Property.*

= ▢   *Add within the parentheses.*

The expression _____ represents how much they spent on apples.

REFLECT

1a. Suppose that apples sold for $0.90 per pound. Evaluate the original expression to find how much Alex and Derrick spent on apples. Then evaluate the simplified expression. Are the amounts the same?

_____

_____

TRY THIS!

1b. Simplify $2(n-5) + 7.4n$.

$$2(n-5) + 7.4n = 2n - \boxed{} + \boxed{}\, n \quad \cdot \quad \text{_____ Property}$$

$$= 2n + \boxed{}\, n - \boxed{} \quad \text{_____ Property}$$

$$= \left(\boxed{} + \boxed{}\right) - \boxed{} \quad \text{_____ Property}$$

$$= \left(\boxed{} + \boxed{}\right)n - \boxed{} \quad \text{_____ Property}$$

$$= \boxed{}\, n - \boxed{} \quad \text{Simplify.}$$

2 EXAMPLE   Writing and Simplifying Two-Variable Expressions

Devin bought $2\frac{1}{2}$ pounds of mixed nuts and $1\frac{3}{4}$ pounds of cheese for the class party. At the same store, Kim bought $1\frac{1}{2}$ pounds of cheese and $1\frac{1}{4}$ pounds of mixed nuts. Write and simplify an expression that represents how much they spent in all.

A Write expressions for how much Devin and Kim spent.
Let m represent the cost per pound for mixed nuts. Let c represent the cost per pound for cheese.

Devin: ▢ $m +$ ▢ c Kim: ▢ $c +$ ▢ m

B Add both expressions to represent the total amount they spent.

▢ $m +$ ▢ $c +$ ▢ $c +$ ▢ m

$\left(2\frac{1}{2}m +$ ▢ $m\right) + \left(1\frac{3}{4}c +$ ▢ $c\right)$ _____ and _____ $Properties$

$\left($ ▢ $+$ ▢ $\right)m + \left($ ▢ $+$ ▢ $\right)c$ _____ $Property$

$\left($ ▢ $+$ ▢ $\right)m + \left($ ▢ $+$ ▢ $\right)c$ $Write\ mixed\ numbers\ as\ improper\ fractions.$

$\left(\frac{5}{2}\cdot$ ▢ $+$ ▢ $\right)m + \left($ ▢ $+ \frac{3}{2}\cdot$ ▢ $\right)c$ $Multiply\ by\ fractions\ equal\ to\ 1.$

$\left($ ▢ $+$ ▢ $\right)m + \left($ ▢ $+$ ▢ $\right)c$ $Rewrite\ with\ a\ common\ denominator.$

▢ $m +$ ▢ c $Simplify.$

The expression _____ represents how much Devin and Kim spent on mixed nuts and cheese.

REFLECT

2a. What are the advantages of the simplified expression over the original expression? Of the original expression over the simplified expression?

_____

_____

2b. How is simplifying expressions with *two or more* variables like simplifying expressions with *one* variable?

_____

_____

2c. Simplify $5\left(x + 2\frac{1}{5}y\right) + 3y - \frac{3}{4}x$. Tell what properties you used.

_____

_____

PRACTICE

Simplify each algebraic expression.

1. $4w + 5 - 1.5w$

2. $7b + 5 - 9b + c$

3. $x + 2.3(x - y)$

4. $3(n + 4) - \frac{2}{3}n$

5. $\frac{3}{8}(k + 24) + 2\left(r - \frac{1}{4}\right)$

6. $5.2(3 - x) - 3x$

7. $4.2y + 8.1y + 1.8y + 3(y + 0.5)$

8. $9w + 6 - 2.5w$

Read each description. Then define and use variables to write and simplify an algebraic expression that represents it.

9. Krin buys 3 headbands and 2 wristbands. His brother Clay buys 4 headbands and 1 wristband. What is the total cost?

_____

10. Lemons cost x¢ per pound and limes cost y¢ each. Ellie buys 3.5 pounds of lemons and a dozen limes. What is the total cost?

_____

11. Jerome and Claire make the same hourly rate. Jerome worked for three-quarters of an hour on Tuesday and for one and one-half hours on Wednesday. On Tuesday, Claire worked twice as long as Jerome did. On Wednesday she worked for one-third of an hour. What is their total income?

_____

12. Mara bought $2\frac{1}{2}$ pounds of sliced turkey and half a pound of roast beef. Leah bought 2 pounds of roast beef, $1\frac{3}{4}$ pounds of sliced turkey, and half a pound of coleslaw. What the total cost of the food?

_____

13. The length of a rectangular field is 5 yards less than twice its width.

expression for perimeter: _____

expression for area: _____

Use the table to write a simplified expression for each purchase. Include a 10% tip. *Think*: **The expression will be an amount of money.**

PAT'S PIZZA EXPRESS		
Pie	**Topping**	**Drink**
Small...................$11.00	Mushrooms...........$2.50	Small.....................$1.50
Medium.............$15.50	Onions..................$2.25	Medium................$2.25
Large $18.25	Peppers $2.50	Large $4.00
Gargantuan $22.00	Pineapple..............$3.50	Enormous.............$5.50

14. two small pies with no toppings and two medium pies with mushrooms

_____

15. a small pie with peppers, a large pie with all toppings, and four small drinks

_____

16. two large pies with mushrooms and peppers, one gargantuan pie with pineapple, and three enormous drinks

_____

17. six enormous drinks, two medium pies with all toppings, and two large pies with all toppings

_____

18. Error Analysis Ira says that to simplify $3(2.5n + 3p)$ you would apply the Distributive Property as follows: $3 + 2.5n + 3 + 3p$ and then combine like terms to form $2.5n + 3p + 6$. Explain his error.

_____

_____

19. Simplify $9\left(a + 1\frac{2}{5}b\right) + 8\left(b - 1\frac{3}{5}a\right)$. Tell what properties you used.

_____

_____

Additional Practice

Combine like terms.

1. $8a^3 - 5a^3$

2. $12g + 7g$

3. $4a + 7a + 6$

_____

_____

_____

4. $6x + 3y + 5x$

5. $10k - 3k + 5h$

6. $3p^6 - 7q + 14p^6$

_____

_____

_____

7. $3k + 7k + 5k^2$

8. $5c + 12d - 6$

9. $13 + 4b + 6b - 5$

_____

_____

_____

10. $4f + 6 + 7f - 2$

11. $x^3 + y + 3x^3 + 7y$

12. $9n + 13 - 8n - 6$

_____

_____

_____

Simplify.

13. $4(x + 3) - 5$

14. $6(7 + x) + 5x$

15. $3(5 + 3x) - 4x$

_____

_____

_____

Solve.

16. $6y + 2y = 16$

17. $14b - 9b = 35$

18. $3q + 9q = 48$

_____

_____

_____

19. Gregg has q quarters and p pennies. His brother has 4 times as many quarters and 8 times as many pennies as Gregg has. Write the sum of the number of coins they have, and then combine like terms.

_____

20. If Gregg has 6 quarters and 15 pennies, how many total coins do Gregg and his brother have?

_____

Problem Solving

Write the correct answer.

1. An item costs x dollars. The tax rate is 5% of the cost of the item, or 0.05x. Write and simplify an expression to find the total cost of the item with tax.

2. A sweater costs d dollars at regular price. The sweater is reduced by 20%, or 0.2d. Write and simplify an expression to find the cost of the sweater before tax.

3. Consecutive integers are integers that differ by one. You can represent consecutive integers as x, $x + 1$, $x + 2$ and so on. Write an equation and solve to find three consecutive integers whose sum is 33.

4. Consecutive even integers can be represented by x, $x + 2$, $x + 4$ and so on. Write an equation and solve to find three consecutive even integers whose sum is 54.

Choose the letter for the best answer.

5. In Super Bowl XXXV, the total number of points scored was 41. The winning team outscored the losing team by 27 points. What was the final score of the game?

   A 33 to 8

   B 34 to 7

   C 22 to 2

   D 18 to 6

6. A high school basketball court is 34 feet longer than it is wide. If the perimeter of the court is 268, what are the dimensions of the court?

   F 234 ft by 34 ft

   G 67 ft by 67 ft

   H 70 ft by 36 ft

   J 84 ft by 50 ft

7. Julia ordered 2 hamburgers and Steven ordered 3 hamburgers. If their total bill before tax was $7.50, how much did each hamburger cost?

   A $1.50

   B $1.25

   C $1.15

   D $1.02

8. On three tests, a student scored a total of 258 points. If the student improved his performance on each test by 5 points, what was the score on each test?

   F 81, 86, 91

   G 80, 85, 90

   H 75, 80, 85

   J 70, 75, 80

© Houghton Mifflin Harcourt Publishing Company

Solving Multi-Step Equations
Going Deeper

Essential question: *How do you solve equations by collecting like terms and multiplying expressions?*

CC.8.EE.7b

1 EXPLORE Solving Equations by Collecting Like Terms

A soccer club spent $97.50 on trophies from a custom trophy company. The cost of manufacturing x custom trophies is $18.50 for the setup cost, plus $12.50 per trophy. To ship the trophies, the company charges a standard fee of $4 per order plus $2.50 per trophy. How many trophies did the soccer club order?

A Write an expression representing the **cost of manufacturing**.

Setup cost   +   Cost for x trophies

[   ]   +   12.50x

B Write an expression representing the **cost of shipping**.

Standard fee + Cost for x trophies

[   ]   +   [   ]

C Write an equation that can be solved to find the number of trophies the soccer club ordered.

Cost of manufacturing   +   Cost of shipping   =   Club's total cost

[   ]   +   [   ]   =   [   ]

D Solve your equation for x.

The soccer club ordered _____ trophies.

TRY THIS!

Solve each equation.

1a. $14x + 6 - 10x + 30 = 64$

1b. $2\frac{1}{3}x + 10 + 5\frac{2}{3}x - 9\frac{1}{2} = 12\frac{1}{2}$

2 EXPLORE   Solving Equations by Using the Distributive Property

Carla chose a number between 1 and 50 and then described to Henry how he could determine the number she chose.

Carla says, "If you subtract 5 from my number, multiply that quantity by 4, and then add 7 to the result, you get 35."

Write an equation that Henry can solve to find Carla's number.

A   First write an expression for "subtract 5 from my number."

_____

B   Use your answer to **A** to write an expression for "multiply that quantity by 4."

_____

C   Now use your answer to **B** to write an expression for "then add 7 to the result."

_____

D   Use your answer to **C** and the rest of Carla's description to write an equation that you can solve to find Carla's number.

_____

E   Solve the equation for *x*. Use the Distributive Property to simplify one side of the equation before collecting like terms.

Carla's number is _____.

TRY THIS!

Solve each equation.

2a. $3(x + 2) + 4 = 31$

2b. $4 - 3(x + 2) - 2(x - 4) + 8 = -1$

Solve each equation.

1. $3x + 4 + 2x + 5 = 34$

2. $2.5x - 5 + 3x + 8 = 19.5$

3. $\frac{1}{2}x + 6 - 2x + \frac{1}{2} = \frac{7}{2}$

4. $-10x - 3 - 2.5x + 20 = 67$

5. $2(x + 1) + 4 = 12$

6. $-3(x + 4) + 15 = -12$

7. $15 - 3(x - 1) = 12$

8. $3(x - 2) + 2(x + 1) = -14$

9. $\frac{1}{2}(x + 8) - 15 = -3$

10. $2.5(x + 2) + 4.5 + 1.5(x - 3) = 15$

Solve by writing and solving an equation.

11. The perimeter of a rectangular garden is 4.8 meters. Its length is twice its width. How wide is the garden?

12. Willy and Freddie spent a total of $17.50 on lunch. Willy spent 4 times as much as Freddie did. How much did Freddie spend?

13. Half a number plus 2.5 times that number equals 18. What is the number?

14. Jason is 6 years older than his sister. Their mother is 15 years older than the sum of their ages. If their mother is 39, how old is Jason?

15. Tanya has a certain amount of money in her savings account. Each month, for 6 months, she deposits $50 less than her original savings amount. After 6 months, she has a total of $750 in the account. How much money did she have in the account when she began adding money to it?

_____

16. A class of 24 students hopes to collect 1,200 plastic bottles per week. In the first week, the students collected 34 bottles each. This was not enough. How many more bottles per student must the class collect to meet the weekly goal of 1,200?

_____

17. Six times a number increased by 12 plus 3 times the number increased by 6 is equal to 58.5. What is the number?

_____

18. The larger of two numbers is three times the smaller. The sum of the two numbers is 6. What are the numbers?

_____

19. Consecutive integers are 1 apart. The sum of three consecutive integers is 54. What are the integers?

_____

20. Find the mystery number: When you multiply a number by −4 and then add 3 times the number to the product, the result is 4. What is the number?

_____

21. Jake and Abigail worked on a job together. Jake earned three-fourths of what Abigail did. Together, they earned $140. How much did each earn?

_____

22. Error Analysis Five dollars more than half the price of a sweater comes to $45.49. A student wrote the following equation to find the sweater price: $\frac{n}{2+5} = \$45.49$. What should the correct equation be? What does the sweater cost?

_____

_____

Additional Practice

Solve.

1. $2x + 5x + 4 = 25$

2. $9 + 3y - 2y = 14$

3. $16 = 2(2w + w - 1)$

4. $26 = 3b - 2 - 7b$

5. $31 + 4t - t = 40$

6. $2(7 - x) + 4x = 20$

7. $\dfrac{5m}{8} - \dfrac{6}{8} + \dfrac{3m}{8} = \dfrac{2}{8}$

8. $-4\dfrac{2}{3} = \dfrac{2n}{3} + \dfrac{1}{3} + \dfrac{n}{3}$

9. $7a + 16 - 3a = -4$

10. $\dfrac{x}{2} + 1 + \dfrac{3x}{4} = -9$

11. $7m + 3 - 4m = -9$

12. $\dfrac{2x}{5} + 3 - \dfrac{4x}{5} = \dfrac{1}{5}$

13. $\dfrac{7k}{8} - \dfrac{3}{4} - \dfrac{5k}{16} = \dfrac{3}{8}$

14. $3(2y + 3) - 4y = -3$

15. $\dfrac{5a}{6} - \dfrac{7}{12} + \dfrac{3a}{4} = -2\dfrac{1}{6}$

16. The measure of an angle is 28° greater than its complement. Find the measure of each angle.

17. The measure of an angle is 21° more than twice its supplement. Find the measure of each angle.

18. The perimeter of the triangle is 126 units. Find the measure of each side.

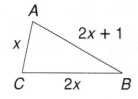

19. The base angles of an isosceles triangle are congruent. If the measure of each of the base angles is twice the measure of the third angle, find the measure of all three angles.

Problem Solving

A taxi company charges $2.25 for the first mile and then $0.20 per mile for each mile after the first, or $F = \$2.25 + \$0.20(m - 1)$ where F is the fare and m is the number of miles.

1. If Juan's taxi fare was $6.05, how many miles did he travel in the taxi?

    _____

2. If Juan's taxi fare was $7.65, how many miles did he travel in the taxi?

    _____

A new car loses 20% of its original value when you buy it and then 8% of its original value per year, or $D = 0.8V - 0.08Vy$ where D is the value after y years with an original value V.

3. If a vehicle that was valued at $20,000 new is now worth $9,600, how old is the car?

    _____

4. A 6-year old vehicle is worth $12,000. What was the original value of the car?

    _____

The equation used to estimate typing speed is $S = \dfrac{1}{5}(w - 10e)$,

where S is the accurate typing speed, w is the number of words typed in 5 minutes and e is the number of errors. Choose the letter of the best answer.

5. Jane can type 55 words per minute (wpm). In 5 minutes, she types 285 words. How many errors would you expect her to make?

    A 0   C 2

    B 1   D 5

6. If Alex types 300 words in 5 minutes with 5 errors, what is his typing speed?

    F 48 wpm   H 59 wpm

    G 50 wpm   J 60 wpm

7. Johanna receives a report that says her typing speed is 65 words per minute. She knows that she made 4 errors in the 5-minute test. How many words did she type in 5 minutes?

    A 285   C 365

    B 329   D 1825

8. Cecil can type 35 words per minute. In 5 minutes, she types 255 words. How many errors would you expect her to make?

    F 2   H 6

    G 4   J 8

Solving Equations with Variables on Both Sides
Going Deeper

video tutor

Essential question: *How can you give examples of equations with a given number of solutions?*

So far, when you solved a linear equation in one variable, you found one value of x that makes the equation a true statement. When you simplify some equations, you may find that they do not have one solution.

CC.8.EE.7a

1 EXPLORE | Determining the Number of Solutions

Use the properties of equality to simplify each equation. Tell whether the final equation is a true statement.

A $4x - 3 = 2x + 13$

$$4x - 3 = \quad 2x + 13$$

$$\underline{} \quad \underline{}$$

$$= \quad 2x + \boxed{}$$

$$\underline{}$$

$$2x = 16$$

$$\frac{2x}{\boxed{}} = \frac{16}{\boxed{}}$$

$$x = \boxed{}$$

The statement is true / false.

B $4x - 5 = 2(2x - 1) - 3$

$$4x - 5 = 2(2x - 1) - 3$$

$$4x - 5 = \boxed{} x - \boxed{} - 3$$

$$4x - 5 = \quad 4x - \boxed{}$$

$$\underline{} \quad \underline{}$$

$$-5 = \boxed{}$$

The statement is true / false.

C $4x + 2 = 4x - 5$

$$4x + 2 = 4x - 5$$

$$\underline{\boxed{}} \quad \underline{\boxed{}}$$

$$4x = \quad 4x - 7$$

$$\underline{\boxed{}} \quad \underline{\boxed{}}$$

$$\boxed{} = \boxed{}$$

The statement is true / false.

REFLECT

1. What happens when you substitute any value for x in the original equation in **B** ? In the original equation in **C** ?

_____

_____

When you simplify an equation using the properties of equality, you will find one of three results.

Result	What does this mean?	How many solutions?
$x = a$	When the value of x is a, the equation is a true statement.	1
$a = a$	Any value of x makes the equation a true statement.	Infinitely many
$a = b$	There is no value of x that makes the equation a true statement.	0

2 EXPLORE   Writing Equations with a Given Number of Solutions

Write a linear equation in one variable that has no solutions.

You can use the strategy of working backward:

A   Start with a false statement such as $3 = 5$. Add the same variable term to both sides.

_____

B   Next, add the same constant to both sides and combine like terms on each side of the equation.

_____

C   Verify that your equation has no solutions by using properties of equality to simplify your equation.

REFLECT

2a.   Explain why the result of the process above is an equation with no solutions.

_____

_____

_____

TRY THIS!

Tell whether each equation has one, zero, or infinitely many solutions.

2b. $6 + 3x = x - 8$

2c. $8x + 4 = 4(2x + 1)$

_____   _____

Complete each equation so that it has the indicated number of solutions.

2d.   No solutions: $3x + 1 = 3x + \boxed{}$

2e.   Infinitely many: $2x - 4 = 2x - \boxed{}$

3 EXPLORE **Solving Equations with Variables on Both Sides**

At Silver Gym, membership is $25 per month, and personal training sessions are $30 each. At Fit Factor, membership is $65 per month, and personal training sessions are $20 each. In one month, how many personal training sessions would Sarah have to buy to make the total cost at the two gyms equal?

A Write an expression representing the **total monthly cost at Silver Gym**.

Monthly   +   Cost for x
membership   training sessions

[   ]   + $30x$

B Write an expression representing the **total monthly cost at Fit Factor**.

Monthly   +   Cost for x
membership   training sessions

[   ]   +   [   ]

C How can you find the number of personal training sessions in one month that would make the total costs of the gyms equal?

_____

D Write an equation that can be solved to find the number of training sessions in one month that makes the total costs equal.

Total cost at Silver Gym   =   Total cost at Fit Factor

[   ]   =   [   ]

E Solve the equation for x. Use inverse operations to get all variable terms on one side of the equation and all constants on the other side.

Sarah would have to buy _____ personal training sessions to make the total cost at the two gyms equal.

TRY THIS!

Solve each equation.

3a. $10x + 5 = 20 - 20x$

3b. $\frac{1}{4}x + 4 = \frac{3}{4}x - 8$

PRACTICE

Tell whether each equation has one, zero, or infinitely many solutions.

1. $4 + 5y = y - 8$

_____

2. $4.5n + 3 = 4.5(n + 3)$

_____

3. $3.1n = 2(1.55n)$

_____

4. $\frac{3}{8}w + 5 = 9w$

_____

Complete each equation so that it has the indicated number of solutions.

5. No solutions: $5k + 2 = 5k + $ ▨

6. Infinitely many: $2b - 3 = 2b - $ ▨

Solve by writing and solving an equation.

7. When 15 is added to twice a number, the result is the same as when 3 is added to 5 times the number. What is the number?

_____

8. Albert's father is 24 years older than Albert is. In 8 years, his father will be twice as old as Albert. How old is Albert now? How old is his father?

_____

9. Cal's Carriage Rides charges $20 plus $4.50 an hour for rides in the park. Hal's Horse & Buggy charges $30 plus $2.50 an hour for the same service. For how many hours would you pay the same total fee for a ride? What is that fee?

_____

10. Mr. Guerrero left his house and drove north at an average speed of 40 mph. Two hours later, his daughter Miranda left the house and drove the same route as her father, but at an average speed of 48 mph. How far from home were they when Miranda overtook her father?

_____

11. **Error Analysis** A student solved an equation as shown. Explain the error the student made. Then solve the equation correctly.

$$3n + 4 - n = 12 + n$$
$$3n + 4 = 12$$
$$3n = 8$$
$$n = \frac{8}{3}$$

_____

_____

Additional Practice

Solve.

1. $7x - 11 = -19 + 3x$

2. $11a + 9 = 4a + 30$

3. $4t + 14 = \dfrac{6t}{5} + 7$

_____

4. $\dfrac{3y}{8} - 9 = 13 + \dfrac{y}{8}$

5. $\dfrac{3k}{5} + 44 = \dfrac{12k}{25} + 8$

6. $15 - x = 2(x + 3)$

_____

7. $15y + 14 = 2(5y + 6)$

8. $14 - \dfrac{w}{8} = \dfrac{3w}{4} - 21$

9. $\dfrac{1}{2}(6x - 4) = 4x - 9$

_____

10. $4(3d - 2) = 8d - 5$

11. $\dfrac{y}{3} + 11 = \dfrac{y}{2} - 3$

12. $\dfrac{2x - 9}{3} = 8 - 3x$

_____

13. Forty-eight decreased by a number is the same as the difference of four times the number and seven. Find the number.

14. The square and the equilateral triangle at the right have the same perimeter. Find the length of the sides of the triangle.

 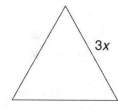

$3x$

$x + 5$

15. The equation $V = \dfrac{1}{3}Bh$ gives the volume V of a pyramid, where B is the area of the base and h is the height. Solve this equation for B.

_____

Problem Solving

The chart below describes three long-distance calling plans.
Round to the nearest minute. Write the correct answer.

1. For what number of minutes will plan A and plan B cost the same?

_____

Long-Distance Plans

Plan	Monthly Access Fee	Charge per minute
A	$3.95	$0.08
B	$8.95	$0.06
C	$0	$0.10

2. For what number of minutes per month will plan B and plan C cost the same?

_____

3. For what number of minutes will plan A and plan C cost the same?

_____

Choose the letter for the best answer.

4. Carpet Plus installs carpet for $100 plus $8 per square yard of carpet. Carpet World charges $75 for installation and $10 per square yard of carpet. Find the number of square yards of carpet for which the cost including carpet and installation is the same.

    A 1.4 yd²   C 12.5 yd²

    B 9.7 yd²   D 87.5 yd²

5. One shuttle service charges $10 for pickup and $0.10 per mile. The other shuttle service has no pickup fee but charges $0.35 per mile. Find the number of miles for which the cost of the shuttle services is the same.

    F 2.5 miles

    G 22 miles

    H 40 miles

    J 48 miles

6. Joshua can purchase tile at one store for $0.99 per tile, but he will have to rent a tile saw for $25. At another store he can buy tile for $1.50 per tile and borrow a tile saw for free. Find the number of tiles for which the cost is the same. Round to the nearest tile.

    A 10 tiles   C 25 tiles

    B 13 tiles   D 49 tiles

7. One plumber charges a fee of $75 per service call plus $15 per hour. Another plumber has no flat fee, but charges $25 per hour. Find the number of hours for which the cost of the two plumbers is the same.

    F 2.1 hours   H 7.5 hours

    G 7 hours   J 7.8 hours

Systems of Equations
Going Deeper

Essential question: *How can you solve a system of equations algebraically?*

A **system of equations** is a set of equations that have the same variables. An ordered pair is a solution of a system if it satisfies every equation in the system.

video tutor

CC.8.EE.8b

1 EXAMPLE **Solving Systems Algebraically**

Solve each system algebraically.

A $\begin{cases} y = 7x + 10 \\ y = 9x + 38 \end{cases}$

$$7x + 10 = 9x + 38$$

$$\underline{} \quad \underline{}$$

$$\underline{} = \underline{} + 38$$

$$\underline{} \quad \underline{}$$

$$\underline{} = \underline{}$$

$$\underline{} = x$$

Substitute the expression for y given in the first equation for the value of y in the second equation.

Then use properties of equality to solve the equation for x.

Substitute the value of x into one of the original equations to solve for y.

The solution of the system is (_____, _____).

B $\begin{cases} 3x + 4y = 31 \\ 2x - y = 6 \end{cases}$

$$2x - y = 6$$

$$\underline{} \quad \underline{}$$

$$-y = 6 - \underline{}$$

$$-y(-1) = \left(6 - \boxed{}\right)(-1)$$

$$\boxed{} = -6 + \boxed{}$$

Solve one equation for one of the variables. Because y is by itself in the second equation, solving that equation for y is a good place to start.

$$3x + 4y = 31$$

$$3x + 4\left(\boxed{}\right) = 31$$

$$3x + (-24) + \boxed{} = 31$$

$$11x - 24 = 31$$

$$\underline{} \quad \underline{}$$

$$11x = \boxed{}$$

$$x = \boxed{}$$

Substitute the expression for y into the first equation and solve for x.

Substitute the value of x into one of the original equations to solve for y.

The solution of the system is (_____, _____).

1. How can you check your answer?

_____

_____

You can use a graph to estimate the solution of a system of equations before solving algebraically.

CC.8.EE.8b

2 EXAMPLE Using a Graph to Estimate the Solution of a System

Solve the system $\begin{cases} x - 4y = 4 \\ 2x - 3y = -3 \end{cases}$.

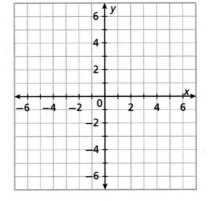

A Sketch a graph of each linear function by substituting some values for x and generating values of y.

B The lines appear to intersect near $(-5, -2)$. How can you tell whether $(-5, -2)$ is the solution of the system?

_____

_____

_____

_____

C Solve the system algebraically.

The solution is (_____, _____).

D Use the estimate you made using the graph to judge the reasonableness of your solution.

_____

_____

REFLECT

2. How can you determine that the system $\begin{cases} 5x - 2y = 8 \\ 5x - 2y = -3 \end{cases}$ has no solution without graphing or using algebraic methods?

_____

CC.8.EE.8c

3 EXAMPLE **Problem Solving with Systems of Equations**

Aaargh! There's pirate treasure to be found,
So search on the island, all around.
Draw a line through A and B.
Then a second line through C and D.
Dance a jig, "X" marks the spot,
If the lines intersect, that's the treasure's plot!

A Give the coordinates of each point and find the slope of the line through each pair of points.

A: (_____, _____) C: (_____, _____)

B: (_____, _____) D: (_____, _____)

Slope: Slope:

B Use the slopes of the lines to determine whether they will intersect.

_____

_____

C Write equations in slope-intercept form describing the line through points A and B and the line through points C and D.

Line through A and B: Line through C and D:

D Solve the system algebraically.

The solution is (_____, _____).

PRACTICE

Solve each system of equations algebraically.

1. $\begin{cases} y = \frac{2}{3}x - 5 \\ y = -x + 10 \end{cases}$

2. $\begin{cases} 3x + 2y = 9 \\ y = 4x - 1 \end{cases}$

3. $\begin{cases} 5x - 2y = 4 \\ 2x - y = 1 \end{cases}$

_____

_____

_____

4. Error Analysis Zach solves the system $\begin{cases} x + y = -3 \\ x - y = 1 \end{cases}$ and finds the solution $(1, -2)$.

Use a graph to explain whether Zach's solution is reasonable.

_____

_____

_____

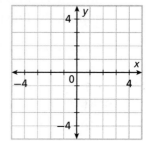

5. Error Analysis Angelica solves the system $\begin{cases} 3x - y = 0 \\ \frac{1}{4}x + \frac{3}{4}y = \frac{5}{2} \end{cases}$

and finds the solution $(1, 3)$. Use substitution to explain whether Angelica's solution is correct.

_____

_____

Angelo bought apples and bananas at the fruit stand. He bought 20 pieces of fruit and spent $11.50. Apples cost $0.50 and bananas cost $0.75 each.

6. Write a system of equations to model the problem. (Hint: One equation will represent the number of pieces of fruit. A second equation will represent the money spent on the fruit.)

_____

7. Solve the system algebraically. Tell how many apples and bananas Angelo bought.

_____

Additional Practice

Solve each system of equations.

1. $y = 2x - 4$
   $y = x - 1$

   _____

2. $y = -x + 10$
   $y = x + 2$

   _____

3. $y = 2x - 1$
   $y = -3x - 6$

   _____

4. $y = 2x$
   $y = 12 - x$

   _____

5. $y = 2x - 3$
   $y = 2x + 1$

   _____

6. $y = 3x - 1$
   $y = x + 1$

   _____

7. $x + y = 0$
   $5x + 2y = -3$

   _____

8. $2x - 3y = 0$
   $2x + y = 8$

   _____

9. $2x + 3y = 6$
   $4x + 6y = 12$

   _____

10. $6x - y = -14$
    $2x - 3y = 6$

    _____

11. The sum of two numbers is 24. The second number is 6 less than the first. Write a system of equations and solve it to find the number.

    _____

    _____

12. Kerry and Luke biked a total of 18 miles in one weekend. Kerry biked 4 miles more than Luke. Write a system of equations and solve it to find how far each boy biked.

    _____

    _____

Problem Solving

After college, Julia is offered two different jobs. The table summarizes the pay offered with each job. Write the correct answer.

1. Write an equation that shows the pay *y* of Job A after *x* years.

   _____

Job	Yearly Salary	Yearly Increase
A	$20,000	$2500
B	$25,000	$2000

2. Write an equation that shows the pay *y* of Job B after *x* years.

   _____

3. Is (8, 35,000) a solution to the system of equations in Exercises 1 and 2?

   _____

4. Solve the system of equations in Exercises 1 and 2.

   _____

5. If Julia plans to stay at this job only a few years and pay is the only consideration, which job should she choose?

   _____

A travel agency is offering two Orlando trip plans that include hotel accommodations and pairs of tickets to theme parks. Use the table below. Choose the letter for the best answer.

6. Find an equation about trip A where *x* represents the hotel cost per night and *y* represents the cost per pair of theme park tickets.

   A $5x + 2y = 415$ C $8x + 6y = 415$

   B $2x + 3y = 415$ D $3x + 2y = 415$

Trip	Number of nights	Pairs of theme park tickets	Cost
A	3	2	$415
B	5	4	$725

7. Find an equation about trip B where *x* represents the hotel cost per night and *y* represents the cost per pair of theme park tickets.

   F $5x + 4y = 725$

   G $4x + 5y = 725$

   H $8x + 6y = 725$

   J $3x + 4y = 725$

8. Solve the system of equations to find the nightly hotel cost and the cost for each pair of theme park tickets.

   A ($50, $105)

   B ($125, $20)

   C ($105, $50)

   D ($115, $35)

CHAPTER 7

Problem Solving Connections

Shirts for Sale! Emerson Middle School is having its annual spring fair. A group of students have decided to sell t-shirts at the fair to raise money for the school. The students plan to sell tie-dyed shirts and hand-painted shirts. How many of each type of shirt should they make, and how much money will they raise?

COMMON CORE

CC.8.EE.7a
CC.8.EE.7b
CC.8.EE.8b
CC.8.EE.8c

1 Order the Shirts

Mikiko is in charge of ordering the t-shirts that will be dyed and painted. She plans to spend $150 on plain white shirts that are printed with the name of the school. She gathers pricing information from two companies that make custom shirts.

Company Name	Price per Shirt	Setup Fee	Shipping Fee
The Shirt Shoppe	$4.25	$16.75	$5.75
Tee Town	$4.75	$25.50	$8 plus $0.75 per shirt

A Write and simplify an expression that represents the total cost of ordering x t-shirts from The Shirt Shoppe.

B Write and solve an equation to find the number of t-shirts Mikiko can order from The Shirt Shoppe.

C Write and simplify an expression that represents the total cost of ordering x t-shirts from Tee Town.

D Mikiko has a coupon for 20% off the total cost of her order at Tee Town. What percent of the total cost does Mikiko pay? How do you write this as a decimal?

E Write an expression that represents the final cost of ordering x t-shirts at Tee Town after the discount is taken.

F Write and solve an equation to find the number of t-shirts Mikiko can order from Tee Town. Show the steps in solving the equation.

G Mikiko wants to get the greatest number of shirts possible. Which company should she choose and how many shirts should she order?

2 Order Gift Bags

The group decides to package the t-shirts in gift bags that are printed with the name of the school. Jamal is in charge of ordering the bags. He gets pricing information from a company that prints custom bags.

Type of Bag	Price per Bag	Shipping Fee
Regular Paper	$1.05	$5
Heavy Paper	$0.95	$8 plus $0.10 per bag

A Write expressions that represent the total cost of ordering b bags made from regular paper and the total cost of ordering b bags made from heavy paper.

B Jamal wants to compare the cost of regular paper versus heavy paper. He decides to find out how many bags he would have to order so that the costs are equal. Show how to write and solve an equation to find this number of bags.

C What do your results tell you about the prices of the bags?

D Jamal orders the less-expensive bags and he orders just enough of them to package the t-shirts. What is the total cost of the bags?

3 Determine the Number of Each Type of Shirt

The table shows the prices the group will charge at the fair for tie-dyed shirts and hand-painted shirts. The group wants to know how many of each type of shirt they should make so that their total income from the sales will be $550.

Type of Shirt	Price
Tie-Dyed	$15
Hand-Painted	$20

A Let t be the number of tie-dyed shirts that the group makes and let h be the number of hand-painted shirts that the group makes. Write an equation that relates the number of each type of shirt to the total number of shirts.

B Write an equation that relates the amount of money the group makes from sales of each type of shirt to the total income the group makes from the sales.

C Solve the system of equations to find out how many of each type of shirt the group should make.

4 Answer the Question

In previous years, other groups of students sold t-shirts at the fair. Emma looks up information about the cost of supplies, such as dye and paint, in those years so that she can estimate costs for this year. The table shows her findings.

Year	Number of Tie-Dyed Shirts	Number of Hand-Painted Shirts	Total Cost of Supplies
2010	4	2	$10
2011	6	1	$10

A Let x represent the cost of supplies for making one tie-dyed shirt and let y represent the cost of supplies for making one hand-painted shirt. Use the data in the table to write a system of equations for x and y.

B Sketch a graph of each equation in the system by substituting some values of x and generating values of y. Make the graphs on the coordinate plane at right.

C Use your graph to estimate the solution of the system of equations

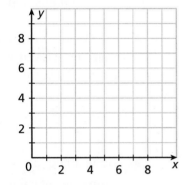

D Solve the system algebraically.

E What is the cost of supplies for making one tie-dyed shirt? What is the cost of supplies for making one hand-painted shirt?

F What is the total cost of supplies for making the tie-dyed shirts and hand-painted shirts for the fair?

G What is the total amount of money the group will raise at the fair? (Look back at your work to find the total income from the sales of the shirts. Then subtract the cost of the shirts, the cost of the gift bags, and the cost of the supplies.)

CHAPTER 7

Performance Task

COMMON CORE

CC.8.EE.7
CC.8.EE.7b
CC.8.EE.8
CC.8.EE.8b
CC.8.EE.8c

⭐ **1.** Pete's Pizza charges $13 for a pizza, and a soda costs $1.50. Mama's House charges $15 for a pizza, and a soda costs $1.

    a. Write an expression for the cost of two pizzas and x sodas at each restaurant.

    b. Set your expressions from part **a** equal to each other. Solve the equation. Explain what the solution means.

⭐ **2.** Eloise goes to the mall to buy 4 t-shirts and 2 pairs of pants. Each shirt costs the same price, as do the pants. The total price is $126, but she only has $85. Eloise returns a shirt and a pair of pants. The total price is now $81.

    a. Write a system of equations to represent this situation. Define the variables that you use.

    b. Solve the system from part **a** to find the prices of a shirt and a pair of pants.

3. Hannah got a perfect score on 3 more spelling quizzes this quarter than last quarter. If she doubles the number of perfect quizzes she had this quarter, she will tie the school record. The record is 3 times the number of spelling quizzes Hannah scored perfectly on last quarter.

   a. Write an expression for the number of perfect spelling quizzes Hannah had this quarter. What does your variable represent?

   b. Write an expression for the record number of perfect spelling quizzes.

   c. Use your expressions from parts a and b to write and solve an equation to find the number of perfect spelling quizzes Hannah had last quarter.

4. A coin purse has only nickels and quarters in it. The total value of the coins is $1.05.

   a. Millie claims that there are 10 coins in the purse. Write and solve a system of equations for this situation.

   b. Is Millie's claim correct? Explain how you know.

Name _____ **Class** _____ **Date** _____

SELECTED RESPONSE

1. Which value of x makes the equation $5(x - 2) - 4 = 6$ true?

   A. 2   **C.** 4

   B. 3   **D.** 5

2. Which has the same solution as $2(x + 4) = -7 - 3x$?

   F. $5x = 15$

   G. $-5x = 15$

   H. $-x = 11$

   J. $x = 15$

3. How many solutions does the equation $2(x - 5) = 2x + 3$ have?

   A. 0   **C.** 2

   B. 1   **D.** infinitely many

4. How many solutions does the equation $4x + 28 = 4(x + 3) + 16$ have?

   F. 0   **H.** 2

   G. 1   **J.** infinitely many

5. Solve.
$3(9 - 8x - 4x) + 8(3x + 4) = 11$

   A. $x = 3$ **C.** $x = 24$

   B. $x = 4$ **D.** $x = 5$

6. Solve $2d - 7 = 8 - 3d$.

   F. $d = -\frac{1}{5}$

   G. $d = \frac{1}{5}$

   H. $d = 3$

   J. $d = -15$

7. A hockey season ticket holder pays $72.48 for her tickets plus $6.00 for a program each game. A second person pays $18.08 for a ticket to every game, but doesn't buy programs. In how many games will they have paid the same amount?

   A. 5   **C.** 13

   B. 4   **D.** 6

8. Which of the following equations has infinitely many solutions?

   F. $b + 2 = b + 2$

   G. $b = -b + 2$

   H. $b + 2 = b - 2$

   J. $b + b = 2$

9. Which of the following equations has only one solution?

   A. $c + 2 = c + 2$

   B. $c = -c + 2$

   C. $c + 2 = c - 2$

   D. $c - c = 2$

10. Which equation can you use to solve the system of equations shown?

$$\begin{cases} -4x + y = 3 \\ 11x - 5y = 16 \end{cases}$$

F. $11(4x + 3) - 5y = 16$

G. $11x - 5(4x + 3) = 16$

H. $-4(11x - 5y) = 3$

J. $-4x + 16 - 11x = 3$

11. Students from Thornebrooke Elementary are going on a field trip to an amusement park. Those who have annual passes will pay $10. Other students will pay $35. The school collected $1,375 for 50 students.

Which system of linear equations models this situation?

A. $\begin{cases} 10x + 35y = 50 \\ x + y = 1{,}375 \end{cases}$

B. $\begin{cases} 10x + 35y = 1{,}375 \\ x + y = 50 \end{cases}$

C. $\begin{cases} 10x + y = 50 \\ 35x + y = 1{,}375 \end{cases}$

D. $\begin{cases} 10x + y = 1{,}375 \\ x + 35y = 50 \end{cases}$

12. Which ordered pair is a solution of the system shown?

$$\begin{cases} -4x + 5y = 14 \\ 7x + 3y = -1 \end{cases}$$

F. $(1, 2)$

G. $(1, -2)$

H. $(-1, 2)$

J. $(-1, -2)$

CONSTRUCTED RESPONSE

13. Dani solves the system of equations shown graphically and finds that the solution is $(2, 7)$. Explain whether Dani is correct.

$$\begin{cases} 7x - y = 7 \\ -3x + 2y = 8 \end{cases}$$

_____

_____

_____

_____

_____

14. Solve the equation $5(x - 2) + 3 = 7x - 9$.

© Houghton Mifflin Harcourt Publishing Company

Graphing Lines

Chapter Focus

You will find a rate of change and show that the slope of a line is the same between any two points on the line. You will use slopes and intercepts to write and graph linear equations. The slope-intercept form and point-slope form of an equation will be developed. You will learn to identify a direct variation, and finally, you will solve a system of equations by graphing.

Chapter at a Glance

COMMON
CORE

Lesson		Standards for Mathematical Content
8-1	Graphing Linear Equations	CC.8.F.4
8-2	Slope of a Line	CC.8.EE.6
8-3	Using Slopes and Intercepts	CC.8.EE.6, CC.8.F.3, CC.8.F.4
8-4	Point-Slope Form	CC.8.F.4
8-5	Direct Variation	CC.8.EE.5
8-6	Solving Systems of Linear Equations by Graphing	CC.8.EE.8a, CC.8.EE.8c
	Problem Solving Connections	
	Performance Task	
	Assessment Readiness	

Unpacking the Standards

Understanding the standards and the vocabulary terms in the standards will help you know exactly what you are expected to learn in this chapter.

COMMON CORE CC.8.EE.8a

Understand that solutions to a system of two linear equations in two variables correspond to points of intersection of their graphs, because points of intersection satisfy both equations simultaneously.

Key Vocabulary

system of equations *(sistema de ecuaciones)* A set of two or more equations that contain two or more variables.

What It Means to You

You will understand that the points of intersection represent the solutions to a system of linear equations.

EXAMPLE

Solve each linear system by graphing.

$$-x = -1 + y$$
$$x + y = 4$$

The lines are parallel, so the system has no solution.

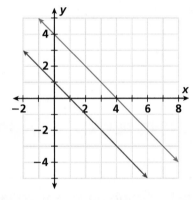

$$-x + y = 8$$
$$y - 8 = x$$

The lines are the same, so the system has infinitely many solutions.

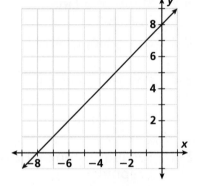

$$2y + x = 1$$
$$y - 2 = x$$

The lines intersect at one point, so the solution is (–1, 1).

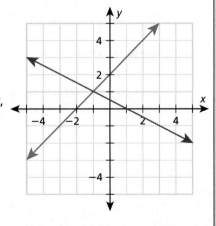

COMMON CORE CC.8.F.4

Construct a function to model a linear relationship between two quantities. Determine the rate of change and initial value of the function from a description of a relationship or from two (x, y) values, including reading these from a table or from a graph. Interpret the rate of change and initial value of a linear function in terms of the situation it models, and in terms of its graph or a table of values.

Key Vocabulary

linear function *(función lineal)* A function whose graph is a straight line.

What It Means to You

You will learn to identify the slope of a line and the *y*-intercept.

EXAMPLE

The cash register deducts $2.50 from a $25 Java Café gift card for every medium coffee the customer buys. The linear equation $y = -2.50x + 25$ represents the number of dollars *y* on the card after *x* medium coffees have been purchased. Explain the meaning of the slope and the *y*-intercept.

The slope represents the rate of change, −$2.50 per medium coffee.

The *y*-intercept represents the initial amount on the card, $25.

COMMON CORE CC.8.EE.5

Graph proportional relationships, interpreting the unit rate as the slope of the graph. Compare two different proportional relationships represented in different ways.

Key Vocabulary

unit rate *(tasa unitaria)* A rate in which the second quantity in the comparison is one unit.

slope *(pendiente)* A measure of the steepness of a line on a graph; the rise divided by the run.

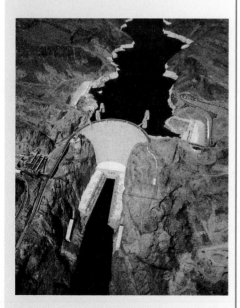

What It Means to You

You will recognize constant rates and apply your understanding of rates to analyzing real-world situations.

EXAMPLE

The table shows the volume of water released by Hoover Dam over a certain period of time. Use the data to make a graph. Find the slope of the line and explain what it shows.

Water Released from Hoover Dam	
Time (s)	Volume of Water (m³)
5	75,000
10	150,000
15	225,000
20	300,000

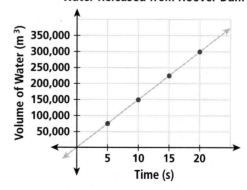

The slope of the line is 15,000. This means that for every second that passed, 15,000 m³ of water was released from Hoover Dam.

CHAPTER 8

Key Vocabulary

direct variation *(variación directa)* A linear relationship between two variables, x and y, that can be written in the form $y = kx$, where k is a nonzero constant.

rate of change *(tasa de cambio)* A ratio that compares the amount of change in a dependent variable to the amount of change in an independent variable.

slope *(pendiente)* A measure of the steepness of a line on a graph; the rise divided by the run.

slope-intercept form *(forma de pendiente-intersección)* A linear equation written in the form $y = mx + b$, where m represents slope and b represents the y-intercept.

y-intercept *(intersección con el eje y)* The y-coordinate of the point where the graph of a line crosses the y-axis.

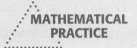
MATHEMATICAL PRACTICE

The Common Core Standards for Mathematical Practice describe varieties of expertise that mathematics educators at all levels should seek to develop in their students. Opportunities to develop these practices are integrated throughout this program.

1. Make sense of problems and persevere in solving them.
2. Reason abstractly and quantitatively.
3. Construct viable arguments and critique the reasoning of others.
4. Model with mathematics.
5. Use appropriate tools strategically.
6. Attend to precision.
7. Look for and make use of structure.
8. Look for and express regularity in repeated reasoning.

CHAPTER 8

Graphing Linear Equations
Reasoning: Rates of Change

Essential question: *How do you find a rate of change?*

A **rate of change** is a ratio of the amount of change in the output to the amount of change in the input.

PREP FOR CC.8.F.4

1 EXAMPLE Investigating Rates of Change

Eve keeps a record of the number of lawns she mows and the money she earns.

	Day 1	Day 2	Day 3	Day 4	Day 5
Number of Lawns	1	3	6	8	13
Amount Earned ($)	15	45	90	120	195

Input variable: _____   Output variable: _____

Find the rates of change:

Day 1 to Day 2 $\dfrac{\text{change in \$}}{\text{change in lawns}} = \dfrac{45 - \boxed{}}{3 - 1} = \dfrac{\boxed{}}{2} = \boxed{}$

Day 2 to Day 3 $\dfrac{\text{change in \$}}{\text{change in lawns}} = \dfrac{\boxed{} - 45}{6 - \boxed{}} = \dfrac{\boxed{}}{3} = \boxed{}$

Day 3 to Day 4 $\dfrac{\text{change in \$}}{\text{change in lawns}} = \dfrac{\boxed{} - \boxed{}}{\boxed{} - 6} = \dfrac{\boxed{}}{2} = \boxed{}$

Day 4 to Day 5 $\dfrac{\text{change in \$}}{\text{change in lawns}} = \dfrac{\boxed{} - \boxed{}}{\boxed{} - \boxed{}} = \dfrac{\boxed{}}{\boxed{}} = \boxed{}$

The rates of change are constant / variable.

TRY THIS!

1. The table shows the approximate height of a football after it is kicked.

Time (s)	0	0.5	1.5	2
Height (ft)	0	18	31	26

Input variable: _____   Output variable: _____

Find the rates of change:

The rates of change are constant / variable.

You can also use a graph to find rates of change.

2 EXPLORE Using Graphs to Find Rates of Change

The graph shows the distance Nathan bicycled over time. What is Nathan's rate of change?

A Find the rate of change from 1 hour to 2 hours.

$$\frac{\text{change in distance}}{\text{change in hours}} = \frac{30 - \boxed{}}{2 - 1} = \frac{\boxed{}}{1} = \boxed{} \text{ miles per hour}$$

B Find the rate of change from 1 hour to 4 hours.

$$\frac{\text{change in distance}}{\text{change in hours}} = \frac{60 - \boxed{}}{4 - \boxed{}} = \frac{\boxed{}}{\boxed{}} = \boxed{} \text{ miles per hour}$$

C Recall that the graph of a proportional relationship is a straight line through the origin. Explain whether the relationship between Nathan's time and distance appears to be a proportional relationship.

_____

_____

D Find Nathan's unit rate.

_____

E Compare the rate of change to the unit rate.

_____

REFLECT

2a. Does it matter what interval you use when you find the rate of change of a proportional relationship? Explain.

_____

_____

2b. **Conjecture** Do you think that the value of r in the point $(1, r)$ is always the unit rate for any situation? Explain.

_____

_____

_____

Additional Practice

Determine whether the rates of change are constant or variable.

1.

x	0	1	2	4	5
y	3	4	5	6	7

_____

2.

x	2	4	6	8	12
y	7	9	11	13	17

_____

The graph shows the commission a real estate agent earns based on his total sales.

3. What is the rate of change of the real estate agent's commission?

_____

4. Explain whether the relationship between sales and commissions is proportional.

_____

_____

_____

5. Find the unit rate of the real estate agent's commission.

_____

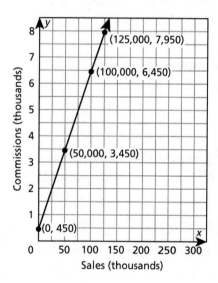

Problem Solving

The graph shows the distance Alisha drove over time.

1. What is Alisha's rate of change?

   _____

2. Explain whether the relationship between Alisha's time and distance appears to be a proportional relationship.

   _____

   _____

Wind chill is the temperature that the air feels like with the effect of the wind. The graph below shows the wind chill equation for a wind speed of 25 mph. For Exercises 3–6, refer to the graph.

3. If the temperature is 40° with a 25 mph wind, what is the wind chill?

   A 6°   C 29°

   B 20°   D 40°

4. If the temperature is 20° with a 25 mph wind, what is the wind chill?

   F 3°   H 13°

   G 10°   J 20°

5. If the temperature is 0° with a 25 mph wind, what is the wind chill?

   A −30°   C −15°

   B −24°   D 0°

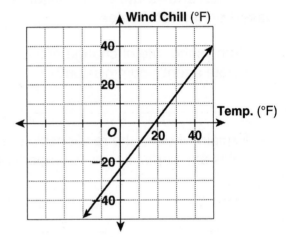

6. If the wind chill is 10° and there is a 25 mph wind, what is the actual temperature?

   F −11°   H 15°

   G 0°   J 25°

8-2

Slope of a Line
Reasoning

Essential question: *How can you show that the slope of a line is the same between any two points on the line?*

video tutor

CC.8.EE.6

1 **EXPLORE**   **Investigating Slope**

The graph shows the linear function $y = -\frac{2}{3}x + 4$.

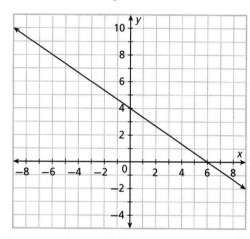

A Find the slope of the line using the points (0, 4) and (−3, 6).

$$m = \dfrac{6 - \boxed{}}{\boxed{} - 0} = \dfrac{\boxed{}}{\boxed{}} = \boxed{}$$

B Find the slope of the line using a different pair of points on the line.

_____

C Find the slope of the line using another pair of points on the line.

_____

REFLECT

1a. What does slope represent?

_____

1b. Does it matter which pair of points you use when finding the slope of a line? Explain.

_____

_____

© Houghton Mifflin Harcourt Publishing Company

The **slope** of a line is the ratio of the change in *y*-values (rise) for a segment of the graph to the corresponding change in *x*-values (run).

2 EXPLORE   Using Similar Triangles to Explain Slope

Use similar triangles to show that the slope of a line is constant.
Use this space to make your drawing:

A Draw line ℓ that is not a horizontal line. Label four points on the line as *A*, *B*, *C*, and *D*.

You need to show that the slope between points *A* and *B* is the same as the slope between points *C* and *D*.

B Draw the rise and run for the slope between points *A* and *B*. Label the intersection as point *E*. Draw the rise and run for the slope between points *C* and *D*. Label the intersection as point *F*.

C Write expressions for the slope between *A* and *B* and between *C* and *D*.

Slope between *A* and *B*: $\dfrac{BE}{}$

Slope between *C* and *D*: $\dfrac{}{CF}$

D Extend $\overleftrightarrow{AE}$ and $\overleftrightarrow{CF}$ across your drawing. $\overleftrightarrow{AE}$ and $\overleftrightarrow{CF}$ are both horizontal lines, so they are parallel. Line ℓ is a transversal that intersects parallel lines.

E Complete the following statements:

∠*BAE* and _____ are corresponding angles and are _____.

∠*BEA* and _____ are right angles and are _____.

300

F By Angle-Angle Similarity, $\triangle ABE$ and _____ are similar triangles.

G Use the fact that the lengths of corresponding sides of similar triangles are proportional to complete the following ratios: $\dfrac{BE}{DF} = \dfrac{\boxed{}}{CF}$.

H Recall that you can also write the proportion so that the ratios compare parts of the same triangle: $\dfrac{\boxed{}}{AE} = \dfrac{DF}{\boxed{}}$.

I The proportion you wrote in step **H** shows that the ratios you wrote in **C** are equal. So, the slope of the line is constant.

PRACTICE

The graph shows how gas in the fuel tank in Ed's car changes in relation to how far he drives. Use the graph for Questions 1–6.

1. Is the slope of the line positive or negative? How do you know?

   _____

   _____

2. To find the slope of the line, you would choose the coordinates of two points along it, and then divide the change in the _____ values by the change in the _____ values. Another way to describe the process is to divide the _____ by the _____ .

3. Will the choice of points affect the slope you find for the line? Explain.

   _____

   _____

4. What is the slope of the line? _____

5. So, the amount of gas decreases by 1 gallon for every _____ miles driven.

6. If the slope of the line were 0 or positive, would it make sense as a way of describing this real-world situation? Why?

   _____

   _____

Solve.

7. Which roof is steeper: one with a rise of 8 and a run of 4, or one with a rise of 12 and a run of 7? Explain.

_____

_____

_____

8. How would you describe a line that has a slope of 0? A line that has *no* slope?

_____

_____

_____

9. Which hill is steeper: one with a rise of 5 and a run of 4, or one with a rise of 4 and a run of 5? Explain.

_____

_____

_____

10. **Error Analysis** A student says that the slope of a line that passes through the points (1, 3) and (7, 5) is 3. What error did the student make? What is the correct slope?

_____

_____

_____

11. Right triangle ABC has coordinates $A(0, 4)$, $B(6, 10)$, and $C(6, 4)$. Similar right triangle ADE has coordinates $A(0, 4)$, $D(3, 7)$, and $E(3, 4)$. What can you say about the slopes of the hypotenuses of the two triangles?

_____

_____

_____

Additional Practice

Find the slope of each line.

1.

2.

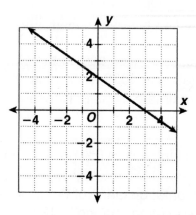

_____   _____

Find the slope of the line that passes through each pair of points.

3. (–2, –8), (1, 4)   4. (–2, 0), (0, 4),   5. (0, 4), (4, 4)   6. (3, –6), (2, –4)

_____   _____   _____   _____

7. (–3, 4), (3, –4)   8. (3, 0), (0, –6),   9. (3, 2), (3, –2)   10. (–4, 4), (3, –1)

_____   _____   _____   _____

11. The table shows the distance Ms. Long had traveled as she went to the beach. Use the data to make a graph. Find the slope of the line and explain what it shows.

Time (min)	Distance (mi)
8	6
12	9
16	12
20	15

_____

_____

_____

_____

Problem Solving

Write the correct answer.

1. The state of Kansas has a fairly steady slope from the east to the west. At the eastern side, the elevation is 771 ft. At the western edge, 413 miles across the state, the elevation is 4039 ft. What is the approximate slope of Kansas?

   _____

2. The Feathered Serpent Pyramid in Teotihuacan, Mexico, has a square base. From the center of the base to the center of an edge of the pyramid is 32.5 m. The pyramid is 19.4 m high. What is the slope of each triangular face of the pyramid?

   _____

3. On a highway, a 6% grade means a slope of 0.06. If a highway covers a horizontal distance of 0.5 miles and the elevation change is 184.8 feet, what is the grade of the road? (Hint: 5280 feet = 1 mile.)

   _____

4. The roof of a house rises vertically 3 feet for every 12 feet of horizontal distance. What is the slope, or pitch of the roof?

   _____

Use the graph for Exercises 5–8.

5. Find the slope of the line between 1990 and 1992.

   A $\dfrac{2}{11}$ C $\dfrac{11}{2}$

   B $\dfrac{35}{3982}$ D $\dfrac{11}{1992}$

6. Find the slope of the line between 1994 and 1996.

   F $\dfrac{7}{2}$ H $\dfrac{2}{7}$

   G $\dfrac{37}{3990}$ J $\dfrac{7}{1996}$

7. Find the slope of the line between 1998 and 2000.

   A 1   C $\dfrac{1}{1000}$

   B $\dfrac{1}{999}$ D 2

Number of Earthquakes Worldwide with a Magnitude of 7.0 or Greater

8. What does it mean when the slope is negative?

   F The number of earthquakes stayed the same.

   G The number of earthquakes increased.

   H The number of earthquakes decreased.

   J It means nothing.

Using Slopes and Intercepts
Going Deeper

8-3

Essential question: *How can you use slopes and intercepts to write and graph linear equations?*

The graph of every non-vertical line crosses the y-axis. The **y-intercept** is the y-coordinate of the point where the graph intersects the y-axis. The x-coordinate of this point is always 0.

To write the equation of a line or to graph a line, you just need to know its slope and y-intercept.

CC.8.EE.6

1 EXPLORE Deriving the Slope-Intercept Formula

A Let L be a line with slope m and y-intercept b. Circle the point that must be on the line. Justify your choice.

$(b, 0)$ $(0, b)$ $(0, m)$ $(m, 0)$

_____

Let (x, y) be a point on line L other than the point containing the y-intercept.

B Write an expression for the change in y values between the point that includes the y-intercept and the point (x, y). _____

C Write an expression for the change in x values between the point that includes the y-intercept and the point (x, y). _____

D Recall that slope is the ratio of change in y to change in x. Complete the equation for the slope m of the line.

$$m = \frac{y - \boxed{}}{\boxed{} - 0}$$

E In an equation of a line, we often want y by itself on one side of the equation. Solve the equation from **D** for y.

$$m = \frac{y - b}{x}$$ *Simplify the denominator.*

$$m \cdot \boxed{} = \frac{y - b}{x} \cdot \boxed{}$$ *Multiply both sides of the equation by _____.*

$$m\boxed{} = y - b$$

$$mx + \boxed{} = y - b + \boxed{}$$ *Add _____ to both sides of the equation.*

$$mx + \boxed{} = y$$

$$y = mx + \boxed{}$$ *Write the equation with y on the left side.*

REFLECT

1. Write the equation of a line with slope m that passes through the origin.

_____

The equation $y = mx + b$ is called the **slope-intercept form** of the equation of a line. In this form, it is easy to see the slope and the y-intercept. When the equation of a line is in slope-intercept form, you can quickly graph the line.

CC.8.F.3

2 E X A M P L E Using Slope-Intercept Form to Graph a Line

Graph $y = -2x + 5$.

Step 1 Identify the slope and the y-intercept.

slope: $m = \boxed{} = \dfrac{\boxed{}}{1}$

y-intercept: $b = \boxed{}$

Step 2 The point that contains the y-intercept is $\left(0, \boxed{}\right)$. Plot this point.

Step 3 Use the slope to find a second point on the line. Count down _____ unit(s) and right _____ unit(s). Plot this point.

Step 4 Draw a line connecting the two points.

TRY THIS!

Write an equation for the line with the given slope and y-intercept.

2a. slope: -4; y-intercept: 6

_____

2b. slope: $\frac{5}{2}$; y-intercept: -3

_____

Graph each equation.

2c. $y = \frac{1}{2}x + 1$

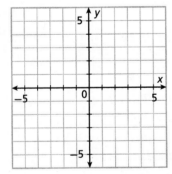

2d. $y = -3x + 4$

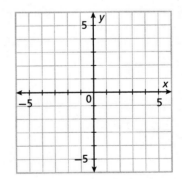

3 EXPLORE Writing an Equation for a Function from a Table

Elizabeth can choose from several monthly cell phone plans. The cost of each plan is a linear function of the number of minutes that are included in the plan. Write an equation in slope-intercept form that represents the function.

Minutes Included, x	100	200	300	400	500
Cost of Plan ($), y	18	28	38	48	58

A Choose any two ordered pairs from the table to find the slope.

$$m = \frac{y_2 - y_1}{x_2 - x_1} = \frac{\boxed{} - \boxed{}}{\boxed{} - \boxed{}} = \frac{\boxed{}}{\boxed{}} = \boxed{}$$

B Use the equation $y = mx + b$ and any point from the table. Substitute values for y, m, and x into the equation and solve for b.

$y = mx + b$

$\boxed{} = \boxed{} \cdot \boxed{} + b$ *Substitute for y, m, and x.*

$\boxed{} = \boxed{} + b$ *Simplify on the right side.*

$\dfrac{-\boxed{} \qquad -\boxed{}}{\boxed{} = \qquad b}$ *Subtract the number that is added to b from both sides.*

C Use the slope and y-intercept values to write an equation in slope-intercept form.

$y = \boxed{}\ x + \boxed{}$

REFLECT

3a. Use the equation to predict the cost of a cell phone plan that includes 175 minutes.

_____

3b. What is the base price for any cell phone plan, regardless of how many minutes are included?

_____

TRY THIS!

3c. **What If?** Elizabeth's cell phone company changed the prices for each of their plans. Write an equation in slope-intercept form that represents the function.

Minutes Included, x	100	200	300	400	500
Cost of Plan ($), y	30	35	40	45	50

4 EXPLORE Writing an Equation for a Function from a Graph

Kate is planning a trip to the beach. She used an estimated average speed to make a graph showing the progress she expects to make on her trip. Write an equation in slope-intercept form that represents the function.

A Choose two points on the graph to find the slope.

$$m = \frac{y_2 - y_1}{x_2 - x_1} = \frac{\boxed{} - \boxed{}}{\boxed{} - \boxed{}} = \frac{\boxed{}}{\boxed{}} = \boxed{}$$

B Read the *y*-intercept from the graph.

$b =$ ☐

C Use your slope and *y*-intercept values to write an equation in slope-intercept form.

_____

REFLECT

4a. What does the value of the slope represent in this context?

_____

_____

4b. Is the slope positive or negative? What does the sign of the slope mean in this context?

_____

_____

4c. Describe the meaning of the *y*-intercept.

_____

_____

TRY THIS!

The graph shows the distance Norma skateboarded over a period of time.

4d. Write an equation in slope-intercept form that represents the function.

_____

4e. Describe the meaning of the *y*-intercept.

_____

_____

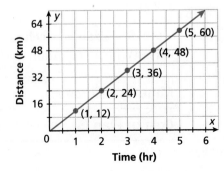

5 **EXPLORE** **Writing an Equation for a Function from a Description**

The rate at which crickets chirp is a linear function of temperature. At 59 °F, they chirp 76 times per minute, and at 65 °F, they chirp 100 times per minute. Write an equation in slope-intercept form that represents the function.

A Identify the input and output variables in this relationship.

Input variable: _____   Output variable: _____

B Write the information given in the problem as ordered pairs.

At 59 °F, crickets chirp 76 times per minute: $\left(\begin{array}{cc} \square & \square \end{array}\right)$

At 65 °F, crickets chirp 100 times per minute: $\left(\begin{array}{cc} \square & \square \end{array}\right)$

C Find the slope.

$$m = \frac{y_2 - y_1}{x_2 - x_1} = \frac{\boxed{} - \boxed{}}{\boxed{} - \boxed{}} = \frac{\boxed{}}{\boxed{}} = \boxed{}$$

D Use the equation $y = mx + b$ and one of the ordered pairs. Substitute values for y, m, and x into the equation and solve for b.

$y = mx + b$

$\boxed{} = \boxed{} \cdot \boxed{} + b$ *Substitute for y, m, and x.*

$\boxed{} = \boxed{} + b$ *Simplify on the right side.*

$\dfrac{-\boxed{}}{} \quad \dfrac{-\boxed{}}{}$ *Subtract the number that is added to b from both sides.*

$\boxed{} = b$

E Write an equation in slope-intercept form.

_____

REFLECT

5a. Predict the number of chirps per minute when the temperature is 72 °F.

_____

5b. Without graphing, tell whether the graph of this function rises or falls from left to right. What does the sign of the slope mean in this context?

_____

_____

_____

The table shows the temperature at different altitudes. The temperature is a linear function of the altitude.

Altitude (ft), x	0	2,000	4,000	6,000	8,000	10,000	12,000
Temperature (°F), y	59	51	43	35	27	19	11

1. Find the slope of the function.

2. Find the y-intercept of the function.

3. Write an equation in slope-intercept form that represents the function.

4. Use your equation to determine the temperature at an altitude of 5,000 feet.

The graph shows a scuba diver's ascent over time.

5. Use the graph to find the slope of the line. Tell what the slope means in this context.

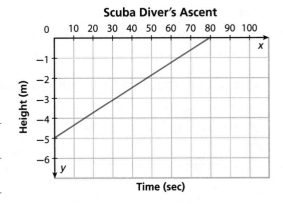

6. Identify the y-intercept. Tell what the y-intercept means in this context.

7. Write an equation in slope-intercept form that represents the function.

The formula for converting Celsius temperatures to Fahrenheit temperatures is a linear function. Water freezes at 0 °C, or 32 °F, and it boils at 100 °C, or 212 °F.

8. Find the slope and y-intercept. Then write an equation in slope-intercept form that represents the function.

9. Average human body temperature is 37 °C. What is this temperature in degrees Fahrenheit?

Additional Practice

Find the *x*-intercept and *y*-intercept of each line. Use the intercepts to graph the equation.

1. $x - y = -3$

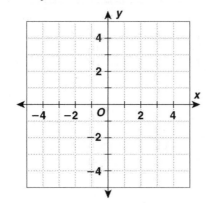

_____

_____

2. $2x + 3y = 12$

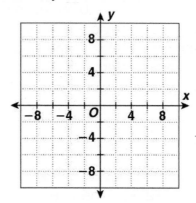

_____

_____

Write each equation in slope-intercept form, and then find the slope and *y*-intercept.

3. $3x + y = 0$

_____

_____

4. $2x - y = -15$

_____

_____

5. $x - 5y = 10$

_____

_____

Write the equation of the line that passes through each pair of points in slope-intercept form.

6. $(3, 4), (4, 6)$

_____

7. $(-1, -1), (2, -10)$

_____

8. $(6, 5), (-9, -20)$

_____

9. A pizzeria charges $8 for a large cheese pizza, plus $2 for each topping. The total cost for a large pizza is given by the equation $C = 2t + 8$, where *t* is the number of toppings. Graph the equation for *t* between 0 and 5 toppings, and explain the meaning of the slope and *y*-intercept.

_____

_____

Problem Solving

Write the correct answer.

1. Jaime purchased a $20 bus pass. Each time she rides the bus, $1.25 is deducted from the pass. The linear equation $y = -1.25x + 20$ represents the amount of money on the bus pass after x rides. Identify the slope and the x- and y-intercepts. Graph the equation at the right.

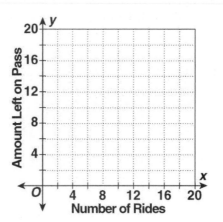

_____

_____

2. The rent charged for space in an office building is related to the size of the space rented. The rent for 600 square feet of floor space is $750, while the rent for 900 square feet is $1150. Write an equation for the rent y based on the square footage of the floor space x.

_____

Choose the letter of the correct answer.

3. A limousine charges $35 plus $2 per mile. Which equation shows the total cost of a ride in the limousine?

   A $y = 35x + 2$ C $y = 2x - 35$

   B $y = 2x + 35$ D $2x + 35y = 2$

4. A newspaper delivery person earns $75 each day plus $0.10 per paper delivered. Which equation shows the daily earnings of a delivery person?

   F $y = 0.1x + 75$ H $x + 0.1y = 75$

   G $y = 75x + 0.1$ J $0.1x + y = 75$

5. A friend gave Ms. Morris a $50 gift card for a local car wash. If each car wash costs $6, which equation shows the number of dollars left on the card?

   A $50x + 6y = 1$ C $y = -6x + 50$

   B $y = 6x + 50$ D $y = 6x - 50$

6. Antonio's weekly allowance is given by the equation $A = 0.5c + 10$, where c is the number of chores he does. If he received $16 in allowance one week, how many chores did he do?

   F 10   H 14

   G 12   J 15

8-4

Point-Slope Form
Going Deeper

Essential question: *How can you develop the point-slope form of an equation of a line?*

video tutor

CC.8.F.4

1 EXPLORE **Developing the Point-Slope Form**

A Let L be a line with slope m that passes through the points (x, y) and (x_1, y_1).

Recall that slope is the ratio of change in y to change in x. Complete the equation for the slope m of the line.

$$\dfrac{y - \boxed{}}{\boxed{} - x_1} = m \qquad\qquad \textit{Use the formula for slope.}$$

$$(x - x_1)\left(\dfrac{y - \boxed{}}{\boxed{} - x_1}\right) = m(x - x_1) \qquad\qquad \textit{Multiply both sides by _____.}$$

$$y - \boxed{} = m\left(\boxed{}\right) \qquad\qquad \textit{Point-slope form of an equation}$$

B What is the point-slope form of the equation of a line with $m = 5$ that passes through $(4, 2)$?

If you know the slope of a line and a point on the line, you can use substitution to write the point-slope form of the equation for that line.

$$y - y_1 = m(x - x_1) \qquad\qquad \textit{Write the point-slope form.}$$

$$y - \boxed{} = \boxed{}\,(x - \boxed{}\,) \qquad \textit{Substitute } \boxed{} \textit{ for } y_1, \boxed{} \textit{ for } m, \textit{ and } \boxed{} \textit{ for } x_1.$$

The point-slope form of a line with $m = 5$ that passes through $(4, 2)$ is

_____

REFLECT

1. How would you contrast the point-slope form of the equation for a line with the slope-intercept form of the equation for a line?

_____

_____

_____

Write the point-slope form of the equation of a line with the given slope that passes through the indicated point.

1. the line with slope 5 passing through $(4, -2)$

2. the line with slope 3 passing through $(2, -3)$

3. the line with slope 2.5 passing through $(1, -3)$

4. the line with slope -2 passing through $(-3, -5)$

5. the line with slope -1 passing through $(6, 4)$

6. the line with slope 3.5 passing through $(2, 2)$

Use the point-slope form of each equation to identify a point the line passes through and the slope of the line.

7. $y + 2.5 = 2(x - 3.5)$

8. $y - 4 = 2.2(x + 3.1)$

9. $y - 1 = -4(x + 4)$

10. $y + 1.8 = 0.7(x - 2.4)$

Solve.

11. A stretch of highway has a 4% uphill grade. This means that the road rises 1 foot for every 25 feet of horizontal distance. The beginning of the highway $(x = 0)$ has an elevation of 2,225 feet. Write an equation for this stretch of roadway in point-slope form.

12. What is the highway's elevation a mile from its beginning? Explain how to find that elevation.

13. Write the point-slope form of an equation with $m = 2$ that passes through the point $(2, 5)$. Then graph the equation on the coordinate plane.

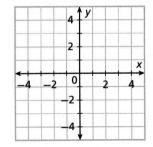

Additional Practice

Use the point-slope form of each equation to identify a point the line passes through and the slope of the line.

1. $y - 2 = 4(x - 1)$

2. $y + 1 = 2(x - 3)$

3. $y - 4 = -3(x + 1)$

_____

_____

_____

_____

_____

_____

4. $y + 5 = -2(x + 6)$

5. $y + 4 = -9(x + 3)$

6. $y - 7 = -7(x - 7)$

_____

_____

_____

_____

_____

_____

7. $y - 10 = 6(x - 8)$

8. $y + 12 = 2.5(x + 4)$

9. $y + 8 = \frac{1}{2}(x - 3)$

_____

_____

_____

_____

_____

_____

Write the point-slope form of the equation with the given slope that passes through the indicated point.

10. the line with slope −1 passing through (2, 5)

11. the line with slope 2 passing through (−1, 4)

_____

_____

12. the line with slope 4 passing through (−3, −2)

13. the line with slope 3 passing through (7, −6)

_____

_____

14. the line with slope −3 passing through (−6, 4)

15. the line with slope −2 passing through (5, 1)

_____

_____

16. Michael was driving at a constant speed of 60 mph when he crossed the Sandy River. After 1 hour, he passed a highway marker for mile 84. Write an equation in point-slope form, and find which highway marker he will pass 90 minutes after crossing the Sandy River.

_____

Problem Solving

Write the correct answer.

1. A 1600 square foot home in City A will sell for about $102,000. The price increases about $43.41 per square foot. Write an equation that describes the price y of a house in City A, based on the square footage x.

_____

2. Write the equation in Exercise 1 in slope-intercept form.

_____

3. Wind chill is a measure of what temperature feels like with the wind. With a 25 mph wind, 40 °F will feel like 29 °F. Write an equation in point-slope form that describes the wind chill y based on the temperature x, if the slope of the line is 1.337.

_____

4. With a 25 mph wind, what does a temperature of 0 °F feel like?

_____

From 2 to 13 years, the growth rate for children is generally linear. Choose the letter of the correct answer.

5. The average height of a 2-year old boy is 36 inches, and the average growth rate per year is 2.2 inches. Write an equation in point-slope form that describes the height of a boy y based on his age x.

  A $y - 36 = 2(x - 2.2)$

  B $y - 2 = 2.2(x - 36)$

  C $y - 36 = 2.2(x - 2)$

  D $y - 2.2 = 2(x - 36)$

6. The average height of a 5-year old girl is 44 inches, and the average growth rate per year is 2.4 inches. Write an equation in point-slope form that describes the height of a girl y based on her age x.

  F $y - 2.4 = 44(x - 5)$

  G $y - 44 = 2.4(x - 5)$

  H $y - 44 = 5(x - 2.4)$

  J $y - 5 = 2.4(x - 44)$

7. Write the equation from Exercise 6 in slope-intercept form.

  A $y = 2.4x - 100.6$

  B $y = 44x - 217.6$

  C $y = 5x + 32$

  D $y = 2.4x + 32$

8. Use the equation in Exercise 6 to find the average height of a 13-year old girl.

  F 56.3 in.

  G 63.2 in.

  H 69.4 in.

  J 97 in.

© Houghton Mifflin Harcourt Publishing Company

Direct Variation
Going Deeper

Essential question: *How can you identify a direct variation?*

A **direct variation** is a linear function that has an equation of the form $y = kx$, in which k is a fixed nonzero constant called the *constant of variation*.

video tutor

CC.8.EE.5

1 EXAMPLE Identifying Direct Variations

Does each equation represent a direct variation between *x* and *y*?

A $-3x + y = 0$

Write the equation in $y = kx$ form, if possible.

$$-3x + y = \quad 0$$
$$+\boxed{} \qquad +\boxed{}$$
$$y = \boxed{}$$

Make a table of values. Then find the ratios of y to x.

x	−1	1	2	3
y				

Graph the equation.

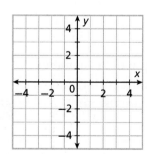

Can $-3x + y = 0$ be written as $y = kx$? _____

Do the ratios of y to x form a constant? _____

Is the graph a straight line passing through the origin? _____

Does $-3x + y = 0$ represent a direct variation between x and y? _____

The constant of variation is _____.

B $-3x + y = 2$

Write the equation in $y = kx$ form, if possible.

$$-3x + y = \quad 2$$
$$+\boxed{} \qquad +\boxed{}$$
$$y = \boxed{}$$

Make a table of values. Then find the ratios of y to x.

x	−1	1	2	3
y				

Graph the equation.

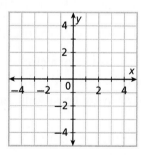

Can $-3x + y = 2$ be written as $y = kx$? _____

Do the ratios of y to x form a constant? _____

Is the graph a straight line passing through the origin? _____

Does $-3x + y = 2$ represent a direct variation between x and y? _____

1a. Does the equation $2.5x - y = 0$ represent a direct variation between x and y? If so, what is the constant of variation? What is the slope of the line?

_____

1b. Is the equation for finding the perimeter of a square P given the length of a side s an example of direct variation? Explain.

_____

_____

_____

PRACTICE

Tell whether the function represented by each table is or is not a direct variation. Explain your reasoning.

1.

x	1	2	3	4
y	−3	−6	−9	−12

2.

x	1	2	3	4
y	4	5	6	7

_____   _____

_____   _____

Use the graph for 3–5.

3. Does the graph represent a direct variation between x and y? _____

4. Write an equation for the graph. _____

5. What is the value of y when $x = 6$? _____

6. The circumference of a circle varies directly with the length of its diameter. How would you describe the relationship between circumference C and diameter d? What equation can you write to show this relationship?

_____

7. Explain how the constant of variation k affects the appearance of the graph of an equation that is a direct variation.

_____

8. **Error Analysis** A classmate claims that the score you'll get on a test varies directly with the amount of time you spend studying. What do you think?

_____

_____

Additional Practice

Determine whether the data sets show direct variation.

1.

x	y
6	9
4	6
0	0
−2	−3
−8	−12

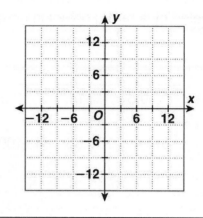

_____

2. Write the equation of direct variation for Exercise 1.

_____

Find each equation of direct variation, given that _y_ varies with _x_.

3. _y_ is 32 when _x_ is 4

4. _y_ is −10 when _x_ is −20

_____   _____

5. _y_ is 63 when _x_ is −7

6. _y_ is 40 when _x_ is 50

_____   _____

7. _y_ is 87.5 when _x_ is 25

8. _y_ is 90 when _x_ is 270

_____   _____

9. The table shows the length and width of various U.S. flags. Determine whether there is direct variation between the two data sets. If so, find the equation of direct variation.

Length (ft)	2.85	5.7	7.6	9.88	11.4
Width (ft)	1.5	3	4	5.2	6

_____

_____

_____

Problem Solving

Determine whether the data sets show direct variation. If so, find the equation of direct variation.

1. The table shows the distance in feet traveled by a falling object in certain times.

Time (s)	0	0.5	1	1.5	2	2.5	3
Distance (ft)	0	4	16	36	64	100	144

_____

_____

2. The R-value of insulation gives the material's resistance to heat flow. The table shows the R-value for different thicknesses of fiberglass insulation.

Thickness (in.)	1	2	3	4	5	6
R-value	3.14	6.28	9.42	12.56	15.7	18.84

_____

_____

3. The table shows the lifting power of hot air.

Hot Air (ft^3)	50	100	500	1000	2000	3000
Lift (lb)	1	2	10	20	40	60

_____

_____

4. The table shows the relationship between degrees Celsius and degrees Fahrenheit.

° Celsius	−10	−5	0	5	10	20	30
° Fahrenheit	14	23	32	41	50	68	86

_____

_____

Your weight on Earth varies directly with your weights on other planetary bodies. The table below shows how much a person who weighs 100 lb on Earth would weigh on the moon and different planets.

5. Find the equation of direct variation for the weight on earth e and on the moon m.

   A $m = 0.166e$ C $m = 6.02e$

   B $m = 16.6e$ D $m = 1660e$

Planetary Bodies	Weight (lb)
Moon	16.6
Jupiter	236.4
Pluto	6.7

6. How much would a 150 lb person weigh on Jupiter?

   F 63.5 lb   H 354.6 lb

   G 286.4 lb   J 483.7 lb

7. How much would a 150 lb person weigh on Pluto?

   A 5.8 lb   C 12.3 lb

   B 10.05 lb   D 2238.8 lb

8-6

Solving Systems of Linear Equations by Graphing
Going Deeper

Essential question: *How can you solve a system of equations by graphing?*

CC.8.EE.8a

1 EXPLORE Investigating Systems of Equations

A Graph the system of linear functions: $\begin{cases} y = 3x - 2 \\ y = -2x + 3 \end{cases}$.

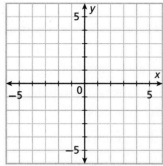

B Explain how to tell whether the ordered pair $(2, -1)$ is a solution of the equation $y = 3x - 2$ without using the graph.

_____

_____

C Explain how to tell whether the ordered pair $(2, -1)$ is a solution of the equation $y = -2x + 3$ without using the graph.

_____

_____

D Explain how to use the graph to tell whether the ordered pair $(2, -1)$ is a solution of either equation.

_____

_____

E Find an ordered pair that is a solution of both equations. Test the coordinates in each equation to verify your hypothesis.

The point _____ is a solution of both equations.

An ordered pair (x, y) is a solution of an equation in two variables if substituting the x- and y-values into the equation results in a true statement. Recall that *a system of equations* is a set of equations that have the same variables. An ordered pair is a solution of a system if it is a solution of every equation in the system.

Since the graph of a function represents all ordered pairs that are solutions of the related equation, if a point lies on the graphs of two functions, the point is a solution of both related equations.

2 EXAMPLE Solving Systems Graphically

Solve each system by graphing.

A $\begin{cases} y = -x + 4 \\ y = 3x \end{cases}$

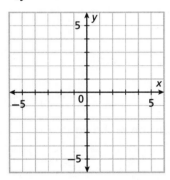

Start by graphing each function.

Identify if there are any ordered pairs that are solutions of both equations.

The solution of the system appears to be

_____.

To check your answer, you can substitute the values for x and y into each equation and make sure the equations are true statements.

B $\begin{cases} y = 2x - 2 \\ y = 2x + 4 \end{cases}$

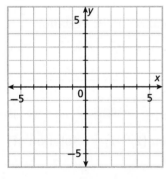

Start by graphing each function.

Identify if there are any ordered pairs that are solutions of both equations.

The graphs are parallel, so there is no ordered pair that is a solution of both equations. The system has

_____.

C $\begin{cases} y = 3x - 3 \\ y = 3(x - 1) \end{cases}$

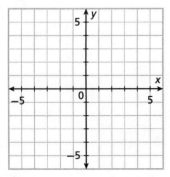

Start by graphing each function.

Identify if there are any ordered pairs that are solutions of both equations.

The graphs overlap, so every ordered pair that is a solution of one equation is also a solution of the other equation. The system has

_____.

3 **EXAMPLE** Solving a Real-World Problem by Graphing

Keisha and her friends visit the concession stand at a football game. The stand charges $2 for a hot dog and $1 for a drink. The friends buy a total of 8 items for $11. Tell how many hot dogs and how many drinks they bought.

A Let x represent the number of hot dogs they bought and y represent the number of drinks they bought.

Write an equation representing the **number of items they purchased**.

Number of hot dogs   +   Number of drinks   =   Total items

     ☐   +   ☐   =   ☐

Write an equation representing the **money spent on the items**.

Cost of 1 hot dog times   +   Cost of 1 drink times   =   Total cost
number of hot dogs   number of drinks

     ☐   +   ☐   =   ☐

B Write your equations in slope-intercept form.

_____

C Graph the solutions of both equations.

D Use the graph to identify the solution of the system of equations. Check your answer by substituting the ordered pair into both equations.

The point _____ is a solution of both equations.

E Interpret the solution in the original context.

Keisha and her friends bought _____ hot dog(s) and _____ drink(s).

REFLECT

3. **Conjecture** Why do you think the graph is limited to the first quadrant?

_____

_____

Solve each system by graphing.

1. $\begin{cases} 2x - 4y = 10 \\ x + y = 2 \end{cases}$ _____

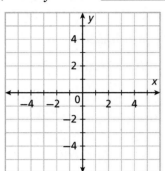

2. $\begin{cases} 2x - y = 0 \\ x + y = -6 \end{cases}$ _____

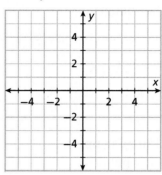

Graph each system and tell how many solutions the system has.

3. $\begin{cases} x - 3y = 2 \\ -3x + 9y = -6 \end{cases}$

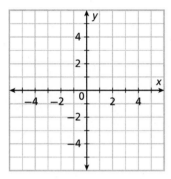

4. $\begin{cases} 2x - y = 5 \\ 2x - y = -1 \end{cases}$

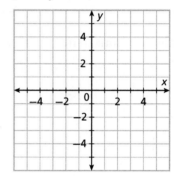

_____ solutions   _____ solutions

Mrs. Morales wrote a test with 15 questions covering spelling and vocabulary. Spelling questions (x) are worth 5 points and vocabulary questions (y) are worth 10 points. The maximum number of points possible on the test is 100.

5. Write an equation in slope-intercept form to represent the number of questions on the test.

   _____

6. Write an equation in slope-intercept form to represent the total points on the test.

   _____

7. Graph the solutions of both equations.

8. Use your graph to tell how many of each question type are on the test.

   _____ spelling questions; _____ vocabulary questions

Additional Practice

Solve each linear system by graphing. Check your answer.

1. $y = -1$
   $y = 2x - 7$

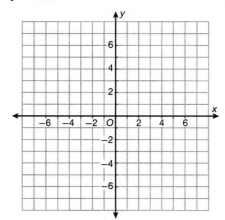

_____

2. $x - y = 6$
   $2x = 12 + 2y$

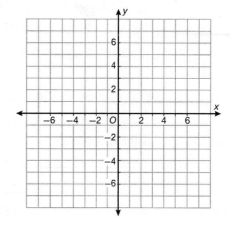

_____

3. $\frac{1}{2}x - y = 4$
   $2y = x + 6$

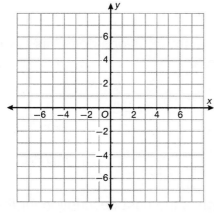

_____

4. $y = 4x - 3$
   $2y - 3x = -4$

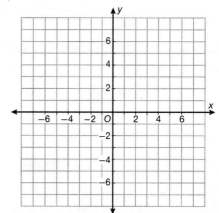

_____

5. Two skaters are racing toward the finish line of a race. The first skater has a 40 meter lead and is traveling at a rate of 12 meters per second. The second skater is traveling at a rate of 14 meters per second. How long will it take for the second skater to pass the first skater?

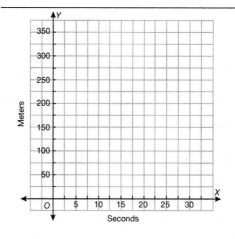

_____

Problem Solving

Write the equations for each system. Graph the system to solve each problem.

Kelly needs to order lunch for the 6 people at a business meeting. Her menu choices are chicken salad for a cost of $5 per person and egg salad for a cost of $4 per person. She only has $28 to spend. More people want chicken salad. How many of each lunch can she order?

1. Write one equation in a system for this situation. _____

2. Write a second equation in the system.
   _____

3. What do x and y represent?
   _____
   _____

4. How many of each type of lunch can she order?
   _____
   _____

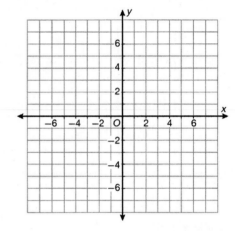

Solve each problem.

5. How many solutions does this system have?
$$y = -3x + 6$$
$$9x + 3y = 18$$

   A 0   C 2

   B 1   D infinite

6. How many solutions does this system have?
$$5x - y = 1$$
$$2x = 3y$$

   F 0   H 2

   G 1   J infinite

7. For which system is the ordered pair (2, –2) a solution?

   A $y = x$
   $y = \dfrac{1}{2}x - 3$

   C $y = -x$
   $y = \dfrac{1}{2}x - 3$

   B $y = -\dfrac{1}{2}x$
   $y = 2x - 4$

   D $2y = -x$
   $2y = 2x$

8. Which is the best description for the graph of this system of equations?
$$x + y = 4$$
$$4x + 4y = 8$$

   F same line

   G parallel lines

   H intersecting lines

   J coinciding lines

Name_____ Class_____ Date_____

Problem Solving Connections 🌐

Is the Price Right? Travelers who arrive at an aiport usually have transportation options for getting to their next destination. Most travelers can choose between taxi or shuttle services to get to their hotels.

COMMON CORE

CC.8.EE.7a,
CC.8.EE.7b,
CC.8.EE.8a,
CC.8.EE.8b,
CC.8.EE.8c

1 Writing Equations

Jackie just arrived at the Orlando International Airport. There are two routes from the airport to Jackie's hotel:

- If the driver uses city streets, the distance to the hotel is 29 miles.

- If the driver takes the expressway, the distance is only 23 miles, but Jackie will pay an additional $2.75 in toll charges.

A The first taxi company Jackie talks to charges an initial fee of $2.00 plus $2.40 for each mile. Write an equation to show the total charge y for traveling x miles.

_____

B Calculate the total cost to travel to Jackie's hotel taking each route.

> Streets: Expressway:

Which route should Jackie instruct the driver to take? Why?

_____

C Jackie learns that the taxi can transport up to 4 people to the same destination at the rates given above. There is a $3 charge for each additional person. A shuttle bus company offers transportation to the hotel for $15 per person. Jackie is traveling with 3 friends. Calculate the total cost for Jackie and her friends to take the taxi along the expressway and the shuttle.

> Taxi: Shuttle:

Should Jackie and her friends choose the taxi or the shuttle? Explain.

_____

© Houghton Mifflin Harcourt Publishing Company

2 Graphing a System

Chuck and his family are also vacationing in Florida. He researches taxi rates before they leave home. There are 5 people in Chuck's family (including Chuck).

Company 1: $2 initial fee, plus $2.40 per mile for 1 to 2 passengers and $3 per person for each additional person.

Company 2: $3.75 initial fee, plus $2.00 per mile for 1 to 2 passengers and $1.50 per person for each additional person.

Company 3: $3.85 initial fee, plus $2.20 per mile for up to 5 passengers.

A Write equations in slope-intercept form to model each company's fare y for traveling x miles with 5 passengers.

Company 1:   Company 2:   Company 3:

B Sketch a graph of the system.

C Explain any restrictions that should be placed on the values of x and y.

_____

_____

_____

_____

D The distance from the airport to the hotel where Chuck and his family are staying is 35 miles. Use your graph to determine which company is most expensive for Chuck's family of five to get to their hotel. Which company is least expensive?

_____

_____

E How could you check your answers to **D** ?

_____

_____

3 Solving a System of Equations Algebraically

Chuck's family decides to change their hotel reservation. They also learn that taxi company 1 will not be in operation on they day they need transportation.

A Chuck has not yet determined the distance between the airport and his family's new hotel. Explain how to use the graph from **2** to help Chuck's family choose the best value.

_____

_____

_____

_____

B Can you use the graph to determine which company is less expensive for a distance of 23 miles? If not, what method can you use?

_____

_____

_____

C Use algebraic methods to solve the system of equations representing fares for company 2 and company 3.

D Explain what your solution means in the context of the problem.

_____

_____

_____

_____

E Which company should Chuck's family choose to travel 23 miles to their new hotel?

_____

A What factors do you need to consider when analyzing transportation costs?

_____

_____

_____

B Suppose two companies have the same rate per mile but different initial fees. Describe what the graph representing their fares would look like. What is the solution of the system of equations representing the fares? Which company has the lower fare?

_____

_____

_____

_____

_____

C Suppose two companies have the same initial fees but different rates per mile. Describe what the graph representing their fares would look like. What is the solution of the system of equations representing the fares? Which company has the lower fare?

_____

_____

_____

_____

_____

D Why is it important to put restrictions on the values of x and y in a real-world problem?

_____

_____

_____

_____

_____

Performance Task

COMMON
CORE

CC.8.EE.8
CC.8.F.3
CC.8.F.4
CC.8.F.5

⭐ **1.** Ed begins walking home from the library. After 3 minutes, he has walked 288 yards.

    a. Use the points (0, 0) and (3, 288) to find the rate Ed is walking. Write your final answer in yards per second.

    b. Write and graph a function that gives the distance *d* in yards Ed walks after *t* seconds.

⭐ **2.** Han and James are telling people about their new website. Han e-mails 8 people every day for one week. James calls 20 friends on the first day, and then calls 4 friends every following day for the same week.

    a. Draw graphs that represent the total number of people *p* Han and James have told about the website after *d* days. Let the first day be *d* = 0, and the last day be *d* = 6.

    b. After how many days have Han and James contacted the same number of people? How do you know?

3. The graph shows the number of miles m that Frank is from home, t minutes after starting to prepare for a bike ride.

    a. How long is it before Frank actually starts biking? How do you know?

    b. What is the fastest that Frank bicycles? Explain.

    c. Describe in your own words the significance of the sign of the slope for the 3 different segments of Frank's ride.

4. A farm sells peaches for $2 per pound. If you're a member of the farm co-op, you get 25% off per pound, but you also have to pay a one-time $10 membership fee.

    a. If you're a member, how many pounds of peaches do you have to buy before you start saving money over the regular price? Write your answer as an inequality. Explain your reasoning, and show any graphs or equations you use.

    b. The farm is considering adding another membership plan that has a $20 fee but offers a bigger discount. Choose a discount and write an equation for the plan.

Name _____ **Class** _____ **Date** _____

SELECTED RESPONSE

1. Determine whether the rates of change are constant or variable.

x	−5	−3	2	4
y	13	5	−15	−23

   A. variable   **B.** constant

2. Find the slope of the line.

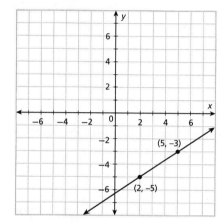

  F. $-\dfrac{3}{5}$ **H.** $\dfrac{3}{2}$

  G. $\dfrac{2}{3}$ **J.** $-\dfrac{2}{3}$

3. Write the equation of the line that passes through (7, 4) and (4, 8) in slope-intercept form.

  A. $y = -\dfrac{4}{3}x + \dfrac{3}{40}$ **C.** $y = -\dfrac{3}{4}x + \dfrac{40}{3}$

  B. $y = -\dfrac{4}{3}x + \dfrac{40}{3}$ **D.** $y = \dfrac{4}{3}x + \dfrac{40}{3}$

4. After it is planted, a tree grows at a rate of 0.3 meters per year. After 4 years the tree is 1.7 meters tall. Write the equation in point-slope form that models the situation. Then, predict the height of the tree after 7 years.

  F. $y - 4 = 0.3(x - 1.7)$; 5.59 meters

  G. $y - 0.3 = 1.7(x - 4)$; 5.4 meters

  H. $y - 1.7 = 0.3(x - 4)$; 2.6 meters

  J. $y - 1.7 = 4(x - 0.3)$; 28.5 meters

5. Write the point-slope form of the equation of the line with slope $\dfrac{2}{3}$ that passes through the point (2, −9).

  A. $y - 9 = \dfrac{2}{3}(x + 2)$ **C.** $y + 9 = \dfrac{2}{3}(x - 2)$

  B. $y + 2 = \dfrac{2}{3}(x - 9)$ **D.** $x - 2 = \dfrac{2}{3}(y + 9)$

6. A remote-control airplane descends at a rate of 2 feet per second. After 3 seconds it is 67 feet above the ground. Write the equation in point-slope form that models the situation. Then, find the height of the plane after 8 seconds.

  F. $y - 67 = -2(x - 3)$; 57 feet

  G. $y - 67 = -3(x - 2)$; 49 feet

  H. $y - 3 = -2(x - 67)$; 121 feet

  J. $y - 2 = 67(x - 3)$; 337 feet

7. Determine whether the data sets show direct variation.

Number of Baskets	Cost
4	$12
5	$15
7	$21
8	$24
9	$27

  A. yes   **B.** no

8. At a summer camp there is one counselor for every 5 campers. Determine whether there is a direct variation between the number of campers, y, and the number of counselors, x. If so, find the equation of direct variation.

  F. direct variation; $y = 5x$

  G. direct variation; $x = 5y$

  H. direct variation; $y = 5x + 5$

  J. no direct variation

© Houghton Mifflin Harcourt Publishing Company

9. Solve the system by graphing.

$$y = 5x + 3$$
$$-5x + y = 8$$

A. This system has infinitely many solutions.

B. $\left(\dfrac{1}{2}, \dfrac{11}{2}\right)$

C. $\left(-\dfrac{1}{2}, \dfrac{1}{2}\right)$

D. This system has no solutions.

CONSTRUCTED RESPONSE

10. A plane taking off follows the path given by the equation $y = 0.5x + 2$. Graph this equation.

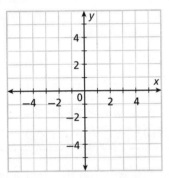

11. A subway pass costs $20.00 and $1.50 is deducted from the balance on the pass every time you use it. Write the equation to represent this situation, and graph it.

_____

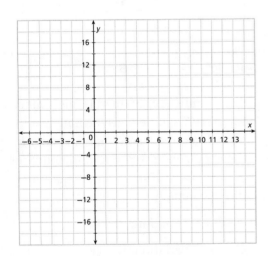

12. The altitude on a ski trail drops 2 feet for every 5 feet of horizontal distance traveled. The end of the trail has an altitude of 4,000 feet and is a horizontal distance of 2000 feet from the start.

a. Write an equation in point-slope form that represents this situation, and graph the equation.

b. Use the graph to find the altitude at the start of the trail.

_____

_____

_____

_____

13. A fast-food restaurant has four sizes of cups as listed in the table below.

Size	Small, 8 oz	Medium, 12 oz	Large, 16 oz	Super, 24 oz
Cost	$0.90	$1.35	$1.80	$2.25

Do the sizes and costs of the beverages show a direct variation? If so, write the equation of variation. If not, explain why not.

_____

_____

_____

Data, Prediction, and Linear Functions

Chapter Focus

You will construct and interpret scatter plots and two-way tables. You will use trend lines to make predictions from scatter plots. Finally, you will graph a linear function and use tables, graphs, and equations to compare functions.

Chapter at a Glance

COMMON CORE

Lesson		Standards for Mathematical Content
9-1	Scatter Plots	CC.8.SP.1, CC.8.SP.2
9-2	Linear Best Fit Models	CC.8.SP.1, CC.8.SP.2, CC.8.SP.3
Ext	Patterns in Two-Way Tables	CC.8.SP.4
9-3	Linear Functions	CC.8.EE.5, CC.8.F.3
9-4	Comparing Multiple Representations	CC.8.EE.5, CC.8.F.2, CC.8.F.4
	Problem Solving Connections	
	Performance Task	
	Assessment Readiness	

CHAPTER 9

Unpacking the Standards

Understanding the standards and the vocabulary terms in the standards will help you know exactly what you are expected to learn in this chapter.

COMMON CORE CC.8.SP.1

Construct and interpret scatter plots for bivariate measurement data to investigate patterns of association between two quantities. Describe patterns such as clustering, outliers, positive or negative association, linear association, and nonlinear association.

Key Vocabulary

scatter plot *(diagrama de dispersión)* A graph with points plotted to show a possible relationship between two sets of data.

positive correlation *(correlación positiva)* Two data sets have a positive correlation when their data values increase or decrease together.

negative correlation *(correlación negativa)* Two data sets have a negative correlation if one set of data values increases while the other decreases.

What It Means to You

You will make and interpret scatter plots. You will describe patterns in two-variable data.

EXAMPLE

The table shows the winning times for the Olympic women's 3000-meter speed skating race. Use the given data to make a scatter plot, and describe the correlation.

Years since 1976	4	8	12	16	18	22	26	30
Winning time (min)	4.54	4.41	4.20	4.33	4.29	4.12	3.96	4.04

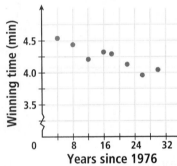

Winning Times

As the number of years increases, the winning times tend to decrease. There is a negative correlation between the two data sets.

COMMON CORE CC.8.SP.2

Know that straight lines are widely used to model relationships between two quantitative variables. For scatter plots that suggest a linear association, informally fit a straight line, and informally assess the model fit by judging the closeness of the data points to the line.

Key Vocabulary

line of best fit *(línea de mejor ajuste)* A straight line that comes closest to the points on a scatter plot.

What It Means to You

You will draw a trend line to model data displayed in a scatter plot. You will use that line to make predictions.

EXAMPLE

Compare the given scatter plots of data and their lines of best fit. Tell which model better fits the data. Explain.

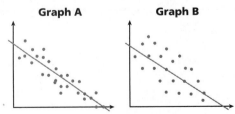

Graph A   **Graph B**

Both data sets have a negative correlation. The points in Graph A are closer to the line of best fit than in Graph B. So the linear model in Graph A fits the data better than the linear model in Graph B.

COMMON CORE CC.8.SP.3

Use the equation of a linear model to solve problems in the context of bivariate measurement data, interpreting the slope and intercept.

Key Vocabulary

bivariate data *(datos bivariado)* Data that involves two variables.

slope *(pendiente)* A measure of the steepness of a line on a graph; the rise divided by the run.

y-intercept *(intersección con el eje y)* The y-coordinate of the point where the graph of a line crosses the y-axis.

What It Means to You

You will write an equation for a trend line that models two-variable data. You will interpret the slope of the line and y-intercept and use the equation to make predictions.

EXAMPLE

Estimate an equation for the line of best fit, and tell what the slope and y-intercept represent in terms of the data it models.

The equation of the line of best fit is $y = 8.7x + 8$.

A slope of 8.7 indicates that the salary would increase by $8,700 for each additional year of post high school education that one receives.

Post High School Education and Salary

A y-intercept of 8 indicates that with no post high school education, an annual salary would begin about $8,000.

COMMON CORE CC.8.F.2

Compare properties of two functions each represented in a different way (algebraically, graphically, numerically in tables, or by verbal descriptions).

Key Vocabulary

function *(función)* An input-output relationship that has exactly one output for each input.

What It Means to You

You will learn to translate between different representations of functions such as tables, graphs, equations, and verbal descriptions.

EXAMPLE

A spider descends a 20-foot drainpipe at a rate of 2.5 feet per minute. Another spider descends a drainpipe as shown in the table. Find and compare the rates of change and initial values of the linear functions in terms of the situations they model.

Spider #1: $f(x) = -2.5x + 20$

Spider #2:

Time (min)	0	1	2
Height (ft)	32	29	26

For Spider #1, the rate of change is −2.5 and the initial value is 20. For Spider #2, the rate of change is −3 and the initial value is 32.

Spider #2 started at 32 feet, which is 12 feet higher than Spider #1. Spider #1 is descending at 2.5 feet per minute, which is 0.5 feet per minute slower than Spider #2.

CHAPTER 9

Key Vocabulary

bivariate data *(datos bivariado)* A data set involving two variables.

clustering *(arracimando)* A condition that occurs when data points in a scatter plot are grouped more in one part of the graph than another.

frequency *(frecuencia)* The number of times the value appears in the data set.

linear equation *(ecuación lineal)* An equation whose solutions form a straight line on a coordinate plane.

linear function *(función lineal)* A function whose graph is a straight line.

relative frequency *(frecuencia relativa)* The frequency of a specific data value divided by the total number of data values in the set.

scatter plot *(diagrama de dispersión)* A graph with points plotted to show a possible relationship between two sets of data.

trend line *(línea de tendencia)* A straight line that comes closest to the points on a scatter plot.

two-way table *(tabla de doble entrada)* A table that displays two-variable data by organizing it into rows and columns.

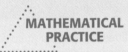 **MATHEMATICAL PRACTICE** The Common Core Standards for Mathematical Practice describe varieties of expertise that mathematics educators at all levels should seek to develop in their students. Opportunities to develop these practices are integrated throughout this program.

1. Make sense of problems and persevere in solving them.
2. Reason abstractly and quantitatively.
3. Construct viable arguments and critique the reasoning of others.
4. Model with mathematics.
5. Use appropriate tools strategically.
6. Attend to precision.
7. Look for and make use of structure.
8. Look for and express regularity in repeated reasoning.

Scatter Plots
Going Deeper

Essential question: *How can you construct and interpret scatter plots?*

A set of **bivariate data** involves two variables. Bivariate data are used to explore the relationship between two variables. You can graph bivariate data on a *scatter plot*. A **scatter plot** is a graph with points plotted to show the relationship between two sets of data.

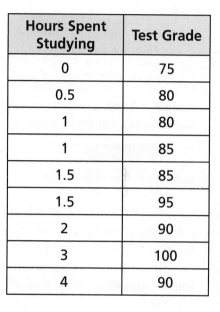

video tutor

CC.8.SP.1

1 EXPLORE Making a Scatter Plot

The final question on a math test reads, "How many hours did you spend studying for this test?" The teacher records the number of hours each student studied and the grade the student received on the test.

Hours Spent Studying	Test Grade
0	75
0.5	80
1	80
1	85
1.5	85
1.5	95
2	90
3	100
4	90

A Make a prediction about the relationship between the number of hours spent studying and test grades.

_____

_____

_____

B Make a scatter plot. Graph hours spent studying as the independent variable and test grade as the dependent variable.

REFLECT

1a. What trend do you see in the data?

_____

_____

_____

1b. Do you think that studying for 10 hours would greatly increase a student's grade?

_____

_____

1c. Why might a student who studied fewer hours make a higher score?

_____

_____

Association tells you how sets of data are related. A positive association means that both data sets increase together. A negative association means that as one data set increases, the other decreases. No association means that changes in one data set do not affect the other data set.

Positive Association

Negative Association

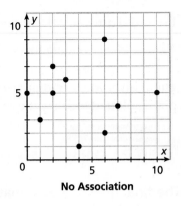

No Association

When data shows a positive or negative association and falls along a line, there is a linear association. When data shows a positive or negative relationship, but does not fall along a line, there is a nonlinear association.

CC.8.SP.1

2 EXPLORE   Determining Association

Susan surveyed 20 people about the price of a cleaning product she developed. She asked each person whether they would buy the cleaner at different prices. A person may answer yes or no to more than one price. Susan's results are shown in the table.

Price ($)	Buyers
2	20
4	19
6	17
8	13
10	8
12	2

A Make a scatter plot of the data.

B Describe the type(s) of association you see between price and number of people who would buy at that price. Explain.

_____

_____

_____

When a scatter plot shows a linear association, you can use a line to model the relationship between the variables. A **trend line** is a straight line that comes closest to the points on a scatter plot. When drawing a trend line, ignore any *outliers*. An **outlier** is a data point that is very different from the rest of the data in the set.

CC.8.SP.2

3 EXPLORE   Drawing a Trend Line

Joyce is training for a 10K race. For some of her training runs, she records the distance she ran and how many minutes she ran.

Distance (mi)	Time (min)
4	38
2	25
1	7
2	16
3	26
5	55
2	20
4	45
3	31

A Make a scatter plot of Joyce's running data.

B To draw a trend line, use a straight edge to draw a line that has about the same number of points above and below it. Ignore any outliers.

C Use your trend line to predict how long it would take Joyce to run 4.5 miles.

_____

REFLECT

3a. How well does your trend line fit the data?

_____

_____

_____

3b. Do you think you can use a scatter plot that shows no association to make a prediction? Explain your answer.

_____

_____

_____

The table shows softball game results.

Hits	8	7	4	11	2	8	5	1
Runs	6	6	2	9	1	8	4	0

1. Use the data table to make a scatter plot.

2. Draw a trend line using a straightedge.

3. Describe the trend your line shows. Is it positive or negative, or is there no trend? How do you know?

_____

_____

4. What does your scatter plot show about the relationship between hits and runs scored for this team?

_____

_____

5. Predict how many runs the softball team would score if its players got 9 hits. What if they got 3 hits?

_____

The table shows age and sleep times for some people.

Age (yr)	6	1	5	15	19	12	3	20
Sleep (h)	9.5	15	11	8.5	7	9.25	12	7

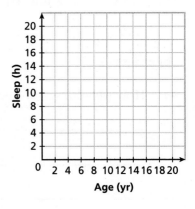

6. Use the data in the table to make a scatter plot.

7. Draw a trend line using a straightedge.

8. What does your scatter plot show about the relationship between age and hours of sleep for this group of people?

_____

_____

9. Predict how many hours of sleep an 18-year old might get nightly. How many hours of sleep might a 4-year old get?

_____

Additional Practice

1. Use the given data to make a scatter plot, and describe the correlation.

Tall Buildings in U.S. Cities

Building	City	Stories	Height (meters)
Sears Tower	Chicago	110	442
Empire State Building	New York	102	381
Bank of America Plaza	Atlanta	55	312
Library Tower	Los Angeles	75	310
Key Tower	Cleveland	57	290
Columbia Seafirst Center	Seattle	76	287
NationsBank Plaza	Dallas	72	281
NationsBank Corporate Center	Charlotte	60	265

Tall Buildings in U.S. Cities

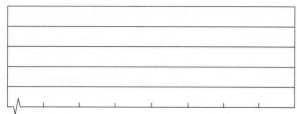

_____

2. Make a scatter plot of the data, and draw a line of best fit. Then use the data to predict the percentage of American homeowners in 1955.

Percent of Americans Owning Homes

Year	1950	1960	1970	1980	1990
Percent	55.0%	61.9%	62.9%	64.4%	64.2%

_____

Problem Solving

Use the data given at the right.

1. Make a scatter plot of the data.

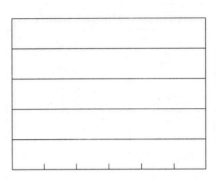

**Percent of Americans Who Have
Completed High School**

Year	Percent
1910	13.5
1920	16.4
1930	19.1
1940	24.5
1950	34.3
1960	41.1
1970	55.2
1980	68.6
1990	77.6
1999	83.4

2. Does the data show a positive, negative or no correlation?

_____

3. Use the scatter plot to predict the percent of Americans who will complete high school in 2010.

_____

Choose the letter for the best answer.

4. Which data sets have a positive correlation?

A   The length of the lines at amusement park rides and the number of rides you can ride in a day

B   The temperature on a summer day and the number of visitors at a swimming pool

C   The square miles of a state and the population of the state in the 2000 census

D   The length of time spent studying and doing homework and the length of time spent doing other activities

5. Which data sets have a negative correlation?

F   The number of visitors at an amusement park and the length of the lines for the rides

G   The amount of speed over the speed limit when you get a speeding ticket and the amount of the fine for speeding

H   The temperature and the number of people wearing coats

J   The distance you live from school and the amount of time it takes to get to school

Linear Best Fit Models
Going Deeper

Essential question: *How can you use a trend line to make a prediction from a scatter plot?*

A **cluster** is a set of closely grouped data. Data may cluster around a point or along a line.

CC.8.SP.1

1 EXAMPLE **Interpreting Clusters and Outliers**

A scientist gathers information about the eruptions of Old Faithful, a geyser in Yellowstone National Park. She uses the data to create a scatter plot. The data shows the length of time between eruptions (interval) and how long the eruption lasts (duration).

A Describe any clusters you see in the scatter plot.

_____

_____

B What do the clusters tell you about eruptions of Old Faithful?

_____

_____

C Describe any outliers you see in the scatter plot.

_____

_____

REFLECT

1a. Suppose the geyser erupts for 2.2 minutes after a 75-minute interval. Would this point lie in one of the clusters? Would it be an outlier? Explain your answer.

_____

_____

_____

1b. Suppose the geyser erupts after an 80-minute interval. Give a range of possible duration times for which the point on the scatter plot would not be considered an outlier.

_____

The scatter plot shows the relationship between the number of chapters and the total number of pages for several books. Draw a trend line, write an equation for the trend line, and describe the meanings of the slope and *y*-intercept.

A Draw a trend line. It will be easier to write an equation for the line if it goes through two of the data points. (Hint: Use (5, 50) as one of the points.)

Identify another point that the trend line goes through:

$$\left(\boxed{}, \boxed{}\right).$$

B What type(s) of association does the scatter plot show?

_____

C Do you expect the slope of the line to be positive or negative?

_____

D Find the slope of the trend line.

$$m = \frac{\boxed{} - 50}{\boxed{} - 5} = \frac{\boxed{}}{\boxed{}} = \boxed{}$$

E Use the equation $y = mx + b$, the slope, and the point (5, 50). Substitute values for *y*, *m*, and *x* into the equation and solve for *b*.

$y = mx + b$

$\boxed{} = \boxed{} \cdot \boxed{} + b$ *Substitute for y, m, and x.*

$\boxed{} = \boxed{} + b$ *Simplify on the right side.*

$\boxed{} = \boxed{} + b$ *Subtract the number that is added to b from both sides.*

$\dfrac{-\boxed{}\quad -\boxed{}}{\boxed{} = \quad b}$

Use your slope and *y*-intercept values to write an equation in slope-intercept form.

$y = \boxed{} x + \boxed{}$

F What is the meaning of the slope in this situation?

_____

_____

G What is the meaning of the *y*-intercept in this situation?

_____

When you use a trend line or its equation to predict a value between data points that you already know, you *interpolate* the predicted value. When you make a prediction that is outside the data that you know, you *extrapolate* the predicted value.

CC.8.SP.2

3 EXPLORE Making Predictions

Refer to the scatter plot and trend line in **2**.

A Use the equation of the trend line to predict how many pages would be in a book with 26 chapters.

Is this prediction an example of interpolation or extrapolation?

_____

$y = $ ☐   *Write the equation for your trend line.*

$y = $ ☐   *Substitute the number of chapters for x.*

$y = $ ☐   *Simplify.*

I predict that a book with 26 chapters would have _____ pages.

B Use the equation of the trend line to predict how many pages would be in a book with 14 chapters.

Is this prediction an example of interpolation or extrapolation?

_____

$y = $ ☐   *Write the equation for your trend line.*

$y = $ ☐   *Substitute the number of chapters for x.*

$y = $ ☐   *Simplify.*

I predict that a book with 14 chapters would have _____ pages.

REFLECT

3a. How well do your new points fit the original data?

_____

3b. Do you think that extrapolation or interpolation is more accurate? Explain.

_____

_____

_____

_____

Twenty-five runners between the ages of 6 and 18 were timed in a mile run. The scatter plot shows the results.

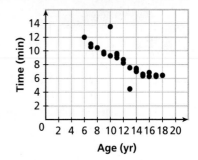

1. In what range of running times does the data appear to cluster?

_____

2. What running times are outliers?

_____

_____

3. Suppose that Juan, who is 17, was timed at 9.5 minutes. Would his time be an outlier? Explain.

_____

_____

The scatter plot shows the circumference and height of a variety of trees.

4. How would you describe the association between circumference and height that the scatter plot shows? Explain.

_____

_____

5. Using (150, 80) as one of the points, draw a trend line using a straightedge. What is the slope of the line? How did you find it?

_____

_____

6. What is the equation for your trend line? _____

7. Why might your classmates' equations for trend lines vary?

_____

_____

8. Error Analysis A student used points (150, 80) and (50, 30) but wrote the equation $y = 5x + 0.5$. What mistake did the student make?

_____

_____

Additional Practice

Use the scatter plot for Exercises 1–6.

Years Worked and Hourly Wage

1. Does the pattern of association between year and pay per hour appear to be linear or nonlinear?

   _____

2. Identify any clustering.

   _____

3. Identify any possible outliers.

   _____

4. Write an equation for the line of best fit.

   _____

5. What does the slope in the scatter plot represent?

   _____

   _____

6. What does the *y*-intercept in the scatter plot represent?

   _____

   _____

Problem Solving

Use the scatter plot for Exercises 1–3.

1. Does the pattern of association between time studied and score appear to be linear or nonlinear?

_____

2. Describe the correlation between the time studied and the scores as positive, negative, or no correlation.

_____

3. Identify any possible outliers.

_____

Studying and Scores

Choose the letter for the best answer. Use the scatter plot for Exercises 4–6.

4. What does the point (0, 400) represent in this scatter plot?

   A the temperature at an elevation of 0 feet

   B the elevation at a temperature of 58°F

   C the elevation at a temperature of 0°F

   D the temperature at an elevation of 500 feet

Temperatures and Elevation

5. Which best describes the correlation between the temperatures and the elevations in the scatter plot?

   F strong positive

   G weak positive

   H strong negative

   J weak negative

6. Which equation best represents the line of best fit?

   A $y = -16x + 400$

   B $y = -15x + 300$

   C $y = 15x - 300$

   D $y = 16x - 400$

© Houghton Mifflin Harcourt Publishing Company

Patterns in Two-Way Tables
Going Deeper

Essential question: *How can you construct and interpret two-way tables?*

The **frequency** is the number of times an event occurs. A **two-way table** shows the frequencies of data that is categorized two ways. The rows indicate one categorization and the columns indicate another.

CC.8.SP.4

1 EXPLORE Making a Two-Way Table

A poll of 120 town residents found that 40% own a bike. Of those who own a bike, 75% shop at the town's farmer's market. Of those who do not own a bike, 25% shop at the town's farmer's market.

	Farmer's Market	No Farmer's Market	TOTAL
Bike			
No Bike			
TOTAL			

A Start in the bottom right cell of the table. Enter the total number of people polled.

B **Fill in the right column.** 40% of those polled own a bike.

40% of 120 is _____.

The remaining people polled do not own a bike. The number who do not own a bike is 120 − _____ = _____.

C **Fill in the top row.** 75% of those who own a bike also shop at the market.

75% of _____ is _____.

The remaining bike owners do not shop at the market. The number of bike owners who do not shop at the market is _____.

D **Fill in the second row.** 25% of those who do not own a bike shop at the market.

25% of _____ is _____.

The remaining people without bikes do not shop at the market. The number without a bike who do not shop at the market is _____.

E **Fill in the last row.** In each column, add the numbers in the first two rows to find the total number of people who shop at the farmer's market and who do not shop at the farmer's market.

F What percent of all the residents polled shop at the farmer's market?

$$\frac{\boxed{}}{120} = \boxed{}$$

_____% of people polled shop at the farmer's market.

REFLECT

1. How can you check that your table is completed correctly?

_____

_____

Relative frequency is the ratio of the number of times an event occurs to the total number of events. In **1**, the relative frequency of bike owners who shop at the market is $\frac{36}{120} = 0.30 = 30\%$. You can use relative frequencies to decide if there is an association between two variables or events.

CC.8.SP.4

2 EXAMPLE Deciding Whether There Is an Association

Determine whether there is an association between the events.

A One hundred teens were polled about whether they are required to do chores and whether they have a curfew. Is there an association between having a curfew and having to do chores?

	Curfew	No Curfew	TOTAL
Chores	16	4	20
No Chores	16	64	80
TOTAL	32	68	100

Find the relative frequency of having to do chores.

Total who have to do chores $\rightarrow$
Total number of teens polled $\rightarrow$ $\dfrac{\boxed{}}{100} = \boxed{} = \boxed{}\%$

Find the relative frequency of having to do chores among those who have a curfew.

Number with a curfew who have to do chores $\rightarrow$
Total number with a curfew $\rightarrow$ $\dfrac{\boxed{}}{32} = \boxed{} = \boxed{}\%$

Compare the relative frequencies. Students who have a curfew are less likely/more likely to have to do chores than the general population.

Is there an association between having a curfew and having to do chores? Explain.

_____

_____

B Data from 200 flights was collected. The flights were categorized as domestic or international and late or not late. Is there an association between international flights and a flight being late?

	Late	Not Late	TOTAL
Domestic	30	120	150
International	10	40	50
TOTAL	40	160	200

Find the relative frequency of a flight being late.

Total flights that are late → $\dfrac{\rule{1cm}{0.4pt}}{\rule{1cm}{0.4pt}}$ = $\boxed{}$ = $\boxed{}$ %
Total number of flights →

Find the relative frequency of a flight being late among international flights.

Number of international flights that are late → $\dfrac{\rule{1cm}{0.4pt}}{\rule{1cm}{0.4pt}}$ = $\boxed{}$ = $\boxed{}$ %
Total number of international flights →

Compare the relative frequencies. International flights are less likely / equally likely / more likely to be late than flights in general.

Is there an association between international flights and a flight being late? Explain.

_____

_____

REFLECT

3a. Compare the relative frequency of having a curfew and having chores to the relative frequency of not having a curfew and having chores. Does this comparison help you draw a conclusion about whether there is an association between having a curfew and having chores? Explain.

_____

_____

_____

3b. Compare the relative frequency of domestic flights being late to the relative frequency of international flights being late. Does this comparison help you draw a conclusion about whether there is an association between international flights and being late? Explain.

_____

_____

Karen asked 150 students at her school if they played sports. She also recorded whether the student was a boy or girl. Of the 150 students, 20% did not play sports, 60% of the total were girls, and 70% of the girls played sports.

	Sports	No Sports	TOTAL
Boys			
Girls			
TOTAL			

1. Complete the two-way table.

2. What is the relative frequency of a student playing sports? _____

3. What is the relative frequency of a boy playing sports? _____

4. Is there an association between being a boy and playing sports at Karen's school? Explain.

_____

_____

_____

_____

Aiden collected data from 80 students about whether they have siblings and whether they have pets.

	Siblings	No Siblings	TOTAL
Pets	49	21	70
No Pets	7	3	10
TOTAL	56	24	80

5. What is the relative frequency of a student having pets? _____

6. What is the relative frequency of a student with siblings having pets? _____

7. Is there an association between having siblings and having pets? Explain.

_____

_____

_____

Linear Functions
Going Deeper

Essential question: *How do you graph a linear function?*

CC.8.EE.5

1 EXPLORE Investigating Change

The U.S. Department of Agriculture defines heavy rain as rain that falls at a rate of 1.5 centimeters per hour.

A The table shows the total amount of rain that falls in various amounts of time during a heavy rain. Complete the table.

Time (h)	0	1	2	3	4	5
Total Amount of Rain (cm)	0	1.5				

B Plot the ordered pairs from the table on the coordinate plane at the right.

C How much rain falls in 3.5 hours?

_____

D Plot the point corresponding to 3.5 hours of heavy rain.

E What do you notice about all of the points you plotted?

_____

Heavy Rainfall

REFLECT

1a. Suppose you continued to plot points for times between those in the table, such as 1.2 hours or 4.5 hours. What can you say about the locations of these points?

_____

_____

1b. The U.S. Department of Agriculture defines excessive rain as rain that falls at a rate of 4 centimeters per hour. How do you think a graph of excessive rainfall would compare to the graph of heavy rainfall?

_____

_____

A **linear function** is a function whose graph is a nonvertical straight line. The function describing heavy rainfall in is a linear function because its graph is a set of points that form a straight line.

A **linear equation** is an equation that represents a linear function. The solutions of a linear equation are ordered pairs that form a straight line on the coordinate plane.

CC.8.F.3

2 EXAMPLE Graphing a Linear Equation

Experts recommend that adult dogs have a daily intake of 50 calories per kilogram of the dog's weight plus 100 calories. Write an equation that gives the recommended number of daily calories y for a dog that weighs x kilograms. Then show that the equation is a linear equation.

Write an equation.

Daily calories equals 50 times weight plus 100.

⬜ = ⬜ + ⬜

Complete the table to find some solutions of the equation.

Weight (kg), x	6	8	10	12	14
Calories, y					

Plot the points, then draw a line through the points to represent all the possible x-values and their corresponding y-values.

The equation is a linear equation because

_____

_____ .

Recommended Daily Intake

TRY THIS!

2. Graph the solutions of the linear equation $y = -2x + 1$. Then explain how the graph is different from the graph in the example.

_____

_____

_____

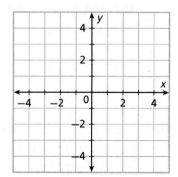

© Houghton Mifflin Harcourt Publishing Company

The linear equation in **2** has the form $y = mx + b$, where m and b are real numbers. Every equation in the form $y = mx + b$ is a linear equation. Equations that cannot be written in this form are not linear equations.

3 EXAMPLE Determining Whether an Equation is Linear

A square tile has a side length of x inches. The equation $y = x^2$ gives the area y of the tile in square inches. Determine whether the equation $y = x^2$ is a linear equation.

Complete the table.

Side Length, x	1	2	3	4
Area, y				

Plot the points, then draw a curve through the points to represent all the possible x-values and their corresponding y-values.

Decide whether the equation $y = x^2$ a linear equation. Explain your reasoning.

_____

_____

_____

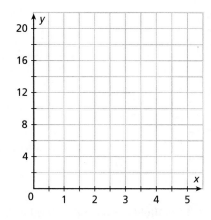

REFLECT

3a. How is the equation $y = x^2$ different from the linear equations you have graphed?

_____

3b. Explain whether you think the equation $y = 2x^2 + 4$ is a linear equation.

_____

3c. Error Analysis A student graphed several solutions of $y = -2x$ as shown. The student concluded that the equation is not a linear equation. Explain the student's error.

_____

_____

_____

_____

Graph solutions of each equation and tell whether the equation is linear or non-linear.

1. $y = 5 - 2x$

Input, x	−1	1	3	5
Output, y				

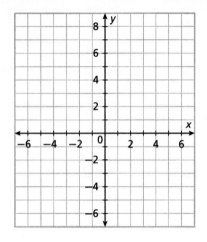

_____

2. $y = 2 - x^2$

Input, x	−2	−1	0	1	2
Output, y					

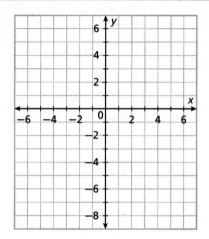

_____

3. Olivia measured several rooms in her house in feet. She wants to express the measurements in inches. Write an equation relating feet x and inches y. Tell whether the equation is linear or non-linear.

_____

4. Seth receives $100 from his grandmother for his birthday. He also saves $20 every month. Write an equation relating months x and total savings y. Tell whether the equation is linear or non-linear.

_____

Explain whether each equation is a linear equation.

5. $y = x^2 - 1$

_____

_____

_____

6. $y = 1 - x$

_____

_____

_____

7. Error Analysis A student claims that the equation $y = 7$ is not a linear equation because it does not have the form $y = mx + b$. Do you agree or disagree? Why?

_____

_____

Additional Practice

Determine whether each function is linear. If so, give the slope and *y*-intercept of the function's graph.

1. $f(x) = -3x + 2$

2. $f(x) = x^2 - 1$

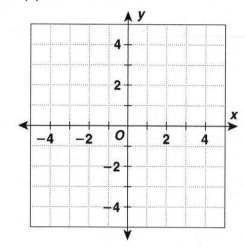

_____   _____

Write a rule for each linear function.

3.

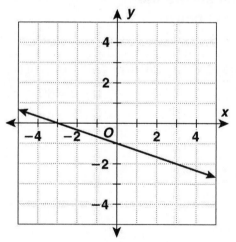

4.

x	y
−3	16
−1	12
3	4
7	−4

_____   _____

5. At the Sweater Store, the price of a sweater is 20% more than the wholesale cost, plus a markup of $8. Find a rule for a linear function that describes the price of sweaters at the Sweater Store. Use it to determine the price of a sweater with a wholesale cost of $24.50.

_____

_____

Problem Solving

Write the correct answer.

1. On April 14–15, 1921 in Silver Lake, Colorado, 76 inches of snow fell in 24 hours, at an average rate of 3.2 inches per hour. Find a rule for the linear function that describes the amount of snow after x hours at the average rate.

_____

2. At the average rate of snowfall from Exercise 1, how much snow had fallen in 15 hours?

_____

3. The altitude of clouds in feet can be found by multiplying the difference between the temperature and the dew point by 228. If the temperature is 75°, find a rule for the linear function that describes the height of the clouds with dew point x.

_____

4. If the temperature is 75° and the dew point is 40°, what is the height of the clouds?

_____

For Exercises 5–7, refer to the table below, which shows the relationship between the number of times a cricket chirps in a minute and temperature.

5. Find a rule for the linear function that describes the temperature based on x, the number of cricket chirps in a minute based on temperature.

   A $f(x) = x + 5$

   B $f(x) = \dfrac{x}{4} + 40$

   C $f(x) = x - 20$

   D $f(x) = \dfrac{x}{2} + 20$

Cricket Chirps/min	Temperature (°F)
80	60
100	65
120	70
140	75

6. What is the temperature if a cricket chirps 150 times in a minute?

   F 77.5 °F   H 130 °F

   G 95 °F   J 155 °F

7. If the temperature is 85 °F, how many times will a cricket chirp in a minute?

   A 61   C 180

   B 105   D 200

Comparing Multiple Representations
Going Deeper

Essential question: *How can you use tables, graphs, and equations to compare functions?*

CC.8.EE.5

1 EXPLORE Comparing a Table and a Graph

The table and graph show how many words Morgan and Brian typed correctly on a typing test. For both students, the relationship between words typed correctly and time is linear.

Morgan's Typing Test					
Time (min)	2	4	6	8	10
Words	30	60	90	120	150

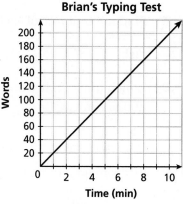
Brian's Typing Test

A Find Morgan's unit rate.

_____

B Find Brian's unit rate.

_____

C Which student types more correct words per minute?

_____

REFLECT

1a. Sketch a graph of Morgan's test results on the same coordinate grid as Brian's results. How are the graphs similar? How are they different?

_____

_____

1b. Katie types 17 correct words per minute. Explain how a graph of Katie's test results would compare to Morgan's and Brian's.

_____

_____

1c. The equation that describes Jen's test results is $y = 24x$. Explain how a graph of Jen's test results would compare to Morgan's and Brian's.

_____

_____

2 EXPLORE Comparing a Table and an Equation

Josh and Maggie buy MP3 files from different music download services. With both services, the monthly charge is a linear function of the number of songs downloaded. The cost at Josh's service is described by $y = 0.50x + 10$ where y is the cost in dollars and x is the number of songs downloaded.

Cost of MP3s at Maggie's Music Service					
Songs, x	5	10	15	20	25
Cost ($), y	4.95	9.90	14.85	19.80	24.75

A Find the unit rate of each function.

Josh: _____   Maggie: _____

B Which function has the greater rate of change? What does that mean in this context?

_____

C Write an equation in slope-intercept form to describe the cost at Maggie's music service.

$y = mx + b$

$\boxed{} = \boxed{} \cdot \boxed{} + b$ *Substitute for y, m, and x.*

$\boxed{} = \boxed{} + b$ *Subtract the number that is added to b from both sides.*

$- \boxed{} \quad - \boxed{}$

$\overline{\boxed{} = \quad b}$

$y = \boxed{} x + \boxed{}$

D Describe each service's cost in words using the meanings of the slopes and y-intercepts.

_____

_____

REFLECT

2a. How much does it cost at each service to download 20 songs?

_____

2b. You are trying to choose between these two music services. How could you decide which service is better for you?

_____

_____

3 EXPLORE Comparing a Graph and a Description

Jamal wants to buy a new game system that costs $200. He only has $100 today, so he compares layaway plans at different stores.

The plan at Store A is shown on the graph.

Store B requires an initial payment of $60 and weekly payments of $20 until the balance is paid in full.

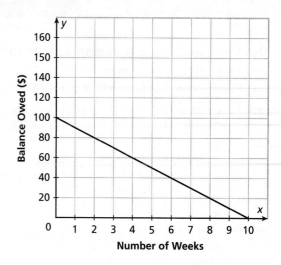

A Use the graph of the layaway plan at Store A to write an equation in slope-intercept form. Let x represent number of weeks and y represent balance owed.

_____

B Use the description of the layaway plan at Store B to write an equation in slope-intercept form. Let x represent number of weeks and y represent balance owed.

_____

C Sketch a graph of the plan at Store B on the same grid as Store A.

D How can you use the graphs to tell which plan requires the greater down payment? How can you use the equations?

_____

_____

E How can you use the graphs to tell which plan requires the greater weekly payment? How can you use the equations?

_____

_____

F Which plan allows Jamal to pay for the game system faster? Explain.

_____

_____

The table and the graph display two different linear functions.

Input, x	Output, y
−3	5
−1	1
2	−5
3	−7
6	−13

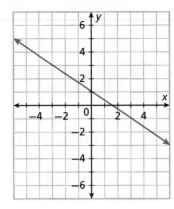

1. Find the slope of each function.

Table: _____   Graph: _____

2. Without graphing the function represented in the table, tell which function's graph is steeper.

_____

_____

3. Write an equation for each function.

Table: _____   Graph: _____

4. Use the equations from **3** to tell which function has the greater *y*-intercept.

_____

Aisha runs a tutoring business. Students may choose to pay $15 per hour or they may follow the plan shown on the graph.

5. Describe the plan shown on the graph.

_____

6. Sketch a graph showing the $15 per hour option.

7. What does the intersection of the two graphs mean?

_____

8. If you wanted to hire Aisha for tutoring, how can you decide which payment option is better for you?

_____

_____

Additional Practice

1. Find and compare the slopes for the linear functions f and g.

$f(x) = \dfrac{1}{2}x - 4$

x	−4	0	4	8
$g(x)$	−3	−2	−1	0

slope of f _____   slope of g _____

Compare _____

_____

2. Find and compare the y-intercepts for the linear functions f and g.

x	−1	0	1	2
$f(x)$	−7	−2	3	8

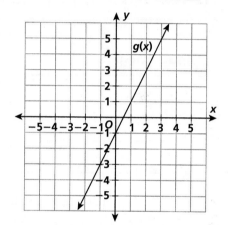

y-intercept of f _____

y-intercept of g _____

Compare _____

_____

Connor and Sheila are in a rock-climbing club. They are climbing down a canyon wall. Connor starts from a cliff that is 200 feet above the canyon floor and climbs down at an average speed of 10 feet per minute. Sheila climbs down the canyon wall as shown in the table.

Time (min)	0	1	2	3
Sheila's height (ft)	242	234	226	218

3. Interpret the rates of change and initial values of the linear functions in terms of the situations they model.

<u>Connor</u>

Initial value _____

Rate of change _____

Compare _____

_____

<u>Sheila</u>

Initial value _____

Rate of change _____

© Houghton Mifflin Harcourt Publishing Company

Problem Solving

Find and compare the rates of change and initial values of the linear functions in terms of the situations they model.

1. Dan and Keri assemble bicycles. So far today, Dan has assembled 3 bikes. He works at a rate of 0.5 bikes per hour. Keri has assembled 4 bikes, so far today, and assembles bicycles as shown in the table.

Time (hr)	0	1	2	3
Bikes Keri Assembled	4	4.75	5.5	6.25

_____

_____

_____

2. Javier and Wendy pay for their cell phone service from their checking accounts according to the equation and graph shown.
Javier: $f(x) = -65x + 450$
Wendy

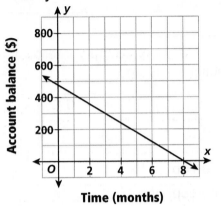

_____

_____

_____

Use the table and the graph for Exercises 3 and 4. Choose the letter for the best answer.

Jane and Alex each start driving from their homes, which are different distances from the warehouse where they both work, to a meeting out of town.

Jane

Time (hr)	2	3	4	5
Distance (mi)	185	240	295	350

3. How much farther from the warehouse was Jane than Alex when she started driving today?

   A 50 miles C 75 miles

   B 60 miles D 200 miles

4. How much faster is Jane driving than Alex?

   A 55 miles per hour

   B 50 miles per hour

   C 25 miles per hour

   D 5 miles per hour

CHAPTER 9

Problem Solving Connections 🌐

Give me a T! Annika asks several of her classmates to make a T with their bodies by standing up straight and putting their arms straight out to their sides. She measures their arm spans and their heights in inches. What associations can be made from the data she collects?

COMMON CORE

CC.8.SP.1
CC.8.SP.2
CC.8.SP.3
CC.8.SP.4

1 Making Scatter Plots

A Annika records her measurements in the table.

Boys		
Name	**Height (in.)**	**Arm Span (in.)**
George	60	$60\frac{1}{2}$
Hank	$52\frac{1}{4}$	50
Peter	60	59
Christopher	65	65
Girls		
Name	**Height (in.)**	**Arm Span (in.)**
Julie	$63\frac{1}{2}$	62
Louisa	55	55
Jan	62	$62\frac{1}{4}$
Kelly	50	$61\frac{3}{4}$

B Make a scatter plot using the data.

C What overall trends do you see in the scatter plot?

_____

_____

_____

D Do you see any outliers? Why might there be an outlier?

_____

_____

_____

2 Finding a Trend line

A Sketch a trend line on the scatter plot. (Hint: Because you will need to write an equation for the line later, it is a good idea to draw your line through data points, if possible.)

B How well does your trend line fit the data?

_____

_____

C Measure your height in inches. Use the trend line to predict your arm span.

_____

_____

D Identify two data points that your trend line goes through.

_____

_____

_____

E Calculate the slope of your trend line.

F Write an equation for the trend line in slope-intercept form.

G Use your trend line to interpolate how wide someone's arm span is if the individual is 58 inches tall.

H Choose a height for which you would have to extrapolate, and use your trend line to predict what the arm span would be.

I Under what circumstances might this trend line not be a good predictor of arm span?

_____

_____

_____

_____

3 Making a Two-Way Table

A Complete the two-way table using Annika's data.

	Arm Span Equal to Height	Arm Span Not Equal to Height	TOTAL
Boys			
Girls			
TOTAL			

B How can you check that you completed the table correctly?

_____

_____

© Houghton Mifflin Harcourt Publishing Company

C What is the relative frequency of boys?

D What is the relative frequency of equal height and arm span for all students?

E What is the relative frequency of equal height and arm span among boys?

4 Answer the Question

A Does there appear to be an association between being a boy and having equal height and arm span? Explain.

_____

_____

_____

_____

B Why might this data set be misleading?

_____

_____

_____

C What conclusions can Annika draw from her data?

_____

_____

_____

Performance Task

COMMON
CORE

CC.8.F.2
CC.8.F.4
CC.8.SP.1
CC.8.SP.2
CC.8.SP.3

1. A restaurant opens its ice cream stand for 5 months each year. The scatter plot shows some ice cream sales data.

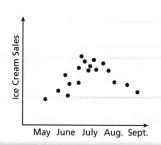

a. Does the data suggest a linear or nonlinear relationship? Explain.

b. Does the scatter plot exhibit any clustering? If so, where?

2. Sara needs to buy eggs. A neighbor sells fresh eggs for 25 cents each. The table shows two options for eggs at the store.

Amount of Eggs	Price
12	$2.29
18	$3.29

a. Write linear functions for the cost per egg for the neighbor's eggs, the 12-pack of eggs, and the 18-pack of eggs. Round to the nearest cent if necessary.

b. Which function has the smallest slope? What does this mean?

3. The scatter plot shows times for the men's 1500-meter Olympic gold medalists for certain years. The times are given in seconds, and $x = 0$ represents 1924.

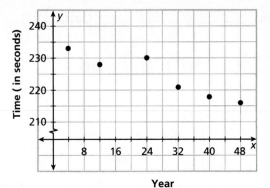

a. Draw a line of best fit and estimate its slope.

b. Write an equation for the line of best fit that you drew.

c. What does your equation predict for a time for 2016? Show your work.

4. The function $C(m) = 7 + 0.20(m - 3)$ gives the cost C for a ride of m miles in Toni's Taxi. A different company, Cozy Cab, has the sign shown.

Cozy Cab
0–5 miles: $7
More than 5 miles: $7 plus $0.15 for every mile after 5 miles

a. Compare the rates of the companies for rides that are 0 to 5 miles. For what distance are the costs the same? For what distance(s) is one company cheaper than the other?

b. Write a linear function for a ride over 5 miles using Cozy Cab. Compare the rates of the companies for rides over 5 miles, and justify your conclusions.

Name _____ Class _____ Date _____

SELECTED RESPONSE

Rebecca played several games of cards with her brother. She made a scatter plot showing how many minutes each game lasted and how many points she scored during that game. Use the scatter plot for 1–3.

1. Using the trend line, how many points can Rebecca expect to score if the game lasts 25 minutes?

　A. 25

　B. 45

　C. 70

　D. 100

2. What is the equation for the trend line?

　F. $y = 2x$

　G. $y = 3x$

　H. $y = 3x - 5$

　J. $y = 3x + 5$

3. Using the equation for the trend line, how many points might Rebecca score in a game that lasts 100 minutes?

　A. 95

　B. 200

　C. 205

　D. 295

A survey of 50 adults asked whether the person had children and whether they had a cat. Use the table for 4–5.

	Cat	No cat	TOTAL
Children	5	27	
No children	16	2	
TOTAL	21	29	50

4. Of those surveyed, 64% said they do have children. Which values complete the last column of the table?

　F. Children: 64
　　No children: 36

　G. Children: 32
　　No children: 18

　H. Children: 25
　　No children: 25

　J. Children: 30
　　No children: 20

5. Which conclusion can be drawn?

　A. There appears to be an association between having no children and having a cat.

　B. The total number of people with cats is 32.

　C. There is no association between having children and having a cat.

　D. The relative frequency of people with no children is 18%.

6. Mr. Radmanovic and Mrs. Chin both fill up their cars with gasoline at the beginning of the week. The equation compares the number of miles driven, x, to the amount of gasoline in the tank, $f(x)$.

Find and compare the y-intercepts for the models and interpret their real-world meanings.

Mr. Radmanovic's Car

$$f(x) = -\frac{1}{20}x + 13.6$$

Mrs. Chin's Car

Miles Driven	0	8
Gasoline Remaining (gallons)	13.2	13

F. The y-intercept for Mr. Radmanovic's car is 20. The y-intercept for Mrs. Chin's car is 13.2. Mr. Radmanovic's car has a larger gasoline tank than Mrs. Chin's car does.

G. The y-intercept for Mr. Radmanovic's car is 13.6. The y-intercept for Mrs. Chin's car is 13.2. Mr. Radmanovic's car has a larger gasoline tank than Mrs. Chin's car does.

H. The y-intercept for Mr. Radmanovic's car is 13.6. The y-intercept for Mrs. Chin's car is 13. Mr. Radmanovic's car has a larger gasoline tank than Mrs. Chin's car does.

J. The y-intercept for Mr. Radmanovic's car is 20. The y-intercept for Mrs. Chin's car is 40. Mrs. Chin's car gets better gas mileage than Mr. Radmanovic's car does.

CONSTRUCTED RESPONSE

Noah researched the weekly high temperature in his city. He chose several weeks between July and December to put in a table. (The first week of July was numbered Week 1 in Noah's source material.) Use this data for Questions 7–10.

Week	High Temp (°F)	Week	High Temp (°F)
16	78	12	78
25	55	7	95
3	100	10	84
17	65	9	90
13	75	15	74
5	90	21	62

7. Use Noah's data to make a scatter plot.

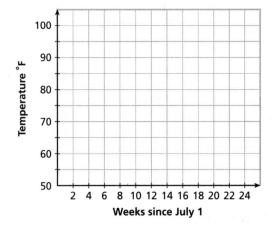

8. What type of association is shown on the scatterplot? Explain.

_____

_____

9. Draw a trend line on the scatter plot.

Correlation of *Explorations in Core Math Grade 8* to the Common Core State Standards

The Number System	Citations
CC.8.NS.1 Understand informally that every number has a decimal expansion; the rational numbers are those with decimal expansions that terminate in 0s or eventually repeat. Know that other numbers are called irrational.	pp. 5–10, 35–38, 39–40, 117–120
CC.8.NS.2 Use rational approximations of irrational numbers to compare the size of irrational numbers, locate them approximately on a number line diagram, and estimate the value of expressions (e.g., π^2).	pp. 111–116, 135–136

Expressions and Equations	Citations
CC.8.EE.1 Know and apply the properties of integer exponents to generate equivalent numerical expressions.	pp. 83–86, 87–92, 131–134, 135–136
CC.8.EE.2 Use square root and cube root symbols to represent solutions to equations of the form $x^2 = p$ and $x^3 = p$, where p is a positive rational number. Evaluate square roots of small perfect squares and cube roots of small perfect cubes. Know that $\sqrt{2}$ is irrational.	pp. 105–110, 135–136
CC.8.EE.3 Use numbers expressed in the form of a single digit times an integer power of 10 to estimate very large or very small quantities, and to express how many times as much one is than the other.	pp. 93–98, 131–134, 135–136
CC.8.EE.4 Perform operations with numbers expressed in scientific notation, including problems where both decimal and scientific notation are used. Use scientific notation and choose units of appropriate size for measurements of very large or very small quantities (e.g., use millimeters per year for seafloor spreading). Interpret scientific notation that has been generated by technology.	pp. 99–104, 131–134, 135–136
CC.8.EE.5 Graph proportional relationships, interpreting the unit rate as the slope of the graph. Compare two different proportional relationships represented in different ways.	pp. 167–168, 317–320, 355–360, 361–366
CC.8.EE.6 Use similar triangles to explain why the slope m is the same between any two distinct points on a non-vertical line in the coordinate plane; derive the equation $y = mx$ for a line through the origin and the equation $y = mx + b$ for a line intercepting the vertical axis at b.	pp. 247–250, 299–304, 305–312
CC.8.EE.7 Solve linear equations in one variable. a. Give examples of linear equations in one variable with one solution, infinitely many solutions, or no solutions. Show which of these possibilities is the case by successively transforming the given equation into simpler forms, until an equivalent equation of the form $x = a$, $a = a$, or $a = b$ results (where a and b are different numbers). b. Solve linear equations with rational number coefficients, including equations whose solutions require expanding expressions using the distributive property and collecting like terms.	pp. 23–28, 29–34, 35–38, 39–40, 265–270, 271–276, 283–286, 287–288, 327–330

CC.8.EE.8 Analyze and solve pairs of simultaneous linear equations. a. Understand that solutions to a system of two linear equations in two variables correspond to points of intersection of their graphs, because points of intersection satisfy both equations simultaneously. b. Solve systems of two linear equations in two variables algebraically, and estimate solutions by graphing the equations. Solve simple cases by inspection. c. Solve real-world and mathematical problems leading to two linear equations in two variables.	pp. 277–282, 283–286, 287–288, 321–326, 327–330, 331–332
Functions	**Citations**
CC.8.F.1 Understand that a function is a rule that assigns to each input exactly one output. The graph of a function is the set of ordered pairs consisting of an input and the corresponding output.	pp. 61–66, 71–74, 75–76
CC.8.F.2 Compare properties of two functions each represented in a different way (algebraically, graphically, numerically in tables, or by verbal descriptions).	pp. 75–76, 361–366, 371–372
CC.8.F.3 Interpret the equation $y = mx + b$ as defining a linear function, whose graph is a straight line; give examples of functions that are not linear.	pp. 305–312, 331–332, 355–360
CC.8.F.4 Construct a function to model a linear relationship between two quantities. Determine the rate of change and initial value of the function from a description of a relationship or from two (x, y) values, including reading these from a table or from a graph. Interpret the rate of change and initial value of a linear function in terms of the situation it models, and in terms of its graph or a table of values.	pp. 67–70, 71–74, 75–76, 295–298, 305–312, 313–316, 331–332, 361–366, 371–372
CC.8.F.5 Describe qualitatively the functional relationship between two quantities by analyzing a graph (e.g., where the function is increasing or decreasing, linear or nonlinear). Sketch a graph that exhibits the qualitative features of a function that has been described verbally.	pp. 55–60, 71–74, 75–76, 331–332
Geometry	**Citations**
CC.8.G.1 Verify experimentally the properties of rotations, reflections, and translations: a. Lines are taken to lines, and line segments to line segments of the same length. b. Angles are taken to angles of the same measure. c. Parallel lines are taken to parallel lines.	pp. 205–208, 217–220
CC.8.G.2 Understand that a two-dimensional figure is congruent to another if the second can be obtained from the first by a sequence of rotations, reflections, and translations; given two congruent figures, describe a sequence that exhibits the congruence between them.	pp. 209–216, 217–220, 221–222
CC.8.G.3 Describe the effect of dilations, translations, rotations, and reflections on two-dimensional figures using coordinates.	pp. 157–162, 163–166, 167–168, 199–204, 217–220, 221–222
CC.8.G.4 Understand that a two-dimensional figure is similar to another if the second can be obtained from the first by a sequence of rotations, reflections, translations, and dilations; given two similar two-dimensional figures, describe a sequence that exhibits the similarity between them.	pp. 163–166, 167–168, 209–216, 217–220, 221–222
CC.8.G.5 Use informal arguments to establish facts about the angle sum and exterior angle of triangles, about the angles created when parallel lines are cut by a transversal, and the angle-angle criterion for similarity of triangles.	pp. 151–156, 179–184, 185–190, 221–222, 247–250
CC.8.G.6 Explain a proof of the Pythagorean Theorem and its converse.	pp. 127–130, 247–250

CC.8.G.7 Apply the Pythagorean Theorem to determine unknown side lengths in right triangles in real-world and mathematical problems in two and three dimensions.	**pp. 121–126, 135–136, 247–250**
CC.8.G.8 Apply the Pythagorean Theorem to find the distance between two points in a coordinate system.	**pp. 121–126, 135–136, 247–250**
CC.8.G.9 Know the formulas for the volumes of cones, cylinders, and spheres and use them to solve real-world and mathematical problems.	**pp. 235–238, 239–242, 243–246, 247–250, 253–254**
Statistics and Probability	**Citations**
CC.8.SP.1 Construct and interpret scatter plots for bivariate measurement data to investigate patterns of association between two quantities. Describe patterns such as clustering, outliers, positive or negative association, linear association, and nonlinear association.	**pp. 339–344, 345–350, 367–370, 371–372**
CC.8.SP.2 Know that straight lines are widely used to model relationships between two quantitative variables. For scatter plots that suggest a linear association, informally fit a straight line, and informally assess the model fit by judging the closeness of the data points to the line.	**pp. 339–344, 345–350, 367–370, 371–372**
CC.8.SP.3 Use the equation of a linear model to solve problems in the context of bivariate measurement data, interpreting the slope and intercept.	**pp. 345–350, 367–370, 371–372**
CC.8.SP.4 Understand that patterns of association can also be seen in bivariate categorical data by displaying frequencies and relative frequencies in a two-way table. Construct and interpret a two-way table summarizing data on two categorical variables collected from the same subjects. Use relative frequencies calculated for rows or columns to describe possible association between the two variables.	**pp. 351–354, 367–370**

HOLT McDOUGAL MATHEMATICS

Explorations in CORE MATH

FOR COMMON CORE

- **Unpacking the Standards** features focus on important academic vocabulary and offer examples and non-examples to clarify learning goals.

- **Interactive lessons** allow you to actively participate and develop a deeper understanding of math concepts.

- **Practice and Problem Solving** pages provide opportunities for mathematical modeling as you practice and apply new concepts in real-world contexts.

- **Leveled Performance Tasks** and **Problem Solving Connections** help you pull together math concepts and skills and apply them to real-world situations.

- **Assessment Readiness** provides you with opportunities to practice and prepare for your high-stakes test.

- **QR codes** make it easy to use your smart phone or tablet to access online resources, including video tutorials, interactive animations, and assessment readiness practice.

HOLT McDOUGAL

HOUGHTON MIFFLIN HARCOURT

ISBN 978-0-547-87643-6

9 780547 876436

90000>

1505936